IMPROVING PERFORMANCE

How to Manage the White Space on the Organization Chart

THIRD EDITION

Geary A. Rummler
Alan P. Brache

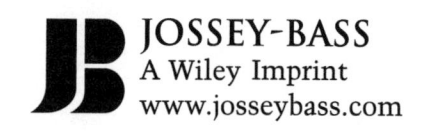

JOSSEY-BASS
A Wiley Imprint
www.josseybass.com

Jacket design by Jeff Puda.

Published by Jossey-Bass
A Wiley Imprint
One Montgomery Street, Suite 1200, San Francisco, CA 94104-4594—www.josseybass.com

Jossey-Bass books and products are available through most bookstores. To contact Jossey-Bass directly call
our Customer Care Department within the U.S. at 800-956-7739, outside the U.S. at 317-572-3986, or fax
317-572-4002.

Wiley publishes in a variety of print and electronic formats and by print-on-demand. Some material
included with standard print versions of this book may not be included in e-books or in print-on-
demand. If this book refers to media such as a CD or DVD that is not included in the version you
purchased, you may download this material at http://booksupport.wiley.com. For more information
about Wiley products, visit www.wiley.com.

Library of Congress Cataloging-in-Publication Data

Rummler, Geary A.
    Improving performance : how to manage the white space on the organization chart / Geary A.
Rummler, Alan P. Brache. — Updated ed., 3rd ed.
        p. cm.
    Includes index.
    ISBN 978-1-118-14370-4 (cloth); ISBN 978-1-118-22559-2 (ebk.); ISBN 978-1-118-23902-5 (ebk.);
ISBN 978-1-118-26367-9 (ebk.)
    1. Industrial productivity. 2. Performance. 3. Organizational effectiveness. I. Brache, Alan P.,
1950– II. Title.
    HD56.R86 2013
    658.4'02—dc23
                            2012030713

Printed in the United States of America
THIRD EDITION

HB Printing   10 9 8 7 6 5 4 3 2 1

Contents

iii

57.60

129767

PART THREE: APPLYING THE THREE LEVELS OF PERFORMANCE 75

LIST OF FIGURES AND TABLES

Figures

Tables

FOREWORD

Improving Performance: How to Manage the White Space on the Organization Chart was the first book written on the mechanics of process improvement, the nuts and bolts of how you actually do it.

The methodology in the book was so embraced by readers that Rummler and Brache became the godfathers of process improvement. They helped spawn a cottage industry of business process management analysts, software vendors, consultants, authors, and conferences.

Today, there are dizzying numbers of process improvement methodologies and technologies competing with one another. But in the light of day, practically all of them owe their origin to their predecessor, the Rummler-Brache methodology.

The Rummler-Brache approach to process improvement is the gold standard. It's a systematic, disciplined framework that does more than just isolate process performance. The methodology addresses all three levels of performance: organization, process, and job performer. And it's all linked to support the strategy and goals of the organization.

Over the years, I've been amazed by the cult-like devotion to the methodology that many of its practitioners have demonstrated. Initially, I thought they were all a little too enthusiastic, sort of like Trekkies at a Star Trek convention. However, since I've seen Rummler-Brache principles applied, I get it. The passion out there for the methodology is really a passion for what it delivers: hard results.

The authors provide a clear blueprint on how to achieve sustainable, tangible improvements. This third edition of the book reveals the latest enhancements to that blueprint: tools to create project deliverables for an accelerated project.

The book is a classic and worth revisiting, especially in the current competitive climate, when organizations must make the right systemic changes in tighter time frames.

Joe Aberger
President, PRITCHETT, LP

PREFACE

Managers face an awesome challenge in this competitive and constantly changing environment, and this is not a passing phenomenon. As customer demands, global competition, and regulatory scrutiny have increased, it has become clear that the current instability in our marketplaces is not going away. Change is and will continue to be the only constant.

The call to arms, chronicled in numerous books and articles, is widely understood by American businesspeople. Our concern is not managers' failure to understand the problem; it is their failure to do anything substantive to address it. We wrote this book because we have a framework and a set of tools that can substantively address the problem. There are plenty of books on management and organization behavior. However, we find that most of them fail to present tools (leaving the reader saying, "I'm a believer, but what do I do tomorrow?") or they provide tools that deal with only one aspect of a multidimensional need. In our review of management literature, training courses, and consultant services, we have encountered some very valuable theories, hints, and tools. However, we have not come across a single methodology for the improvement of organization performance that is conceptually sound, practical, experience-based, and comprehensive. We immodestly believe that our approach, based on Three Levels of Performance, meets these criteria and, by doing so, provides a blueprint for managing change.

Our second reason for writing this book is our desire to capture our fifty years of combined experience in improving organization performance. We both started in the field of training (before it became human resource development). Like many other people in our position, we were quick to realize that training is only one variable that affects human performance. Early in our careers, we began learning about the environmental and managerial variables that influence performance. We then turned our attention to the impact of organization strategy on performance and developed a technology for documenting, improving, and managing the business processes that bridge the gap between organization strategy and the individual.

With the evolution of Process Management, and more recently, of "managing organizations as systems," we believe we have a comprehensive approach that addresses the major variables in the system that influence the quality, quantity, and cost of performance. Through the application of Process Management, we have learned that managers (particularly at senior levels) should concentrate as much or more on the flow of products, paper, and information between departments as on the activities within departments. Process Management provides a methodology for managing this white space between the boxes on the organization chart.

Purpose of the Book

The purpose of this book is to explain the underpinnings of our Three Levels framework and to demonstrate the tools through which the framework is applied and by which the white space can be managed. We have written it for performance improvement specialists (who may be professionals in human resource development, industrial engineering, quality, or systems analysis) and for line and staff managers who want to examine a process that can bring about significant performance improvement. We expect that performance improvement specialists will most often constitute the first wave of readers in an organization and that they will recommend all or part of the book to the managers who are their customers. In addition, business and organization behavior professors may find that our approach presents a different perspective.

American management has a tendency to manage by executive summary. A director gets a one-page summary of an issue, a vice president gets a paragraph, and the president gets a three-item list. At a recent conference on improving American manufacturing's ability to compete in the global market, one conferee criticized a session by saying, "If an idea can't be summarized in one page, it doesn't have any merit." We do not see how U.S. companies will ever beat their global competitors with that view of executive information and analysis.

We are opposed to the "get it to one page" school of management. Managers who are successful over the long haul understand their businesses in detail. As a result, the Three Levels approach has a fair amount of rigor. It is practical, involving a series of straightforward questions and steps. The process has been validated, through application to companies and agencies of all kinds, in all parts of the world. It can even be fun, because teams improve the quality of work life as well as improving productivity and the quality of products and services. But often it is not simple because the challenge is not simple. Any manager or performance improvement specialist who is looking for a quick-fix formula or for the latest program to keep employees stimulated is liable to be disappointed by this book.

Overview of the Chapters

Chapter One contrasts the traditional functional view of the organization (as represented by the organization chart) with the more descriptive and useful systems view. We describe the system components that must be managed to establish an organization that is competitive, adaptive (reactively and proactively), and focused on continuous performance improvement.

The second chapter introduces the Three Levels of Performance and presents the Nine Performance Variables that determine the effectiveness and efficiency of an organization. At each of the Three Levels—the Organization Level, the Process Level, and the Job/Performer Level—this chapter describes the three Performance Needs—Goals, Design, and Management—and shows how they can be used by executives, managers, and analysts.

One of the Three Levels of Performance is explored in each of the next three chapters. Chapter Three provides a set of questions for diagnosing the effectiveness of the Goals, Design, and Management at the Organization Level. It illustrates the use of these questions in a sample company and presents the Relationship Map as a tool for understanding and improving performance at this level.

Chapter Four gives the reader tools for understanding and improving the Goals, Design, and Management of the cross-functional processes through which an organization provides products and services to customers. This chapter continues the examination of the company introduced in Chapter Three and presents the Process Map as a methodology for meeting the needs at this Level of Performance.

Chapter Five uses the sample organization from Chapter Three to explore the role of people in improving organization and process performance. It presents the Human Performance System as a tool for understanding and meeting the Performance Needs (Goals, Design, and Management) of individuals and work teams.

The remaining chapters discuss the application of the systems view of the organization and the Three Levels framework to a variety of performance improvement opportunities faced by most North American corporations today. Chapter Six examines the role of the systems view in ensuring that top management has answered all eleven questions that must be addressed to establish a clear, viable strategy. It goes on to show how the Nine Performance Variables can help in implementing that strategy.

Through four examples, Chapter Seven shows how quality, productivity, cycle time, customer focus, and culture change efforts can fail if they do not address all Three Levels of Performance. It goes on to examine two performance improvement efforts that have benefited from covering all Three Levels.

Chapter Eight provides human resource, industrial engineering, and systems analysts with a comprehensive process for diagnosing organization Performance Needs before prescribing "solutions," such as training, reorganization, and developing management information systems. A case study illustrates each of the fourteen steps in this performance improvement process.

Chapters Nine and Ten describe the Process Improvement methodology that companies such as AT&T, Caterpillar, GTE, and Motorola have used to improve quality and customer satisfaction and reduce cycle time and costs. Chapter Eleven describes the traps we have seen that lessen the return organizations realize on their investment in process redesign.

Measuring performance and designing a performance management system is the focus of Chapter Twelve. This chapter addresses the "what," "why," and "how" of establishing a measurement system that encompasses all Three Levels of Performance. Examples illustrate establishing measures, developing a performance tracking system, and using measures as the basis for planning, feedback, performance improvement, and rewards.

Chapter Thirteen describes how to use measurement as the basis for the continuous management of processes, once they have been redesigned. It then shows how to integrate these Process Management efforts into enterprisewide "managing the organization as a system." Readers are given a description of how the systems culture differs from the traditional hierarchical culture and a set of questions for diagnosing the effectiveness of the organization system in which they work.

Chapter Fourteen presents a nine-step process for designing an organization structure that supports—rather than inhibits—the efficient delivery of high-quality products and services that meet customer needs. Using Relationship and Process Maps (introduced in Chapters Three and Four), a viable organization structure is developed for a sample company.

Chapter Fifteen draws on our experience working with human resource development professionals and shows how the Three Levels approach can help these professionals make a more substantial contribution to organization performance. It describes how the Three Levels tools can help in needs analysis, training design, and evaluation, and how they can transform the training operation into the organization's "performance department."

The final chapter describes a three-step process for getting started on a Three Levels project. It also provides examples of how the Three Levels tools have been unbundled and used to address specific issues and to help develop a customer-focused, participative, low-conflict, accountability-based culture.

How Is This Third Edition Different?

For readers familiar with the previous editions of this book:

- Chapters Nine and Ten are new. These fifty-plus pages are packed with useful, proven process improvement project tools.
- The remaining chapters have changed only moderately or slightly.

THE AUTHORS

Geary A. Rummler was cofounder of the Rummler-Brache Group (RBG). He received his BA degree, his MBA degree, and his PhD degree from the University of Michigan.

Rummler was a pioneer in the application of instructional and performance technologies to organizations, and he brought this experience to the issue of organization effectiveness. His clients in the private sector included the sales, service, and manufacturing functions of the aircraft, automobile, steel, food, rubber, office equipment, pharmaceutical, telecommunications, chemical, and petroleum industries, as well as the retail banking and airline industries. He also worked with such federal agencies as the Internal Revenue Service, the Social Security Administration, the Office of Housing and Urban Development, the General Accounting Office, and the Department of Transportation. His research and consulting took him to Europe, Japan, Korea, Malaysia, China, and Mexico.

Alan P. Brache is cofounder of the Rummler-Brache Group. His consulting, training, and writing have focused on Process Improvement and Management, which is a methodology for implementing strategy and resolving critical issues through the identification, documentation, analysis, design, measurement, and continuous improvement of business processes. Much of his recent work has involved using Process Improvement and Management as a tool for strategy implementation, designing measurement systems, and installing infrastructures for continuous improvement.

Rummler-Brache is a registered trademark. The Rummler-Brache Group is a consulting and training firm specializing in the design and development of organization performance systems for business and governmental organizations. RBG works with large and medium-sized companies in both the manufacturing and service sectors. Its clients include banking, pharmaceutical, telecommunications, insurance, technology, government, health care, utilities, petrochemical, and consumer products companies. Our firm measures the results of a specific project in terms of quality improvement, cost reduction, and/or cycle time reduction. We measure the success of a client relationship not only in terms of project results but also in terms of the degree to which the organization has institutionalized the RBG methodology and has transformed itself into a process-managed company.

We provide a technology, a set of tools, an experience base, and facilitation. Our methodology has been applied to processes that include product development, order fulfillment, hiring, procurement, manufacturing, sales, financial planning, distribution, and accounting.

RBG believes that while an outside consultant can provide tools, experience, best practices, and perspective, the changes and the results should be owned by the client organization. To achieve that objective, RBG works through internal teams and supplements its consulting with training that ultimately enables its clients to be self-sufficient.

The Rummler-Brache Group can be reached at:

800-992-8849

cservice@RummlerBrache.com

www.RummlerBrache.com

PART ONE

A FRAMEWORK FOR IMPROVING PERFORMANCE

CHAPTER ONE

VIEWING ORGANIZATIONS AS SYSTEMS

Adapt or die.

—U<small>NKNOWN</small>

The Traditional (Vertical) View of an Organization

Many managers don't understand their businesses. Given the recent "back
to basics" and "stick to the knitting" trend, they may understand their
products and services. They may even understand their customers and
their competition. However, they often don't understand at a sufficient
level of detail how their businesses get products developed, made, sold,
and distributed. We believe that the primary reason for this lack of understanding is that most managers (and nonmanagers) have a fundamentally
flawed view of their organizations.

When we ask a manager to draw a picture of his or her business (be
it an entire company, a business unit, or a department), we typically get
something that looks like the traditional organization chart shown in
Figure 1.1. While it may have more tiers of boxes and different labels, the
picture inevitably shows the vertical reporting relationships of a series of
functions.

As a picture of a business, what's missing from Figure 1.1? First of
all, it doesn't show the customers. Second, we can't see the products
and services we provide to the customers. Third, we get no sense of
the work flow through which we develop, produce, and deliver the
product or service. Thus, Figure 1.1 doesn't show what we do, whom we
do it for, or how we do it. Other than that, it's a great picture of a business. But, you may say, an organization chart isn't supposed to show those
things. Fine. Where's the picture of the business that does show those
things?

FIGURE 1.1. TRADITIONAL (VERTICAL) VIEW OF AN ORGANIZATION

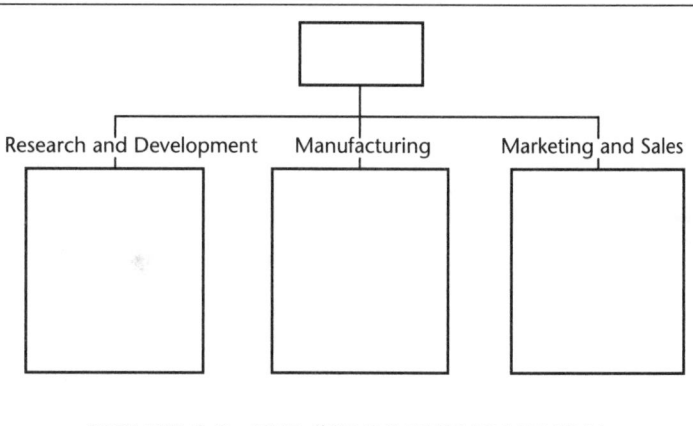

FIGURE 1.2. THE "SILO" PHENOMENON

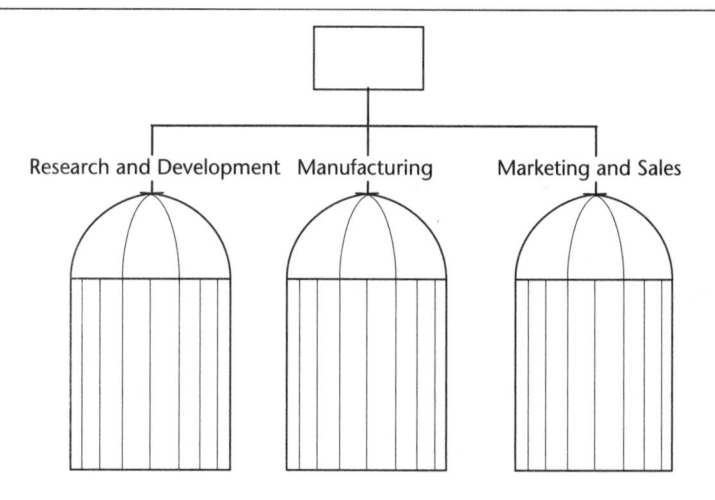

In small or new organizations, this vertical view is not a major problem because everybody in the organization knows each other and needs to understand other functions. However, as time passes and the organization becomes more complex as the environment changes and technology becomes more complicated, this view of the organization becomes a liability.

The danger lies in the fact that when managers see their organizations vertically and functionally (as in Figure 1.1), they tend to manage them vertically and functionally. More often than not, a manager of several units manages those units on a one-to-one basis. Goals are established for each function independently. Meetings between functions are limited to activity reports.

In this environment, subordinate managers tend to perceive other functions as enemies, rather than as partners in the battle against the competition. "Silos"—tall, thick, windowless structures, like those in Figure 1.2—are built around departments. These silos usually prevent interdepartmental issues from being resolved between peers at low and middle levels. A cross-functional issue around scheduling or accuracy, for example, is escalated to the top of a silo. The manager at that level addresses it with the manager at the top of the other silo. Both managers then communicate the resolution down to the level at which the work gets done.

The silo culture forces managers to resolve lower-level issues, taking their time away from higher-priority customer and competitor concerns. Individual contributors, who could be resolving these issues, take less responsibility for results and perceive themselves as mere implementers and information providers. This scenario is not even the worst case. Often, function heads are so at odds that cross-functional issues don't get addressed at all. In this environment, one often hears of things falling between the cracks or disappearing "into a black hole."

As each function strives to meet its goals, it optimizes (gets better and better at "making its numbers"). However, this functional optimization often contributes to the suboptimization of the organization as a whole. For example, marketing and sales can achieve its goals and become a corporate hero by selling lots of products. If those products can't be designed or delivered on schedule or at a profit, that's research and development's, manufacturing's, or distribution's problem; sales did its job. Research and development can look good by designing technically sophisticated products. If they can't be sold, that's sales' problem. If they can't be made at a profit, that's manufacturing's problem. Finally, manufacturing can be a star if it meets its yield and scrap goals. If the proliferation of finished goods sends inventory costs through the roof, that's the concern of distribution, or marketing, or perhaps finance. In each of these situations, a department excels against traditional measures and, in so doing, hurts the organization as a whole.

In the good old days of a seller's market, it didn't matter. A company could introduce products at its own pace, meet only its own internal quality goals, and set prices that guaranteed adequate margins. There were no serious consequences to the evolution of functional silos like those illustrated in the examples. Those days are over. Today's reality requires most organizations to compete in a buyer's market. We need a different way to look at, think about, and manage organizations.

The Systems (Horizontal) View of an Organization

A different perspective is represented by the horizontal, or systems, view of an organization, illustrated in Figure 1.3. This high-level picture of a business:

FIGURE 1.3. SYSTEMS (HORIZONTAL) VIEW OF AN ORGANIZATION

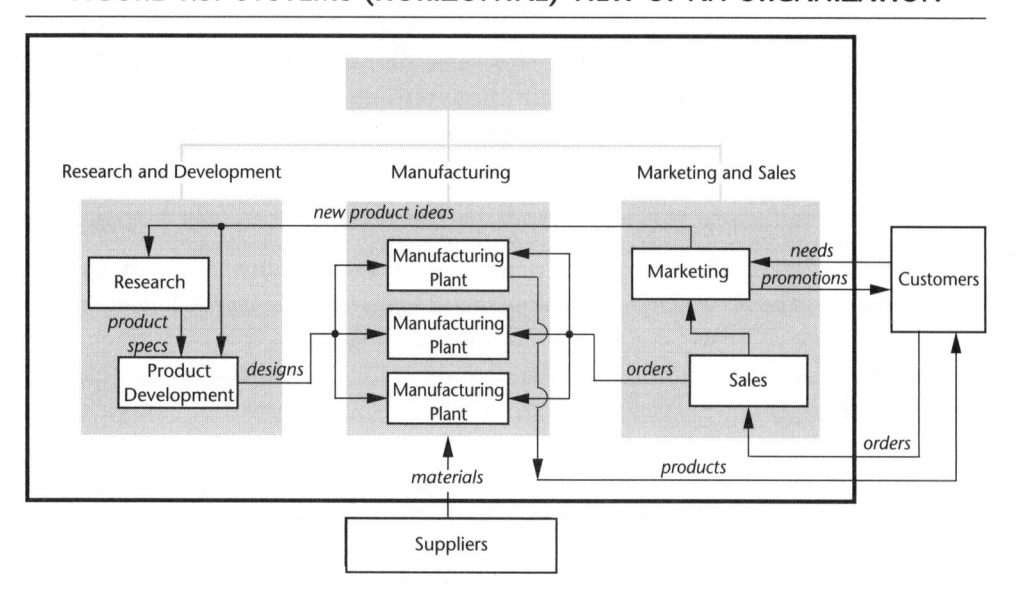

- Includes the three ingredients missing from the organization chart depicted in Figure 1.1: the customer, the product, and the flow of work
- Enables us to see how work actually gets done, which is through processes that cut across functional boundaries
- Shows the internal customer-supplier relationships through which products and services are produced

In our experience, the greatest opportunities for performance improvement often lie in the functional interfaces—those points at which the baton (for example, "production specs") is being passed from one department to another. Examples of key interfaces include the passing of new product ideas from marketing to research and development, the handoff of a new product from research and development to manufacturing, and the transfer of customer billing information from sales to finance. Critical interfaces (which occur in the "white space" on an organization chart) are visible in the horizontal view of an organization.

An organization chart has two purposes:

- It shows which people have been grouped together for operating efficiency and for human resource development.
- It shows reporting relationships.

For these purposes, the organization chart is a valuable administrative convenience. However, it should not be confused with the "what," "why," and "how" of the business; all too often, it's the organization chart, not the business, that's being managed. Managers' failure to recognize the horizontal organization explains their most common answer to the question "What do you do?" They say (to refer to Figure 1.1), "I manage A, B, and C." Assuming that A, B, and C already have competent managers, we have to ask if the senior manager sees his or her job as remanaging those functions. If so, is that a role that justifies his or her salary? We don't believe so. A primary contribution of a manager (at the second level or above) is to manage interfaces. The boxes already have managers; the senior manager adds value by managing the white space between the boxes.

In our experience, the systems view of an organization is the starting point—the foundation—for designing and managing organizations that respond effectively to the new reality of cutthroat competition and changing customer expectations.

The Organization as an Adaptive System

Our framework is based on the premise that organizations behave as adaptive systems. As Figure 1.4—often called a "super-system map"—shows,

FIGURE 1.4. AN ORGANIZATION AS AN ADAPTIVE SYSTEM

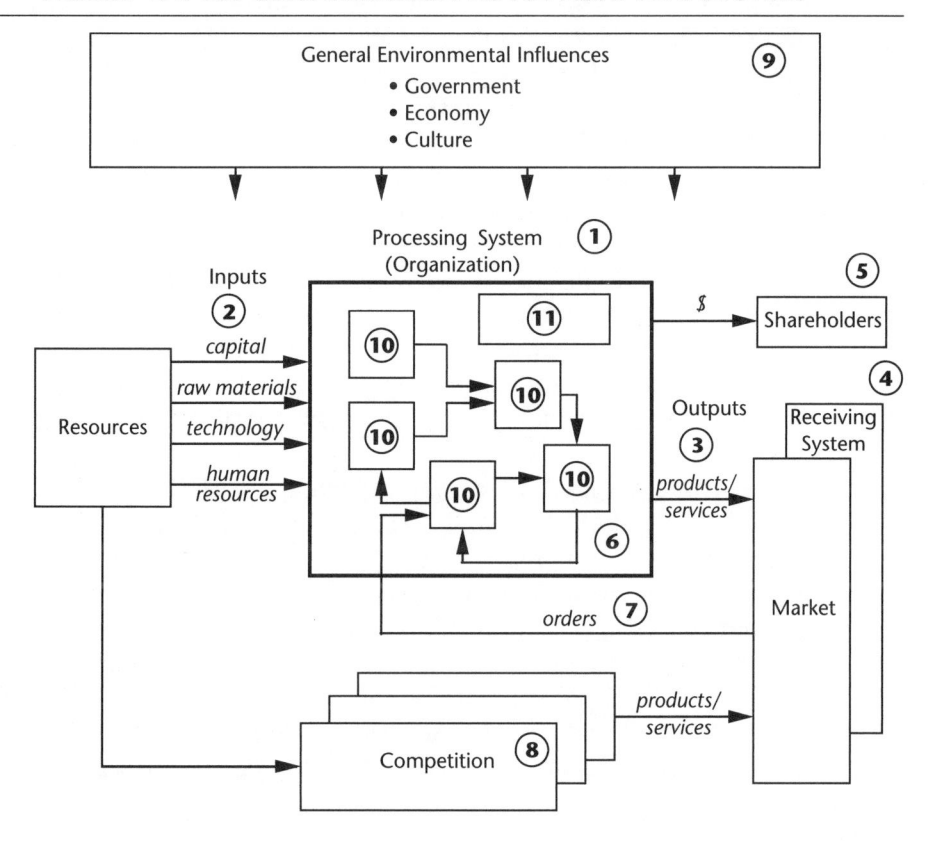

an organization is a processing system (1) that converts various resource inputs (2) into product and service outputs (3), which it provides to receiving systems, or markets (4). It also provides financial value, in the form of equity and dividends, to its shareholders (5). The organization is guided by its own internal criteria and feedback (6) but is ultimately driven by the feedback from its market (7). The competition (8) is also drawing on those resources and providing its products and services to the market. This entire business scenario is played out in the social, economic, and political environment (9). Looking inside the organization, we see functions, or subsystems, that exist to convert the various inputs into products or services (10). These internal functions, or departments, have the same systems characteristics as the total organization. Finally, the organization has a control mechanism—management (11)—that interprets and reacts to the internal and external feedback, so that the organization keeps in balance with the external environment.

To illustrate the systems framework, let us examine a fictitious firm: Computec, Inc. As shown in Figure 1.5, Computec (1) is a software development and systems engineering firm. It takes in capital, staff, technology, and materials (2) and produces products and services (3), which include systems consulting services, custom software, and software packages. It sells its products and services to a primary market—aerospace companies—as well as to other industrial and individual markets (4). It also provides financial value to its shareholders (5). Computec has various internal mechanisms for checking the accuracy and efficiency of its coding, reports, and packages (6). Its customers give it feedback (7) through additional business, complaints, references, and requests for service. Its competitors (8) are other software and systems engineering companies that serve Computec's markets. It conducts its business in the context of the American economic, social, and political environment (9). Inside Computec, such functions (10) as marketing, product development, and field operations serve as internal suppliers and customers, which convert the company inputs into the company outputs. The management team (11) establishes the strategy, monitors the internal and external feedback, establishes goals, tracks performance, and allocates resources.

We contend that this systems perspective describes every organization. Even the systems of monopolies and government entities contain everything, including a modified form of the "competition" (8) component. The markets may change, products and services come and go, but the components of the system remain the same. In fact, the only thing we can say with certainty about the future of an organization (assuming it is still in business) is that the organization will operate in a system that includes the components of the model shown in Figure 1.4. The potential evolution of a business is dramatically illustrated by Primerica, a diversified financial

FIGURE 1.5. THE SUPER-SYSTEM OF COMPUTEC, INC.

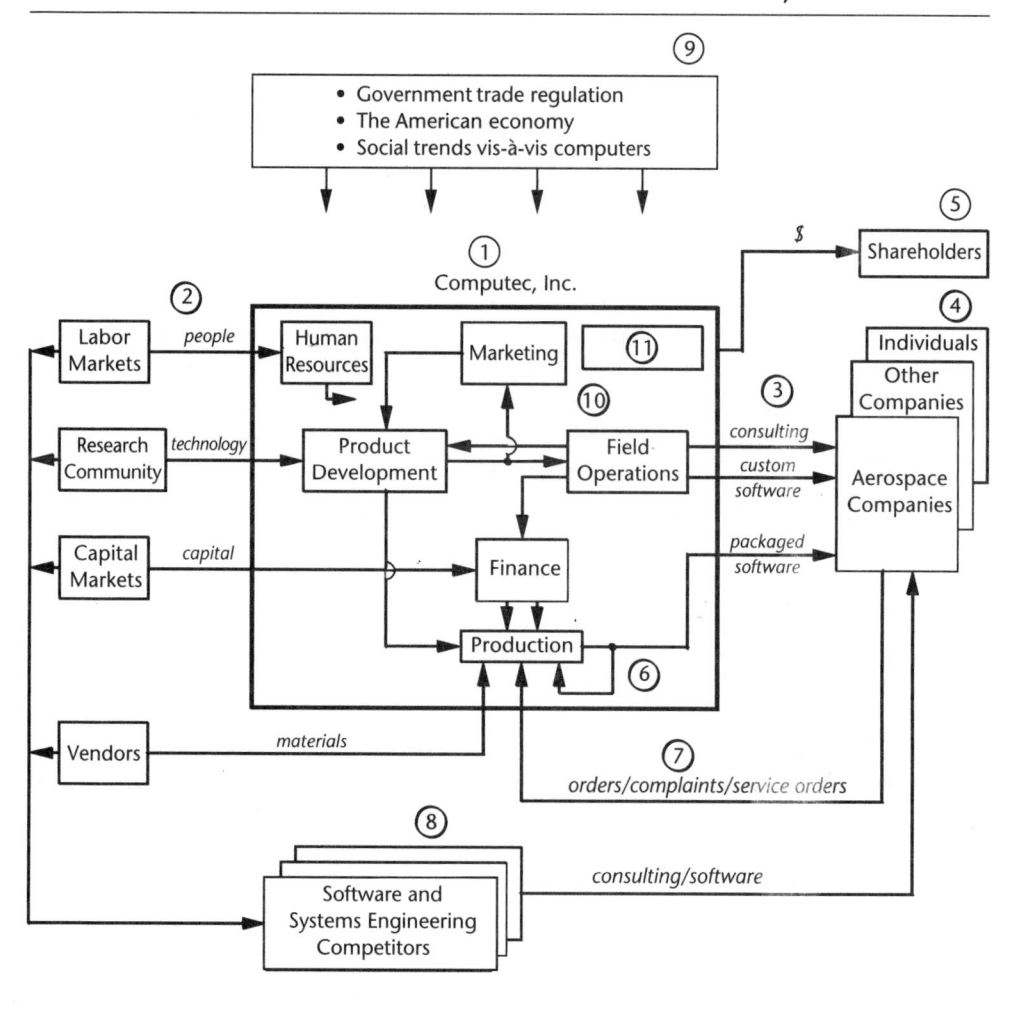

services company, which evolved from American Can, a typical "smoke-stack America" manufacturer.

The Reality of Adaptation

Primerica's transformation illustrates a fundamental element of systems theory applied to organizations—adaptation. A processing system (organization) will either adapt to its environment, especially its receiving system (market), or cease to exist. An organization seeks equilibrium with its external environment.

Not long ago, adaptation was not a burning issue. Organizations adapted to significant changes in key inputs, such as the price of fuel and the cost of capital. With each major disruption, organizations needed to make significant adjustments. However, equilibrium was reestablished in months, or perhaps in a year. Historically, the timing of disruptive events has allowed organizations to adapt before the next change.

Today, the change is more fundamental, more frequent, and less patient. In addition to sporadic fluctuations in critical inputs, such as capital and natural resources, we have an ineradicable change in the receiving system—the marketplace—that seriously threatens both revenue and profit. The primary dimension of that change is the emergence of new forms of competition from foreign and deregulated domestic sources. The market has become destabilized, upsetting the oligopolies and perennial sellers' market. Customers are demanding—and getting—different products and services, better quality, and lower prices, and the changes just keep on coming.

Systems laws and the free market enable and require organizations to adapt to these changing demands. If an organization survives, it has adapted. However, its health is a function of how well it has adapted. In our opinion, the key variable in an organization's ability to effectively and speedily adapt is its management.

What does a manager get out of the systems perspective? To the manager who doesn't take the systems view, the onslaught of change appears chaotic, unpredictable, and out of control. He or she sees a current crisis as a situation-specific event, rather than as part of a never-ending need to adapt. Adaptation is a process, not an event. The systems framework in Figure 1.4 identifies the major generic forces of change and points up the need for continuous adaptation to these constantly changing forces. An effective manager can use the systems framework in Figure 1.4 to predict and proactively cope with change.

Through what-if scenarios around each of the components of the system, the rate and direction of change can be anticipated and built into the organization strategy. Say that we are the top management team in Computec. What will we do if a change in government (component 9) results in lower entry barriers to potential foreign competitors? What if our two major competitors (component 8) merge? What personal computer products might the market (component 4) perceive to be substitutes for our minicomputer software? What computer hardware breakthroughs (component 2) could have a significant effect on our systems integration consulting services?

The rest of this book is dedicated to providing you with tools for analyzing the environments outside and inside your organization. Each of the tools is based on the systems view described here, and on the following fundamental laws of organizational systems:

1. Understanding performance requires documenting the inputs, processes, outputs, and customers that constitute a business. It is interest-

ing to describe an organization as a culture, a set of power dynamics, or a personality. However, it is essential at some point to describe what it does and how it does it. (Chapters Three and Four provide tools for such a description.)

2. Organization systems adapt or die. The success of the survivors depends on the effectiveness and speed with which they adapt to changes in the external environment (customers' needs, competitors' actions, economic fluctuations) and in their internal operations (rising costs, inefficiencies, product development opportunities).

3. When one component of an organization system optimizes, the organization often suboptimizes. (Examples of this law have already been cited.)

4. Pulling any lever in the system will have an effect on other parts of the system. You can't just reorganize, or just train, or just automate, as if you were merely adding some spice to the stew. Each of these actions changes the recipe. (See the discussion of the Three Levels of Performance, Chapter Two.)

5. An organization behaves as a system, regardless of whether it is being managed as a system. If an organization is not being managed as a system, it is not being effectively managed. (Managing organizations as systems is the subject of Chapter Thirteen.)

6. If you pit a good performer against a bad system, the system will win almost every time. We spend too much of our time "fixing" people who are not broken, and not enough time fixing organization systems that are broken. (Chapter Five is devoted to managing the Human Performance Systems in which people work.)

We are performance improvement practitioners. We find the "organizations as systems" model useful because it enables us and our clients to understand the variables that influence performance and to adjust the variables so that performance is improved on a sustained basis. Chapter Two explores the variables—the management levers—that influence each of the Three Levels of Performance.

THREE LEVELS OF PERFORMANCE: ORGANIZATION, PROCESS, AND JOB/PERFORMER

When we try to pick out anything by itself, we find it hitched
to everything else in the universe.

—JOHN MUIR

Nineteenth-century environmentalist John Muir found that each component of the ecosystem is in some way connected to all other components. The brouhaha over the snail darter, which ultimately halted construction on the Clinch River breeder reactor, was not just about a tiny fish that affects very few of us; it was about tampering with a small tile in the environmental mosaic. Each tile that is removed or changed alters, if only in a minute way, the balance of the picture.

Similarly, we have found that everything in an organization's internal and external "ecosystem" (customers, products and services, reward systems, technology, organization structure, and so on) is connected. To improve organization and individual performance, we need to understand these connections. The current mosaic may not present a very pretty picture, but it is a picture. The picture can be changed or enhanced only through a holistic approach that recognizes the interdependence of the Nine Performance Variables. We have found that the way to understand these variables is through the application of the systems view (described in Chapter One) to Three Levels of Performance.

I: The Organization Level

When we take our first, macro "systems" look at the organization, we see the fundamental view and variables discussed in Chapter Two. This level—the *Organization Level*—emphasizes the organization's relationship with its market and the basic "skeleton" of the major functions that comprise the organization. Variables at Level I that affect performance include strategies, organizationwide goals and measures, organization structure, and deployment of resources (see Figure 2.1).

II: The Process Level

The next set of critical variables affecting an organization's performance is at what we call the *Process Level*. If we were to put our organization "body" under a special x-ray, we would see both the skeleton of Level I and the musculature of the cross-functional processes that make up Level II (see Figure 2.2).

When we look beyond the functional boundaries that make up the organization chart, we can see the work flow—how the work gets done. We contend that organizations produce their outputs through myriad cross-functional work processes, such as the new-product design process,

FIGURE 2.1. THE ORGANIZATION LEVEL OF PERFORMANCE

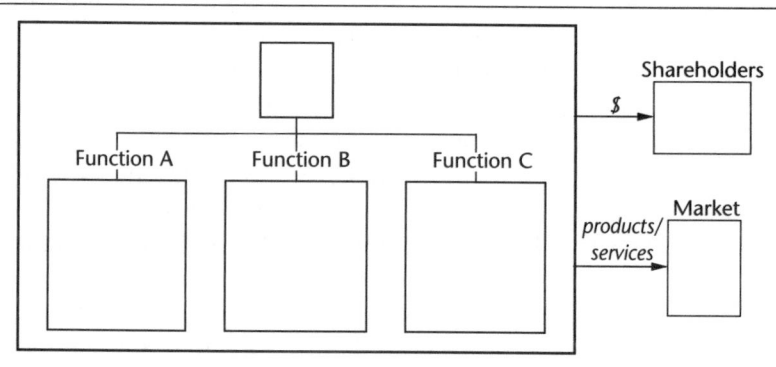

FIGURE 2.2. THE PROCESS LEVEL OF PERFORMANCE

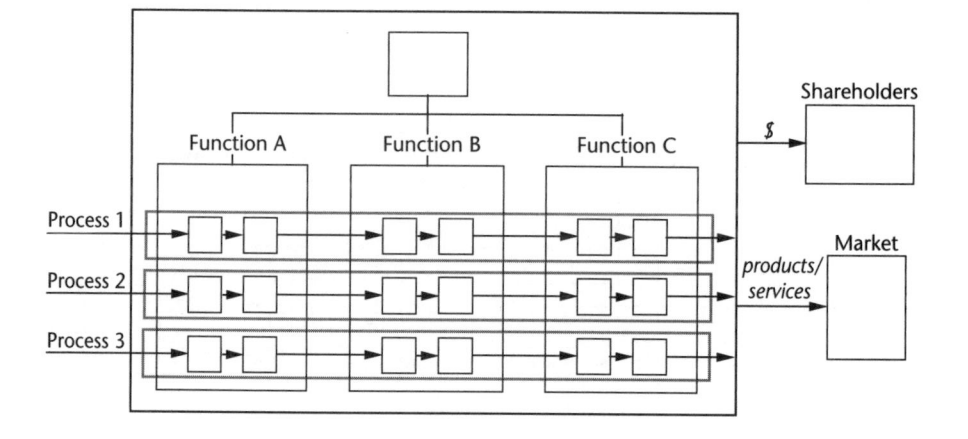

the merchandising process, the production process, the sales process, the distribution process, and the billing process (to name a very few).

An organization is only as good as its processes. To manage the Performance Variables at the Process Level, one must ensure that processes are installed to meet customer needs, that those processes work effectively and efficiently, and that the process goals and measures are driven by the customers' and the organization's requirements.

III: The Job/Performer Level

Organization outputs are produced through processes. Processes, in turn, are performed and managed by individuals doing various jobs. If we increase the power of our x-ray, as in Figure 2.3, we can see this third Level of Performance, which represents the cells of the body. The Performance Variables that must be managed at the Job/Performer Level include hiring and promotion, job responsibilities and standards, feedback, rewards, and training.

Now we have an organization x-ray that depicts the three critical interdependent Levels of Performance. The overall performance of an organization (how well it meets the expectations of its customers) is the result of goals, structures, and management actions at all Three Levels of Performance. If a customer receives a shipment of faulty framuses, for example, the cause may lie in any or all of the Three Levels. The performer may have assembled the framuses incorrectly and/or let faulty framuses be shipped. The processes that influence framus quality (including design, procurement, production, and distribution) may be at fault. The organization—represented by top managers who determine the role of framuses in the organization strategy, provide the budgets for staff and equipment, and establish the goals and measures—may also have caused the problem.

FIGURE 2.3. THE JOB/PERFORMER LEVEL OF PERFORMANCE

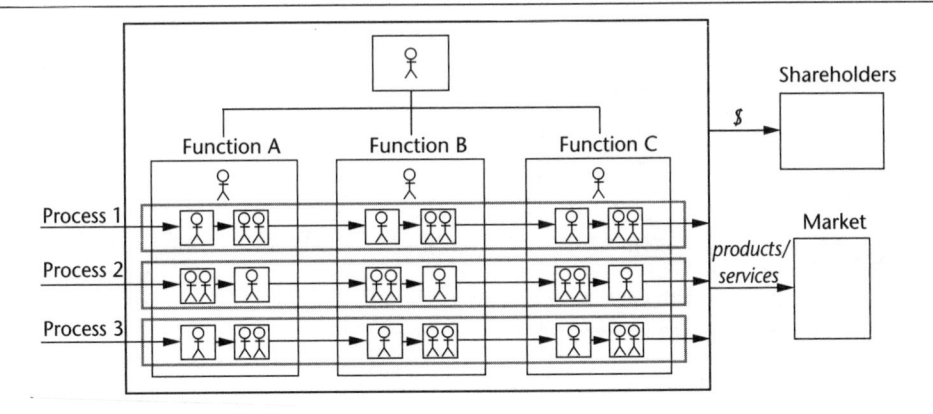

Assembly *performers* can be trained in statistical process control techniques, can be grouped into self-managed work teams, and can be empowered to stop the line if they encounter defects. However, those actions will have little effect if the design *process* has produced a framus that is difficult to assemble correctly, or if the purchasing process can't acquire enough subassemblies, or if out-of-sync sales and forecasting processes lead to product changeovers that require the assembler to follow a different procedure every day. The desire of the assembler to produce a high-quality framus will be further compromised if, in this *organization,* the primary measure and basis of rewards is "the number of units shipped."

The Three Levels framework represents an anatomy of performance. The anatomy of the human body includes a skeletal system, a muscular system, and a central nervous system. Since all of these systems are critical and interdependent, a failure in one subsystem affects the ability of the body to perform effectively. Just as an understanding of human anatomy is fundamental to a doctor's diagnosis and treatment of ailments in a body, an understanding of the Three Levels of Performance is fundamental to a manager's or analyst's diagnosis and treatment of ailments in an organization.

However, our focus is not only on curing such ailments. *Just as enlightened members of the medical community use their knowledge of human anatomy to promote wellness and preventive medicine, enlightened members of the management community use their knowledge of performance anatomy to prevent organization problems and continuously improve performance.* But they can't do it alone. These managers use the talents of their human resource, systems, and management analysts in the same way that veteran doctors benefit from the contributions of their interns, nurses, and laboratory staff.

In Chapter Seven, we describe four performance improvement efforts that are flawed by their failure to address one or more of the Three Levels of Performance. We then present two examples of organizations that have successfully implemented improvement efforts, which included action at all Three Levels.

The Nine Performance Variables

The Three Levels of Performance constitute one dimension of our framework. The second dimension comprises three factors—*Performance Needs*—that determine effectiveness at each level (and the effectiveness of any system):

1. *Goals:* the Organization, Process, and Job/Performer Levels each need specific standards that reflect customers' expectations for product and service quality, quantity, timeliness, and cost.

2. *Design:* the structure of the Organization, Process, and Job/Performer Levels needs to include the necessary components, configured in a way that enables the goals to be efficiently met.

3. *Management:* each of the Three Levels requires management practices that ensure the goals are current and are being achieved.

Combining the Three Levels with the Performance Needs results in the Nine Performance Variables. These variables, which appear in Table 2.1, represent a comprehensive set of improvement levers that can be used by managers at any level.

To illustrate the Three Levels approach, let's take a brief look at the company that we introduced in Chapter One. To refresh your memory, Computec, Inc., is a software development and systems engineering firm, with 70 percent of its business from custom software development and consulting services. The other 30 percent of revenues is generated by off-the-shelf software packages.

Computec was successful for the first thirteen years of its existence. However, during the past two years, it has experienced significant erosion of its market share. Internal problems include high turnover and sinking morale. Senior management is concerned about the situation and has recently studied the organization culture and completed programs on total quality, customer focus, and entrepreneurship. The next program is slated to be on reengineering. So far, company performance has not improved.

Realizing that previous medication may or may not have attacked the disease, we begin by diagnosing Computec. We will use the Nine Performance Variables that make up the framework of the Three Levels approach.

TABLE 2.1.   THE NINE PERFORMANCE VARIABLES

THE THREE PERFORMANCE NEEDS

		Goals	Design	Management
THE THREE LEVELS OF PERFORMANCE	Organization Level	Organization Goals	Organization Design	Organization Management
	Process Level	Process Goals	Process Design	Process Management
	Job/Performer Level	Job Goals	Job Design	Job Management

Organization Level

Before we can effectively analyze the human dimensions of performance, we need to establish a macro-level context. At the Organization Level, we examine the nature and direction of the business and the way it is set up and managed. (In Chapter Three, we will present the specific tools; the following is a discussion of the three Performance Variables at the Organization Level.)

Organization Goals. At the Organization Level, goals are part of the business strategy. All Three Levels and all of the other Performance Variables build on the direction established by the Organization Goals. In this example, our primary question is whether Computec has established clear companywide goals that reflect decisions regarding (1) the organization's competitive advantage(s), (2) new services and new markets, (3) the emphasis it will place on its various products or services and markets, and (4) the resources it is prepared to invest in its operations and the return it expects to realize on these investments. Through this line of questioning, we find that Computec has not established a clear strategy.

Because the company dominated its historic market niche (aerospace project management) until two years ago, top management never spent much time investigating strategic alternatives and preparing for the current competitive environment. The executive team has recently realized the need for a strategy and a set of companywide goals derived from that strategy. While the executives have much more work to do in this area, they have established three clear goals: to aggressively develop new products and services, to provide a level of customer support that differentiates Computec from its competition, and to eliminate the company's competitive disadvantage in the quality and timeliness of filling its orders for standard software products. While these goals are not yet measurable, they provide guidance to employees who otherwise might think that Computec is banking on growth from its existing products, does not intend to feature customer service, and intends to emphasize price (rather than quality and timeliness) as its competitive advantage.

Organization Design. This variable focuses on the structure of the organization. However, our systems view of performance suggests that "structure" should include more than where departmental boundaries have been drawn and who reports to whom. Structure includes the more important dimension of how the work gets done and whether it makes sense. We would begin by developing a Relationship Map, which shows the interfaces among the Computec functions. (The Computec organization chart and Relationship Map appear in Chapter Three.)

We have two key questions: Does Computec have all of the functional components it needs to achieve its strategy? Should any input-output connections (supplier-customer relationships) be added, eliminated, or altered?

Although Computec has occasionally introduced new services, few have been successful. The company relies on two packaged software products and three services, all of which it developed early in its history. The organization structure does not support speedy, effective new-product development and introduction, postsale customer support, or order processing. Given Computec's Organization Goals, the organization structure will have to be realigned to support these three areas of strategic emphasis.

Organization Management. An organization may have appropriate goals and a structure that enables it to function as an efficient system. However, to operate effectively and efficiently, the organization must be managed. At the Organization Level, management includes:

Goal Management: Involves creating functional subgoals that support the achievement of the overall organization goals. Failure to set goals that reflect a function's expected contribution to the entire organization will lead to the silo-based suboptimization discussed earlier.

Performance Management: Involves obtaining regular customer feedback, tracking actual performance along the measurement dimensions established in the goals, feeding back performance information to relevant subsystems, taking corrective action if performance is off target, and resetting goals so that the organization is continually adapting to external and internal reality.

Resource Management: Involves balancing the allocation of people, equipment, and budget across the system. Resource allocation should enable each function to achieve its goals, thereby making its expected contribution to the overall performance of the organization.

Interface Management: Involves ensuring that the "white space" between functions is managed. In this capacity, managers resolve functional "turf" conflicts and establish infrastructures to support the collaboration that characterizes efficient, effective internal customer-supplier relationships.

The Organization Management question is this: Is the Computec executive team managing goals, performance, resources, and interfaces?

Computec is not doing well in this area. Many of its functional goals are in conflict and support short-term profit, rather than the strategic goals around product development, customer service, and order process-ing. The company has no system for performance tracking, feedback, and improvement. Resources are allocated on a "whoever shouts loudest" basis, and the silos around product development, marketing, and opera-tions are tall and well fortified. All four Organization Management areas will have to be addressed if Computec's strategy is to succeed.

Process Level

When we lift the lid and peer inside an organization, the first things we see are the various functions. However, the systems view suggests that this perspective does not enable us to understand the way work actually gets done, which is a necessary precursor to performance improvement. For this understanding, we need to look at processes. Most key dimensions of organization performance result from cross-functional processes, such as order handling, billing, procurement, product development, customer service, and sales forecasting. Chapter Four more fully explores the Process Level; the following is an overview of its three Variables, using Computec as an example.

Process Goals. Since processes are the vehicle through which work gets produced, we need to set goals for processes. The goals for processes that touch the external customer (for example, sales, service, and billing) should be derived from the Organization Goals and other customer requirements. The goals for internal processes (for example, planning, budgeting, and recruiting) should be driven by the needs of the internal customers.

Functional goals, which are part of the Organization Management variable just discussed, should not be finalized until we see the contribu-tion that each function needs to make to the key processes. *Each function exists to serve the needs of one or more internal or external customers. If a func-tion serves external customers, it should be measured on the degree to which its products and services meet those customers' needs. If a function serves only internal customers, it should be measured on the way it meets those customers' needs and on the value it ultimately adds to the external customer. In both cases, the key links to the customer are the processes to which the function contributes.*

The installation process, for example, is critical to any company that installs equipment in a business or a residence. One function that con-tributes to the installation *process* is the sales department. Even though sales may not be part of the installation itself, it is part of the installation process because salespeople usually write orders that include specifica-tions for equipment installations. Because it has a significant impact on the quality and timeliness of an installation, the sales department should be measured on the accuracy, specificity, understandability, and timeliness with which its people provide installation specifications to the department that performs the installation. Installation specification goals are not necessarily part of the sales measurement system. However, when you look at the organization as a set of processes, and at the sales department in terms of the contributions it makes to all the processes it supports, a richer set of goals emerges.

For our overview of Computec's performance in terms of Process Goals, we have two primary questions: Does the company have goals for its processes (particularly those cross-functional processes that influence the strategy)? Are the Process Goals linked to customers' requirements and to the Organization Goals?

Given Computec's strategic thrusts and vulnerabilities, its key processes are the product or service development process, the customer support process, and the order-filling process (for its off-the-shelf software). Not surprisingly, Computec has no goals for these processes. Furthermore, its functional goals do not support the optimal performance of these processes.

Process Design. Once we have Process Goals, we need to make sure that our processes are structured (designed) to meet the goals efficiently. Processes should be logical, streamlined paths to the achievement of the goals. As part of our Computec analysis, we have one simple question that addresses this variable: Do the company's key processes consist of steps that enable it to meet Process Goals efficiently?

Earlier, we determined that Computec has no Process Goals. However, we can still examine its three key processes. The mechanism for product development and introduction is not really a process, by anyone's definition of the term. Products and services eventually emerge from poorly coordinated projects, which are characterized by functional bickering, budget overruns, missed deadlines, and lack of ownership. When the order-filling process is analyzed, the only surprise is that Computec does occasionally meet customers' expectations for quality and timeliness. A customer support process has never really been created. This company has a lot of work to do in the process area. (Examples of Computec processes appear in Chapter Four.)

Process Management. A process with a logical structure will be ineffective if it is not managed. Process Management includes the same ingredients as Organization Management:

> *Goal Management:* Involves establishing subgoals at each critical process step. These goals should drive functional goals.
>
> *Performance Management:* This involves regularly obtaining customer feedback on the process outputs, tracking process performance

along the dimensions established in the goals, feeding back performance information, identifying and correcting process deficiencies, and resetting process goals to reflect the current customer requirements and internal constraints.

Resource Management: Involves supporting each process step with the equipment, staff, and budget it needs to achieve its goals and make its expected contribution to the overall Process Goals.

Interface Management: Involves managing the "white space" between process steps, especially those that pass between functions. As at the Organization Level, where the greatest opportunities for improvement lie between functions, the greatest process improvement opportunities often lie between process steps.

Does Computec manage the goals, performance, resources, and interfaces of its key processes? Since Computec has not established a crossfunctional orientation to its business, it has not established a Process Management infrastructure for its key processes.

Job/Performer Level

The Organization and Process Levels may be beautifully wired in terms of goals, design, and management. However, the electricity will flow only if we address the needs of the people who make or break organization and process performance. If processes are the vehicles through which an organization produces its outputs, people are the vehicles through which processes function. (We address the human dimension of performance through the Job/Performer Level, which is covered in depth in Chapter Five.)

Job Goals. Just as we need to establish Process Goals that support Organization Goals, we need to establish goals for the people in those jobs that support the processes. In examining Computec, we ask what jobs contribute to each key business process, and whether the outputs and standards (goals) of these jobs are linked to the requirements of the key business processes (which are in turn linked to customer and organization requirements).

One of Computec's key processes is the off-the-shelf software order-filling process. A variety of jobs in the sales, production, and finance functions contribute to this process. Like most companies, Computec is not doing a good job of goal setting at the Job/Performer Level. The Job Goals that have been set have not been tied to process requirements. Computec needs to establish process-driven goals for each job in the functions just listed. If the company does not take this step, the odds of achieving the strategic (Organization Level) goals are low.

Job Design. We need to design jobs so that they make the optimum contribution to the Job Goals. The Job Design question is a simple one: Has Computec structured the boundaries and responsibilities of its jobs so that they enable the Job Goals to be met? Again, Computec has never looked at its business through the eyes of Organization, Process, and Job Goals, and so it has never used that perspective as the basis for structuring jobs.

Job Management. The list of ingredients in Job Management does not fall into the goals, performance, resources, and interfaces categories we used when discussing the variables of Organization Management and Process Management. Job Management is really people management. However, this definition supports managers' tendency to overmanage individuals and undermanage the environment in which they work. Therefore, Job Management is more accurately defined as managing the Human Performance System.

While it may sound as if this approach dehumanizes the management of people, the effect is quite the contrary. Human Performance System management is based on the premise that people, for the most part, are motivated and talented. If they don't perform optimally, the cause is most likely in the system (at the Organization, Process, and/or Job/Performer Level) in which they've been asked to perform. The Human Performance System, like the organization system, is composed of inputs, processes, outputs, and feedback, all of which need to be managed.

If Computec is effectively managing the Human Performance System of its key jobs, the managers and incumbents in those jobs would answer yes to these questions:

> *Performance Specifications:* Do the performers understand the outputs they are expected to produce and the standards they are expected to meet? (This question relates to Job Goals.)
>
> *Task Support:* Do the performers have sufficient resources, clear signals and priorities, and a logical set of job responsibilities? (The last part of this question relates to Job Design.)
>
> *Consequences:* Are the performers rewarded for achieving the Job Goals?
>
> *Feedback:* Do the performers know whether they are meeting the Job Goals?
>
> *Skills and Knowledge:* Do the performers have the necessary skills and knowledge to achieve the Job Goals?
>
> *Individual Capacity:* In an environment in which the five questions listed above were answered affirmatively, would the performers have

the physical, mental, and emotional capacity to achieve the Job Goals?

If Computec is to be successful, its managers must create a supportive environment around the people who will determine whether the company strategy becomes reality. For example, one of Computec's Organization Goals is to improve its customer service to the point that it becomes a competitive advantage. Its customer service hotline is currently staffed on a rotating basis by the field operations people, who consider phone duty punishing, believe it takes them away from their real jobs, and do not have the skills to handle customers' complaints effectively and efficiently. If customer service is to be a competitive advantage, then the needs related to Task Support, Consequences, and Skills and Knowledge will have to be addressed.

A Holistic View of Performance

Table 2.2 shows the questions associated with each of the Nine Performance Variables in our framework. This systems view of performance has led us to two conclusions:

- Effective management of performance requires goal setting, designing, and managing each of the Three Levels of Performance—the Organization Level, the Process Level, and the Job/Performer Level.
- The Three Levels are interdependent. For example, a job cannot be properly defined by someone who doesn't understand the requirements of the business process(es) that the job exists to support. Any attempt to implement Organization Goals will fail if those goals are not supported by processes and Human Performance Systems.

The Three Levels framework provides some insight into the short-comings of many attempts to change and improve organizations. For example:

- Most training attempts to improve organization and process performance by addressing only one Level (the Job/Performer Level) and only one dimension of the Job/Performer Level (skills and knowledge). As a result, the training has no significant long-term impact, training dollars are wasted, and trainees are frustrated and confused.
- Automation is generally an attempt to improve the performance of the Process Level. However, the investment in automation rarely

Performance Levels

TABLE 2.2. THE NINE PERFORMANCE VARIABLES WITH QUESTIONS

Performance Needs

	GOALS	DESIGN	MANAGEMENT
ORGANIZATION LEVEL	ORGANIZATION GOALS • Has the organization's strategy or direction been articulated and communicated? • Does this strategy make sense, in terms of the external threats and opportunities and the internal strengths and weaknesses? • Given this strategy, have the required outputs of the organization and the level of performance expected from each output been determined and communicated?	ORGANIZATION DESIGN • Are all relevant functions in place? • Are all functions necessary? • Is the current flow of inputs and outputs between functions appropriate? • Does the formal organization structure support the strategy and enhance the efficiency of the system?	ORGANIZATION MANAGEMENT • Have appropriate function goals been set? • Is relevant performance measured? • Are resources appropriately allocated? • Are the interfaces between functions being managed?
PROCESS LEVEL	PROCESS GOALS • Are goals for key processes linked to customer and organization requirements?	PROCESS DESIGN • Is this the most efficient and effective process for accomplishing the Process Goals?	PROCESS MANAGEMENT • Have appropriate process subgoals been set? • Is process performance managed? • Are sufficient resources allocated to each process? • Are the interfaces between process steps being managed?
JOB/PERFORMER LEVEL	JOB GOALS • Are job outputs and standards linked to process requirements (which are in turn linked to customer and organization requirements)?	JOB DESIGN • Are process requirements reflected in the appropriate jobs? • Are job steps in a logical sequence? • Have supportive policies and procedures been developed? • Is the job environment ergonomically sound?	JOB MANAGEMENT • Do the performers understand the Job Goals (outputs they are expected to produce and standards they are expected to meet)? • Do the performers have sufficient resources, clear signals and priorities, and a logical Job Design? • Are the performers rewarded for achieving the Job Goals? • Do the performers know if they are meeting the Job Goals? • Do the performers have the necessary knowledge and skill to achieve the Job Goals? • If the performers were in an environment in which the five questions listed above were answered "yes," would they have the physical, mental, and emotional capacity to achieve the Job Goals?

realizes its maximum return because the link is not made between the process and the Organization Goals to which it is intended to contribute: the process is inefficient, and so the result is an automated inefficient process; and the automation fails to consider the needs of the Human Performance Systems of the people involved in the process.

- If programs to improve performance in such areas as quality, productivity, and customer focus are just hype, they don't address the needs of any of the Three Levels. Programs that establish Organization Goals and train employees usually fail to address the needs at the Process Level and the goals, feedback, and consequences required at the Job Level.

Using the Three Levels Framework

This framework (summarized in Table 2.2), as well as the process and tools that it has spawned, has evolved over twenty years of research and application in companies, agencies, divisions, departments, and stores. It has been used as:

- A *tool* for diagnosing and eliminating deficient performance (for example, excessive semiconductor chip manufacturing and delivery cycle time; loss of margins in a retail chain)
- An *engine* for continuously improving systems that are performing adequately (for example, increasing responsiveness to airlines' needs for unique aircraft configurations; increasing timeliness of telecommunications customer service)
- A *road map* for guiding an organization in a new direction (for example, toward entering the software business or selling in a newly deregulated environment)
- A *blueprint* for designing a new entity (for example, an electronics "factory of the future"; a marketing department in a public utility)

The Three Levels framework has proved valuable to:

- *Executives,* who provide the vision, leadership, and impetus for change
- *Managers* at all levels, who implement companywide changes by providing vision and leadership on the Organization Level for the departments they manage
- *Analysts,* who design the systems and procedures that enable managers to implement the change

For all three of these forces of change to work efficiently in concert, they must have the same objectives and process. The Three Levels of Performance framework has been designed to meet this need. The remainder of this book addresses the performance improvement responsibilities of all three roles.

PART TWO

EXPLORING THE THREE LEVELS OF PERFORMANCE

CHAPTER THREE

THE ORGANIZATION LEVEL OF PERFORMANCE

All are but parts of one stupendous whole.

—ALEXANDER POPE

A wealthy owner of a baseball franchise will often recruit the most highly skilled (and highly priced) talent and wonder why his or her team doesn't win the World Series. A championship team often pales in position-to-position matchups; it wins because somehow the whole is greater than the sum of its parts. The distinction is usually that the winning team as a whole, not just each individual player and function (hitting, pitching, defense), is being managed.

Similarly, an organization can be greater than the sum of its parts only if the whole organization is managed. An organization may have people with outstanding experiential and academic credentials. Its functions, such as marketing, production, and research, may look good when benchmarked against those departments in other organizations. However, its results may be less than stellar because its executives manage functions and people without placing them in a larger organizational context. This practice is a prescription for suboptimization, a situation in which the whole equals less than the sum of its parts. Our first step in managing organization performance—Level I of the Three Levels—is to acknowledge the viewpoints that often characterize the current situation.

The Customer's View of the Organization. "What is going on with these people? Why can't they give me a product that does what I need it to do and is available when I need it? Where is the follow-up service I was told I'd be getting? Why do I feel that I know more about the product than they do? Why do I have to deal with a different person each time I contact them? Why can't these people get their act together?"

The Supplier's View of the Organization. "Why don't these people ever know what parts they need more than three days ahead of time? Do they realize that because we have to expedite nearly every order, they end up paying top dollar? Why do they keep changing the specifications? Why do they discontinue at least one product every six months, which results in a large number of part returns? Why don't they ever take us up on our offer to visit their plant, at our expense, so we can learn what's happening in their business? Why can't these people get their act together?"

The Employees' View of the Organization. "Why can we match our competitor's quality only by dramatically increasing inspection (which drives our costs through the roof)? Who told sales that we have the capability to offer that service and meet that deadline? Where do the product development people come up with these ideas? So what are our priorities this week? Why don't section managers cooperate with each other? Don't these people realize that if we don't change the way we do business, we won't survive? How does top management expect us to believe that quality comes first when, at the end of every month, they say, 'I don't care; ship it!'? Why are these people, who are paid above the industry average, still not motivated? Why can't we get our act together?"

The Shareholders' View of the Organization. "Why do I continuously see reorganizations, executive shuffles, product launches, and improvement campaigns, but no money in my pocket or increase in the value of my stock? Why can't these people get their act together?"

Exploring the Organization Level

Before we can effectively address the bleak but all-too-common situation just depicted, we have to understand it. The best way we have found for understanding how an organization functions is to see it as an adaptive system. This view, which is described in depth in Chapter One (see Figure 1.4), maintains that every organization operates as a processing system, which converts inputs (such as resources and customer orders) into outputs (products and services) that it provides to its customers. The organization continuously adapts in order to maintain equilibrium with its environment, which includes its market, its competition, its resource pool, and the socioeconomic context in which it functions. As we discussed in Chapter One, an organization that adapts nimbly is likely to succeed; an organization that adapts lethargically is likely to fail.

The systems view does not apply only to an entire company or agency. If we look inside an organization, we see that it is made up of layer upon layer of systems. As Figure 3.1 illustrates, one of the systems in an

FIGURE 3.1. LAYERS OF ORGANIZATION SYSTEMS
IN AN AUTOMOBILE COMPANY

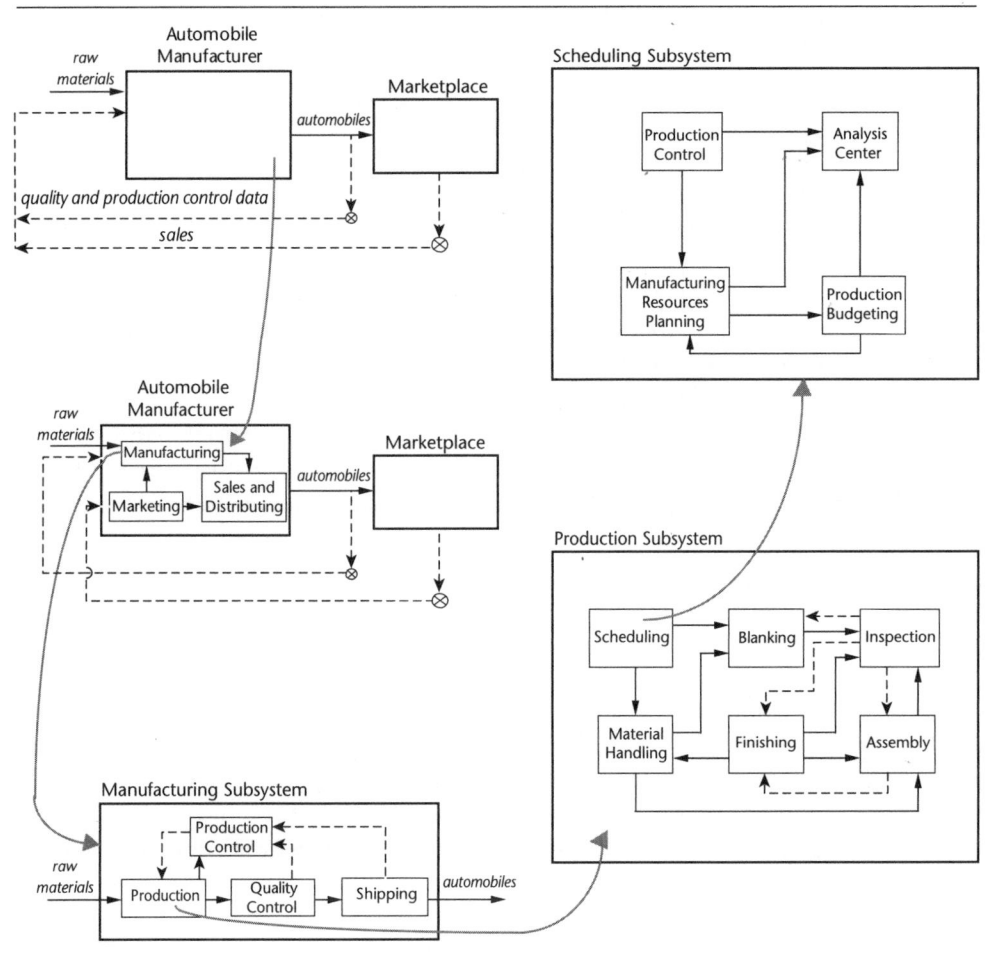

automobile company is its manufacturing system. One of manufacturing's components is its production system. Production is made up of a number of systems, one of which is scheduling. By peeling back the layers of the organization like an onion in this manner, we have found that we can understand how it operates, as well as the variables affecting its performance, at any level of detail.

Understanding and Managing the Organization Level

If executives do not manage performance at the Organization Level, the best they can expect is modest performance improvement. At worst, efforts at other levels will be counterproductive. We have observed a number of companies in which quality improvement is a major thrust. They have embraced Statistical Process Control (SPC) tools, Just-In-Time (JIT) techniques, Manufacturing Resource Planning (MRP II) systems, and employee empowerment practices. They wonder why the quality gains aren't more dramatic. Inevitably, it is because:

- *The various quality efforts are not driven by a clear statement of organization strategy.* The strategy should define the role of quality in the business, the types of quality that represent the competitive advantage, and the organizationwide, customer-driven measures of quality.
- *The organization has not been designed in a way that supports maximum quality.* The impact of the noble efforts in training, tools, systems, and procedures is limited by the organization structure and relationships among departments.
- *The organization is not managed with quality as the driver.* Quality has not been built into tactical goals, performance tracking and feedback, problem solving, or resource allocation. Quality is typically rolled out function by function (there is a design quality program, an engineering quality program, a manufacturing quality program). The tremendous threats and opportunities within the "white space" on the organization chart are ignored.

Each of these shortcomings represents a failure to manage one of the three Performance Variables at the Organization Level. We believe that an organization's managers can "get their act together" (the plea of the customers, suppliers, shareholders, and employees quoted at the beginning of this chapter) only by understanding and pulling the levers of Organization Goals, Organization Design, and Organization Management.

The need to understand the Organization Level is not limited to managers. Analysts (human resource specialists, systems analysts, industrial engineers) also need to understand the nature and dynamics of the Organization Level. With the context that this understanding provides, they are better able to design improvements that have the maximum positive impact on the performance of their organizations.

The Performance Variables at the Organization Level

Organization Goals. At the Organization Level, goals are strategic. A good strategy identifies the organization's:

- Products and services
- Customer groups (markets)

- Competitive advantage(s)
- Product and market priorities (emphasis areas)

Organization Goals, therefore, are stated in terms of how well products and services are expected to do in the various markets to which they are offered. An effective set of Organization Goals includes:

- The values of the organization
- Customers' requirements
- Financial and nonfinancial expectations
- Targets for each product family and market
- Expectations for each competitive advantage to be established or enhanced

Procedurally, Organization Goals should be:

- Based on the Critical Success Factors for the company's industry
- Derived from competitive and environmental scanning information
- Derived from benchmarking information (intelligence on the performance of systems and functions in exemplary organizations)
- Quantifiable whenever possible
- Clear to all who have to understand and be guided by them

Organization Goals for Computec, Inc., the organization we introduced in Chapter One, might include:

- *Never sacrifice quality for short-term net income.*
- *Increase the company's customer satisfaction rating to 98 percent by the end of the year.*
- *Introduce three new software products and two new systems integration services within two years.*
- *Capture 60 percent of the aerospace project management market within three years.*
- *By the end of the year, introduce two new customer services that differentiate Computec from its competitors.*
- *Reduce software package order cycle time to an average of seventy-two hours by the end of next year.*
- *By the end of next year, fill orders with 100 percent accuracy.*
- *Generate $300 million of revenue, $35 million of profit, and $16 million of economic value added (EVA) next year and grow each of these financial measures by 12 percent in each of the following two years.*

These Organization Goals are quantitative, customer oriented, competitive advantage–driven, and easily understood. With these and other goals as a context, Computec can embark on performance improvement efforts in the areas of quality, productivity, total cycle time, and cost control. These Organization Goals will serve as the high-level measures of the success of these efforts.

Most important, the Computec Organization Goals are clearly derived from its strategy. They reflect the executives' tough choices regarding products, markets, competitive advantages, and priorities. (To help identify those tough choices, we have developed a detailed set of questions that need to be answered in applying the systems view and the Three Levels of Performance to strategy development and implementation; those questions are included in Chapter Six.)

In summary, these are the questions for the Organization Goals:

- Has the organization's strategy or direction been articulated and communicated?
- Does this strategy make sense in terms of external threats and opportunities and internal strengths and weaknesses?
- Given this strategy, have the required outputs of the organization and the level of performance expected from each output been determined and communicated?

Since this is our first discussion of goals, it is probably a good place to take a stand. Some of the followers of the late quality-and-productivity guru W. Edwards Deming are avidly against goal setting. They believe that goal achievement leads to complacency, which serves as a barrier to continuous improvement. That can happen. However, we believe that goals should be continually evaluated and reset to fit changing requirements and capabilities. If goals are adapted in this way, they can support rather than hinder the noble pursuit of continuous improvement. (Please note that reestablishment of goals is one of the key steps in Performance Management, which is discussed later in this chapter.)

Organization Design. Unfortunately, establishing clear Organization Goals is only the first step. Managers and analysts need to design an organization that enables the Goals to be met. To find out if the existing organization supports the achievement of the Organization Goals, we develop a Relationship Map. As the name indicates, the purpose of this picture of the business is to depict the customer-supplier relationships among the line and staff functions that make up the business. Because the Relationship Map makes visible the inputs and outputs that flow among functions, it shows what is going on in the "white space" between the boxes on the organization chart. Figure 3.2 contains a traditional organization chart for Computec. Figure 3.3 displays a Computec Relationship Map.

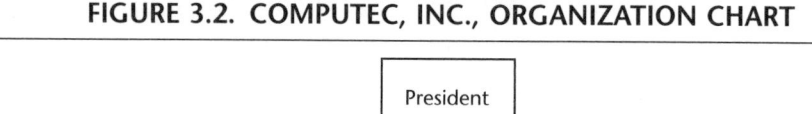

FIGURE 3.2. COMPUTEC, INC., ORGANIZATION CHART

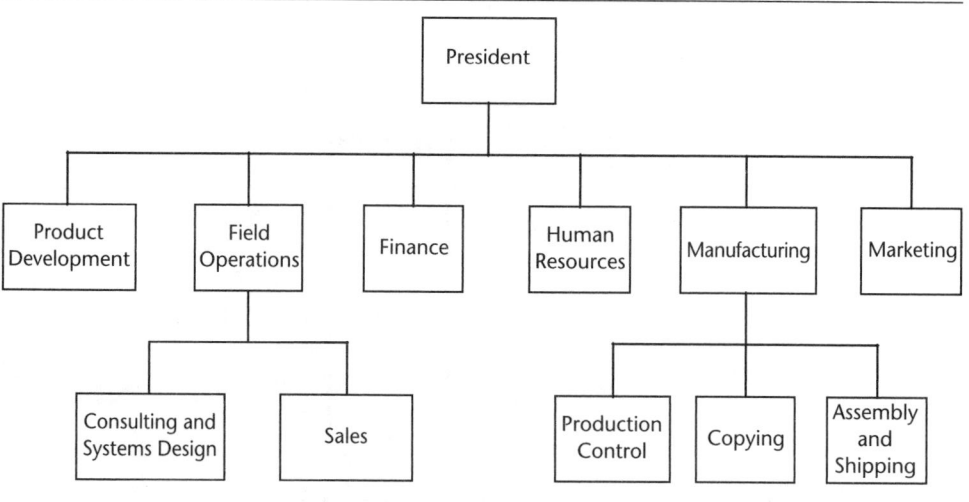

We use the Relationship Map to:

- Understand how work currently gets done (how the organization behaves as a system)
- Identify "disconnects in the organization wiring" (missing, unneeded, confusing, or misdirected inputs or outputs)
- Develop functional relationships that eliminate the disconnects
- Evaluate alternative ways to group people and establish reporting hierarchies

Our initial approach to Organization Design, therefore, is to examine and improve the input-output relationships among functions. To us, the structure depicted by the Relationship Map is most important because that's the structure through which work gets done. *When the focus is placed on the internal and external customer-supplier relationships, the standard organization chart becomes less important.* However, the reporting hierarchy can facilitate or impede the flow of work. (We have devoted Chapter Fourteen to a discussion of organization structure. In that chapter, we address the need for the vertical and horizontal systems to peacefully coexist.)

In summary, these are the questions that underlie the variable of Organization Design:

- Are all relevant functions in place?
- Are all functions necessary?
- Is the current flow of inputs and outputs between functions appropriate?
- Does the formal organization structure support the strategy and enhance the efficiency of the system?

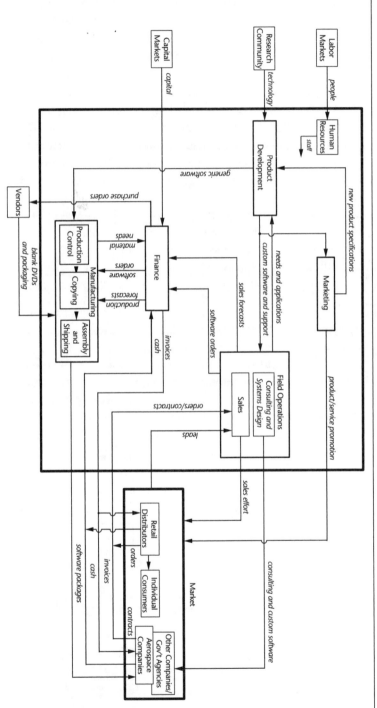

FIGURE 3.3. RELATIONSHIP MAP FOR COMPUTEC, INC.

An examination of Computec's Relationship Map reveals a number of Organization Design disconnects that could hamper the company's ability to achieve its Organization Goals. These disconnects include:

- Marketing does not participate in sales forecasting.
- Marketing is not linked to field operations.
- Marketing does not identify needs through market research.
- No function provides customer service.
- DVD orders have to go through both sales and finance before they go to production to be filled.
- Production forecasts are done by finance.

Unfortunately, identifying disconnects doesn't make them disappear. Computec needs to design an organization that will eliminate the disconnects that are hampering its ability to achieve Organization Goals. (Chapter Twelve discusses the use of the systems view and the Relationship Map to structure an organization. In addition to providing examples of structuring an organization to remove disconnects, Chapter Twelve shows how mapping and derivative tools can be used to support a new strategy, to create a new enterprise or function, and to implement systemic improvements, such as automation and staff reduction. Chapter Thirteen addresses the need to manage the structure that has been created.)

Organization Management. Once the Organization Goals and Organization Design have been established, the organization needs to be managed. Managing the organization—the horizontal organization—as a system includes four dimensions:

1. *Goal Management:* Each function needs to have subgoals, which support the achievement of the Organization Goals. As we discussed in Chapter One, an effective set of subgoals does not permit the optimization of the functional silos, to the detriment of the system as a whole. If each Computec function is to make its maximum contribution to the company as a whole, it will need to be measured against goals that are derived from its strategy (Organization Goals) and that help other functions achieve their goals. For example, Computec's product development department should have goals that:

   - Reflect the Organization Goal of ambitious and speedy new product and service development
   - Ensure that its new products and services are driven by the needs of the marketplace, not by technical wizardry
   - Require it to design products and services that marketing can sell
   - Require it to design products and services that field operations and production can sell, make, and deliver with the quality and timeliness required by customers and the profit required by Computec

2. *Performance Management:* To achieve the goals, performance needs to be managed at the Organization Level. To continue the Computec product development example, Computec senior management needs to:

   - Obtain regular feedback on product effectiveness from Computec's customers
   - Measure the product development, marketing, and field operations departments on their contributions to the Organization Goal of product development and introduction
   - Provide feedback to product development, marketing, and field operations on their product development and product introduction performance
   - Ensure that cross-functional problem-solving teams address product development and product introduction problems
   - Reestablish product development and product introduction goals if there is a change in the market

   Peeling back one layer of the organizational onion, the management of product development needs to:

   - Regularly obtain feedback on product effectiveness from Computec's customers and from product development's internal customers—marketing and field operations
   - Measure performance in terms of the goals it has established (product development will *get* performance in the areas in which it *measures* performance)
   - Feed back performance information to the subunits within product development
   - Solve problems that impede its progress toward the function's goals
   - Reestablish goals to fit the current reality of its internal and external markets

3. *Resource Management:* Computec product development has two resource needs: sufficient people and dollars to meet its goals, and allocation of its resources to those areas of product development that will enable the goals to be met. As with Performance Management, this places responsibility on both the senior management of Computec and the management of product development. If the executive committee members want to reduce costs, they would be foolish to mandate a 10 percent personnel reduction in all departments. They should realize that cutting 10 percent of the product development staff may very well compromise one of Computec's key Organization Goals; perhaps headcounts should not be reduced at all in product development and should be reduced by 20 percent in another department. Since

Organization Goals will be achieved only through the horizontal organization, top management must allocate resources across the entire horizontal organization. Peeling back one layer of the onion, we see that the vice president of product development is responsible for allocating resources across the horizontal organization that exists within his or her department.

4. *Interface Management:* If the senior managers of Computec take the systems view of performance, they will realize that key barriers to and opportunities for Organization Goal achievement reside in the "white space" between functions. They will realize that the product introduction goal will be achieved only if the product development and product introduction system (which includes the functions of marketing, product development, and field operations) works well. The top team (ideally, aided by a Relationship Map) should be clear on the inputs and outputs that flow among these three functions and should spend a significant amount of time ensuring that this flow—this set of interfaces—is smooth.

The vice president of product development has the same responsibility: to ensure that the various subcomponents within that department are effectively and efficiently working together.

In summary, these are the questions for Organization Management:

- Have appropriate functional goals been set?
- Is relevant performance measured?
- Are resources appropriately allocated?
- Are the interfaces between functions being managed?

Summary

If the Organization Level of Performance is not being defined, designed, and managed, there is no context for or driver of human and system performance. In this environment, well-intentioned activities are carried out in a vacuum and are frequently off the mark. Considerations related to the Organization Level are important to any organizational unit, from an entire company or agency to the smallest subdepartment. Variables and tools concerned with the Organization Level can be used by:

- *Executives,* to understand how the business operates, to refine the organization strategy and measures, to establish appropriate departmental relationships, to create a workable organization structure, and to manage the interfaces among departments

- *Managers,* to understand how their businesses operate and how they fit into the big picture, to establish department goals, to strengthen relationships with other departments, to create a workable organization structure, and to manage the interfaces among subunits within their departments
- *Analysts,* to understand how their client organizations currently operate and how they measure results, to identify areas where their efforts will have the greatest payoffs, to determine the impact of system changes and other proposed improvements on the organization as a whole, and to recommend enhancements that will have a positive effect on organizationwide performance

By answering questions such as those listed for each of the three Performance Variables at the Organization Level, and by using tools such as the Relationship Map, one can guide organization performance and bring it under control. This chapter began with a bleak scenario involving customers, suppliers, employees, and shareholders. Effective management of the Organization Level can go a long way toward converting those viewpoints.

The Customer's View of the Organization. "These people are highly responsive to our needs. They frequently know what we want and need before we do. While their product is good, what keeps us coming back is the after-sale service. They don't promise what they can't deliver. We have established a solid, long-term relationship with our account executive. We're proud to have them as a vendor."

The Supplier's View of the Organization. "These people appear to know where they're going. They give us plenty of lead time when they need parts for a new or modified product. They enforce especially tight specifications on those dimensions of our parts that contribute to their competitive edges. And they include us in the process of developing their competitive edges. Because they treat us as a business partner, we'll go the extra mile for them. We're proud to be their vendor."

The Employees' View of the Organization. "Everyone in this organization takes responsibility for doing the job right the first time. We can't afford any mistakes. Before they promise a modified product or a nonstandard delivery schedule to a customer, sales talks to product development, manufacturing, and distribution. I can reach fairly quick agreement with other departments because we all understand the interdependencies and the priorities necessary to keep our customers coming back. Products are developed by a team composed of marketing, manufacturing, and product development. Meetings are frequently attended by customers and prospects. Every employee knows the strategy of the company and how his or her goals contribute to that strategy. I understand my priorities. When they change, I know why. People realize that their role is to serve the needs of internal or external customers. Section managers know that they will not achieve their goals if they don't cooperate with the sections that serve as their suppliers and customers. I am motivated by the challenge provided by my job and by the support I am given. I realize that I am a critical link in the chain. I'm proud to work here."

The Shareholders' View of the Organization. "This company is making me money."

Utopia? Not in our experience. These prevailing views are the natural result of an organization that "has its act together" at each of the Three Levels of Performance, and it all starts at the Organization Level. The Performance Variables and Tools at the Organization Level help identify what needs to get done (goals), the relationships necessary to get it done (design), and the practices that remove the impediments to getting it done (management). With an effective Organization Level as a foundation, we can begin to understand, analyze, and manage performance at the Process and Job/Performer Levels, which are covered in the next two chapters.

CHAPTER FOUR

THE PROCESS LEVEL OF PERFORMANCE

*Looking out upon the future, I do not view the process with
any misgivings. I could not stop it if I wished; no one can stop
it. Like the Mississippi, it just keeps rolling along.*

—WINSTON CHURCHILL

We have found the Process Level to be the least understood and least managed level of performance. Processes are rolling along (or, frequently, stumbling along) in organizations, whether we attend to them or not. We have two choices—we can ignore processes and hope that they do what we wish, or we can understand them and manage them. We have proposed (Chapter One) that the only way to truly understand the way work gets done is to view an organization horizontally (as a system) rather than vertically (as a hierarchy of functions). When you view an organization horizontally, you see business processes.

In Chapter Three, we discussed the systems view at the Organization Level. We introduced the Relationship Map as a tool for viewing an organization as a system. We showed how a tremendous amount of learning and eventual improvement can result from the documentation and examination of the input-output (customer-supplier) linkages depicted in a Relationship Map.

However, between every input and every output is a process. Our understanding and improvement are incomplete if we don't peel back the onion and examine the processes through which inputs are converted to outputs. While the Organization Level provides a perspective, sets a direction, and points to areas of threat and opportunity, our experience strongly suggests that the Process Level is where the most substantive change usually needs to take place. A clear strategy and logical reporting relationships (Organization Level) and skilled, reinforced people (Job/ Performer Level) cannot compensate for flawed business and management processes.

What Is a Process?

A business process is a series of steps designed to produce a product or service. Some processes (such as programming) may be contained wholly within a function. However, most processes (such as order fulfillment) are cross-functional, spanning the "white space" between the boxes on the organization chart.

Some processes result in a product or service that is received by an organization's external customer. We call these *primary processes*. Other processes produce products that are invisible to the external customer but essential to the effective management of the business. We call these *support processes*. The third category of processes—*management processes*—includes actions managers should take to support the business processes. Examples of these types of business processes appear in Table 4.1.

Understanding and Managing the Organization Level

A process can be seen as a "value chain." By its contribution to the creation or delivery of a product or service, each step in a process should add value to the preceding steps. For example, one step in the product development process may be "prototype market-tested." This step adds value by ensuring that the product is appealing to the market before the design is finalized.

Processes are also consumers of resources. They need to be assessed not only in terms of the value they add, but also in terms of the amount of capital, people, time, equipment, and material they require to produce that value.

At the Organization Level, we "peel back the onion" to increase our understanding of the customer-supplier relationships among functions. At the Process Level, we peel back the onion by breaking processes into subprocesses. The manufacturing process, for example, may comprise these subprocesses: scheduling, tooling, fabrication, assembly, and testing.

Why Look at Processes?

An organization is only as effective as its processes. Organization Goals (see Chapter Three) can be achieved only through logical business processes, such as those listed in Table 4.1. For example, one of an automobile manufacturer's Organization Goals may be to reduce the time it takes to deliver a car with the options requested by a customer. The company cannot hope to meet this goal if it has an inefficient ordering process or a convoluted distribution process.

TABLE 4.1.   EXAMPLES OF BUSINESS PROCESSES

Generic Primary Processes

- Business generation
- Product or service development and introduction
- Manufacturing
- Distribution
- Billing
- Order fulfillment
- Customer service
- Warranty administration

Industry-Specific Primary Processes

- Loan processing (banking)
- Claim adjudication (insurance)
- Grant allocation (government)
- Merchandise return (retail)
- Food preparation (restaurant)
- Baggage handling (airline)
- Operator services (telecommunications)
- User-manual writing (computer)
- Reservation handling (hotel)

Generic Support Processes

- Formal strategic and tactical planning
- Budgeting
- Recruiting
- Training
- Facilities management
- Purchasing
- Information management

Generic Management Processes
- Strategic and tactical planning
- Goal setting
- Resource allocation
- Human performance management
- Operations review performance monitoring

When we view the situation from the top down, we see that process effectiveness is a major variable in the achievement of Organization Goals. We can also look at the value of processes from the bottom up. At the Job/Performer Level, we can take a variety of steps to improve performance (see Chapter Five). For example, we can improve our recruiting and promotion practices. We can provide more specific, up-to-date job descriptions, more effective tools, and more attractive incentives. We can drive decision making down in the organization. We can empower teams to solve problems in their work units. However, *even talented and motivated people can improve organization performance only as much as the business processes allow.*

To continue our automobile distribution example, salespeople may be thoroughly completing order forms, data-entry clerks may be accurately coding information, and dock crews may be efficiently loading cars onto trucks. However, the effectiveness of any improvement in their performance could be limited by the logic (or illogic) of the total distribution process, made up of the order entry, production scheduling, and transportation subprocesses.

People in jobs such as these can certainly influence the effectiveness and efficiency of the processes to which they contribute. However, we have found that individual and team problem solving rarely focuses on process improvement. Furthermore, actions taken in a single organizational unit often lead to the reinforcement of the functional silos and the system suboptimization discussed in Chapter One. *The net message is that, over the long haul, strong people cannot compensate for a weak process. All too often, management relies on individual or team heroics to overcome fundamentally flawed processes.* Why not *fix* the processes and enlist our heroes in the battle against the competition?

Finally, the Process Level is important because *process effectiveness and efficiency should drive a multitude of business decisions. For example, a reorganization serves no purpose if it doesn't improve process performance. Jobs should be designed so that people can best contribute to process outputs. Automation is a waste of money if it calcifies an illogical process.* The pivotal link between organization performance and individual performance can be established only through the three variables at the Process Level—Process Goals, Process Design, and Process Management.

The Performance Variables at the Process Level

Process Goals. Each primary process and each support process exists to make a contribution to one or more Organization Goals. Therefore, each process should be measured against Process Goals that reflect the contribution that the process is expected to make to one or more Organization Goals. In our experience, most processes do not have goals. While functions (departments) usually have goals, most key processes cross functional boundaries. If we are working in an organization in which billing is a key process, and if we ask for the goals of the billing process, the response usually is "Oh, you mean the goals of the billing department." When we reply that we really do mean the billing process—including those steps accomplished outside the billing department—we frequently get blank stares.

We believe that measurement is most effective if it is done in relation to targets, or goals. Process Goals are derived from three sources: Organization Goals, customers' requirements, and benchmarking information. Process benchmarking—comparing a process to the same process in an exemplary organization—is particularly useful. Often the organization that is best in its class for a given process is not a competitor and is therefore easy to study. An organization can learn a lot by benchmarking its inventory management process to Wal-Mart's and its product development process to 3M's.

One of the Organization Goals of Computec, Inc., our software and systems engineering company (see Chapter Three), is to introduce three new software products and two new system integration services within two years. As a result, Computec's product development and product introduction process is critical to its strategic success. The goals it might establish for this process include:

- *We will introduce our first new software product within nine months, our second within eighteen months, and our third within twenty-four months.*
- *We will introduce two new system integration services within twelve months.*
- *Our five new products and services will generate a total of $4.4 million in revenues and $660,000 in profits during the first full year after their introduction.*
- *The aerospace industry's need for each new product or service will be supported by current market research.*
- *Each new product and service will have applications outside as well as within the aerospace industry.*
- *New products and services will be unique or will be superior (in the eyes of the customer) to competitors' offerings.*
- *New products and services will use our existing sales and delivery systems.*

These Process Goals are linked both to Organization Goals and to customers' requirements. Note that they are not merely goals for the product development department. These Process Goals also reflect the performance expected of product development's partners in the process of product development and introduction—marketing, sales, manufacturing, and field operations. By meeting these goals, this process will make a significant contribution to the realization of the company's strategic vision.

A second Computec Organization Goal is to reduce the software package's order cycle to an average of seventy-two hours by the end of next year. For this goal, Computec's order-filling process becomes strategically critical. The goals for this process might include:

- *No products will be shipped to incorrect addresses because of Computec's errors.*
- *We will meet our seventy-two-hour goal without increasing the cost of order filling.*
- *We will provide our customers with a single point of contact for order questions and feedback.*

Given Computec's Organization Goals, its managers should also establish Process Goals for the customer support process. (The impact of Process Goals on functions will be discussed in the section on Process Management.) In all cases, the key question for Process Goals is:

> • Are goals for key processes linked to customer and organization requirements?

Process Design. Once Computec has established goals for its critical processes, its managers need to ensure that the processes are designed to achieve those goals efficiently. To determine whether each process and subprocess is appropriately structured, we recommend that a cross-functional team build a Process Map, which displays the way work currently gets done. While the Relationship Map, which is built at the Organization Level (see Chapter Three), shows input-output relationships among departments, a Process Map documents, in sequence, the steps that the departments go through to convert inputs to outputs for a specific process. *All too often, a team finds that there isn't an established process; the work just somehow gets done.*

Figure 4.1 contains an "IS" (current state) Process Map of Computec's order-filling process, as developed by a team representing all functions that contribute to the process. The mapping process starts by identifying the entities involved with the process, listing them on the left-hand axis, and drawing a horizontal band for each. Once this is done, the team (made up of representatives from all the functions listed—possibly including the customer) traces the process of converting the input (orders) through all the intervening steps until the final required output (payment) is produced. The map shows how all functions are involved as the order is processed. This mapping format allows the team to see all the critical interfaces, overlay the time to complete various subprocesses on the map, and identify "disconnects" (illogical, missing, or extraneous steps) in the process.

As the Computec team documented and analyzed the current process for filling an order, it identified a number of disconnects:

- Sales reps take too long to enter orders.
- There are too many entry and logging steps.
- Sales administration slows down the process by batch-processing orders.
- Credit checking is done for both old and new customers.
- Credit checking holds up the process because it is done before (rather than concurrently with) order picking.

The team then created a "SHOULD" Process Map, which reflects a disconnect-free order-filling process. That map appears in Figure 4.2.

As the figure shows, the major changes in the "SHOULD" map are:

- Direct order entry by sales, eliminating sales administration
- Parallel order processing and credit checking
- Elimination of multiple order-entry and order-logging steps

FIGURE 4.1. COMPUTEC ORDER FILLING: AN "IS" PROCESS MAP

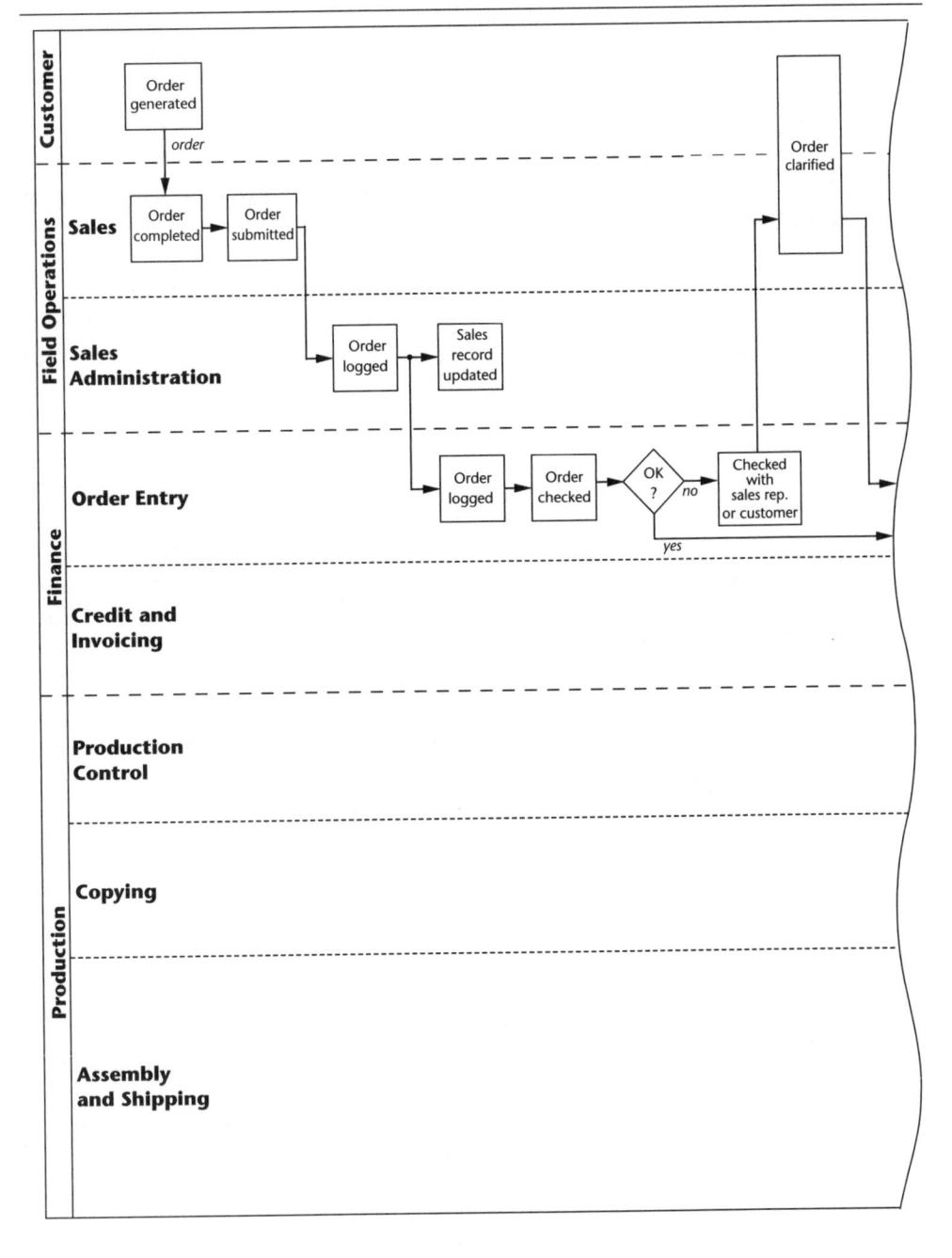

FIGURE 4.1. (*Continued*)

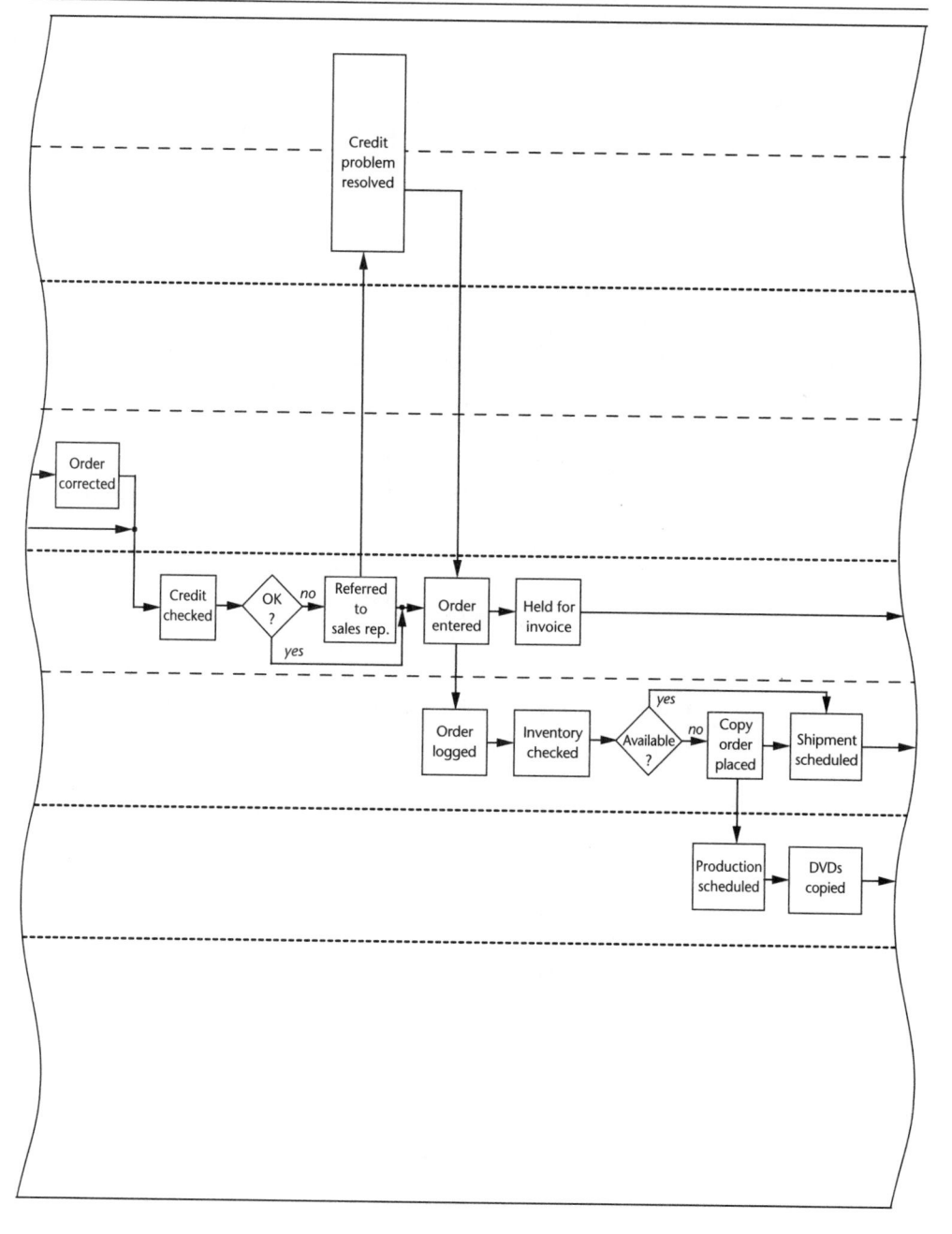

FIGURE 4.1. (*Continued*)

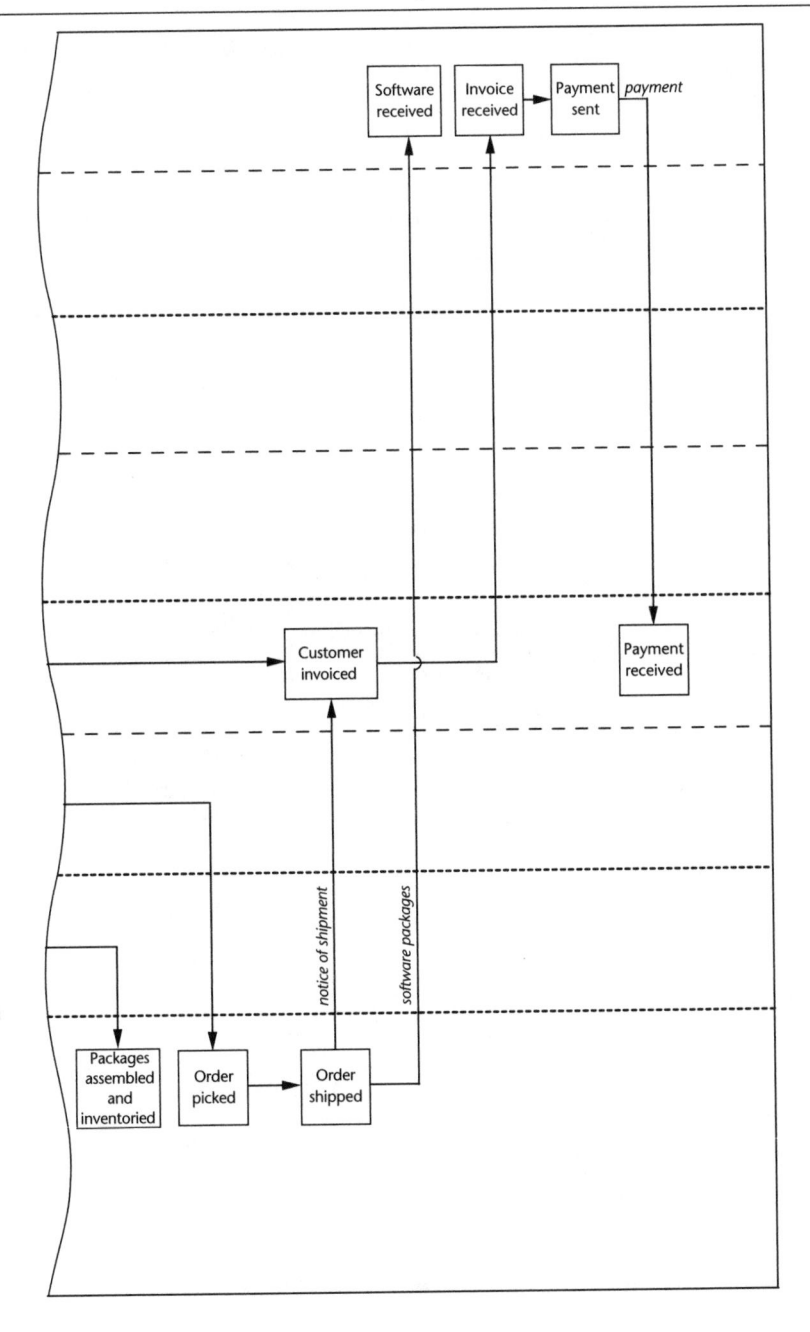

FIGURE 4.2. COMPUTEC ORDER FILLING: A "SHOULD" PROCESS MAP

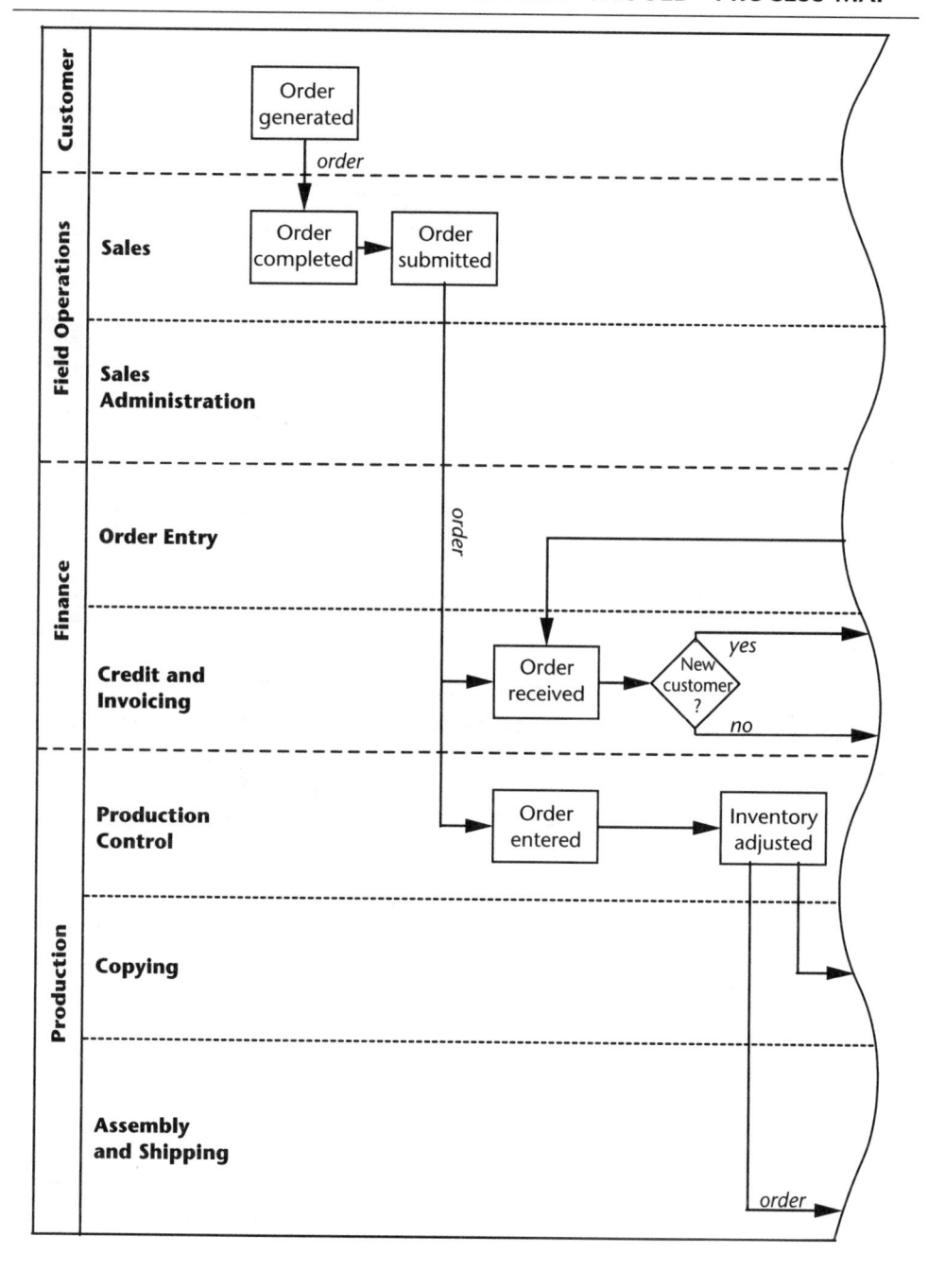

FIGURE 4.2. (*Continued*)

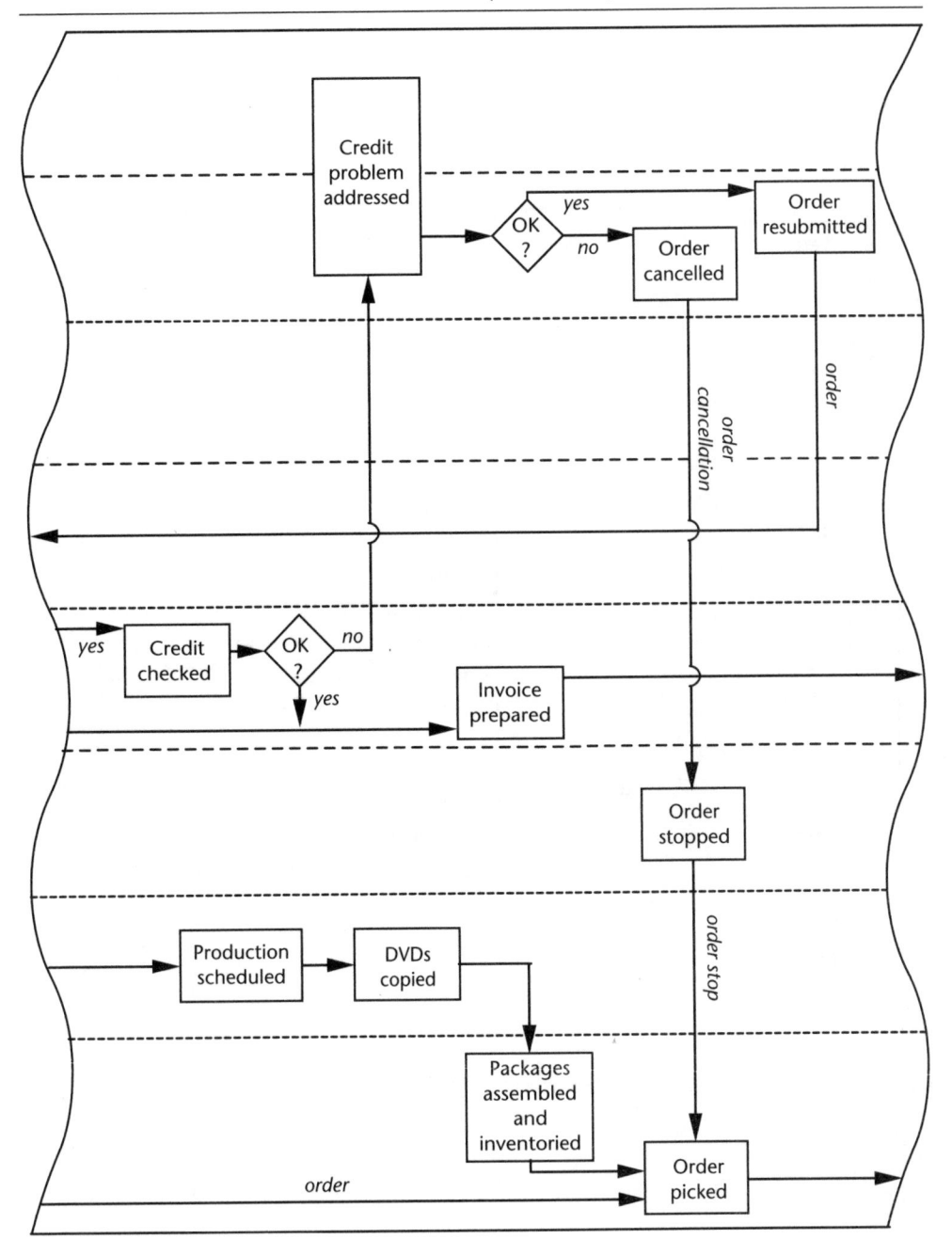

FIGURE 4.2. (*Continued*)

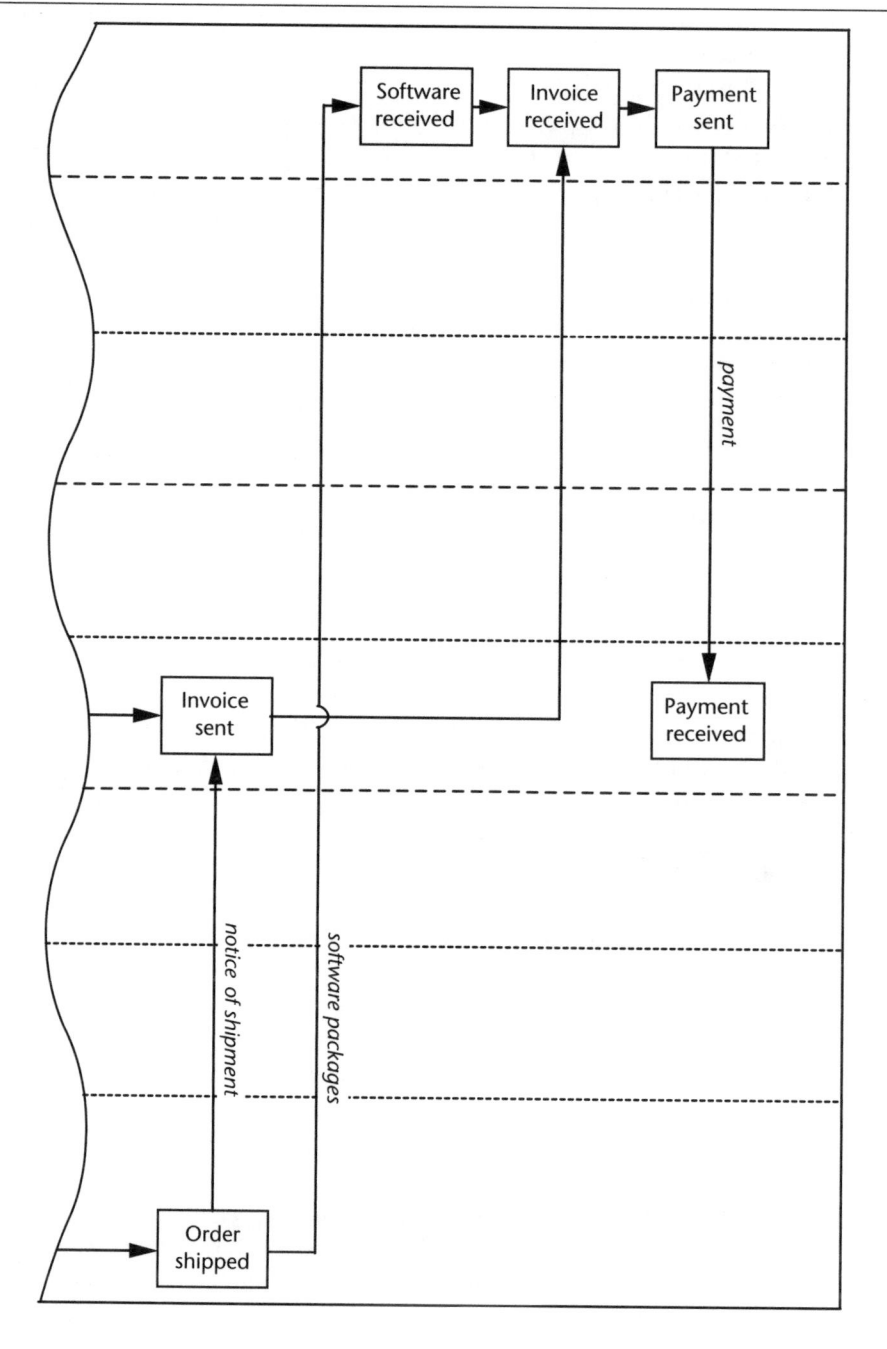

Another possible "SHOULD" process would include a Just-In-Time production system, in which packages are assembled to order and not inventoried.

"IS" and "SHOULD" Process Mapping is a central step in Process Improvement Projects. (A more complete list of Process Improvement Project steps appears in Chapter Nine.) For example, organizations are finding Process Maps to be more useful than procedures manuals as a format for meeting the documentation requirements set forth in the ISO 9000 standards.

A successful Process Improvement Project results in an affirmative answer to the key Process Design question:

• Is this the most efficient and effective process for accomplishing the Process Goals?

Process Management. Unfortunately, even the most logical, goal-directed processes don't manage themselves. These are the four components of effective Process Management:

1. *Goal Management:* The overall Process Goals should serve as the basis for the establishment of subgoals throughout the process. If we managed a natural-gas pipeline, we would want to measure pressure and purity, not only at the end but also at various critical junctures along the line. Similarly, we need to establish process subgoals after each step that has an especially critical impact on the ultimate customer-driven Process Goals. Figure 4.3 shows some examples of process subgoals for Computec's order-filling process.

Many organizations, particularly in manufacturing industries, use Statistical Process Control (SPC) tools. We fully support the use of these tools, such as control charts, to track process performance, reveal problems, and maintain process stability. We have found that the goal-setting approach depicted in Figure 4.3 helps identify *where* SPC tools should be used.

Once process subgoals have been established, functional goals can be developed. Any functional goals established at the Organization Level should be modified, if necessary, to reflect maximum functional contributions to the Process Goals and subgoals. *Since the purpose of a function is to support processes, it should be measured on the degree to which it serves those processes. When we establish functional goals that bolster processes, we ensure that each department meets the needs of its internal and external customers.*

Computec's first step should be to identify each function's contribution to the process. For example, order entry is the first segment (subprocess) of the order-filling process. Three functions contribute to this segment:

- *Sales, which enters the order via telephone*
- *Finance, which determines the customer's credit status*
- *Production control, which determines the inventory status and, if necessary, triggers copying to produce additional DVDs*

FIGURE 4.3. SELECTED PROCESS SUBGOALS FOR COMPUTEC'S ORDER-FILLING PROCESS

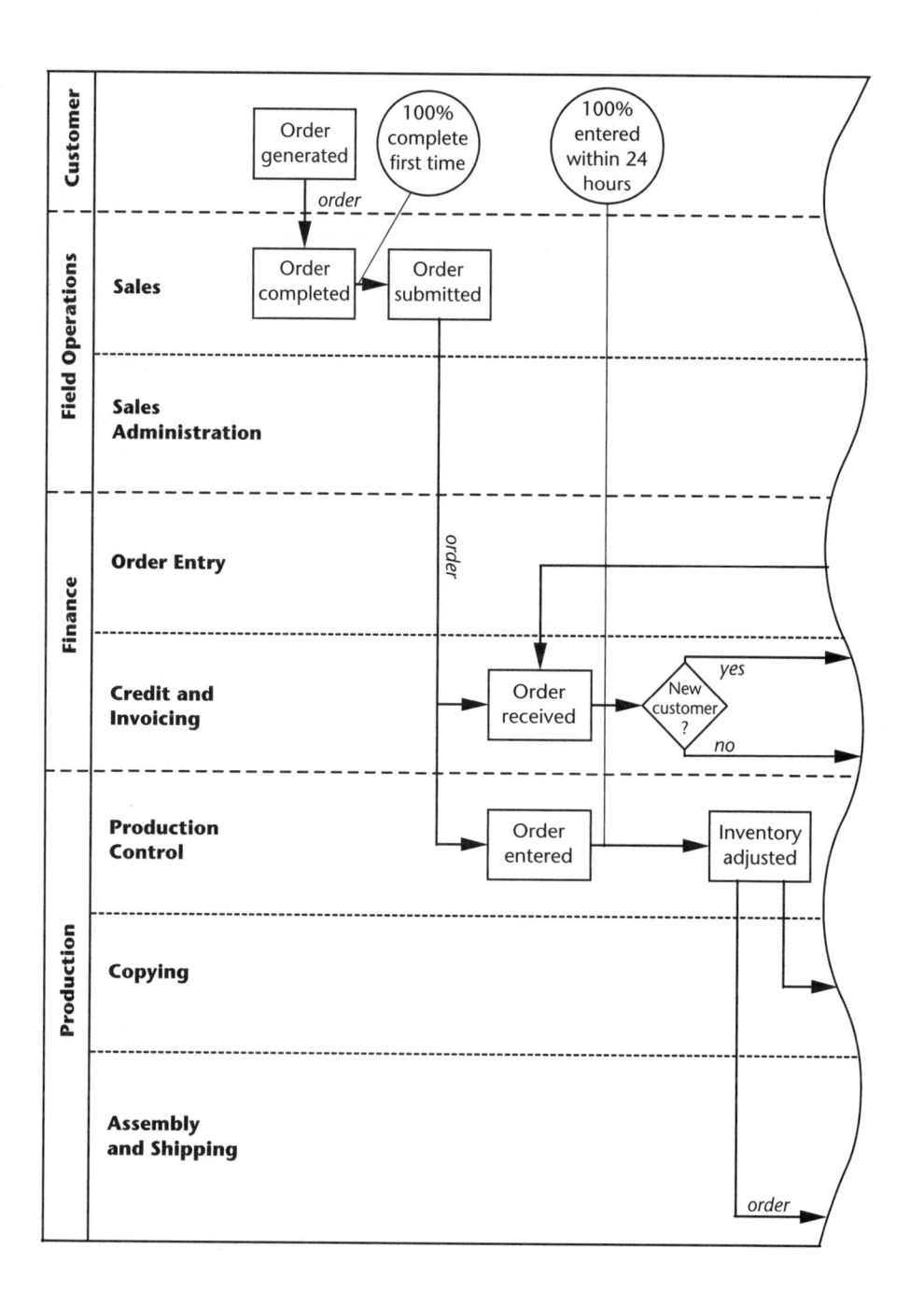

FIGURE 4.3.
(Continued)

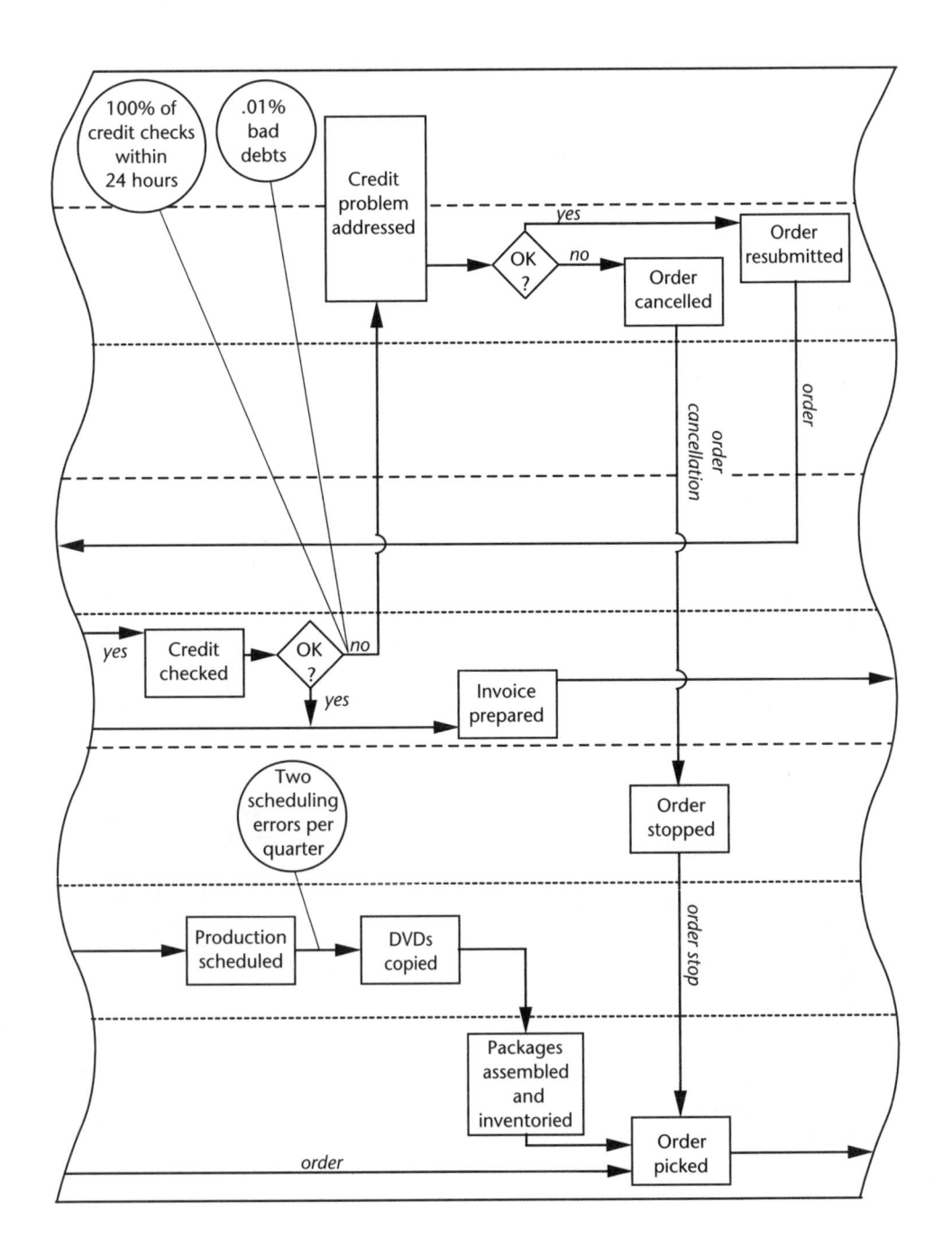

FIGURE 4.3.
(*Continued*)

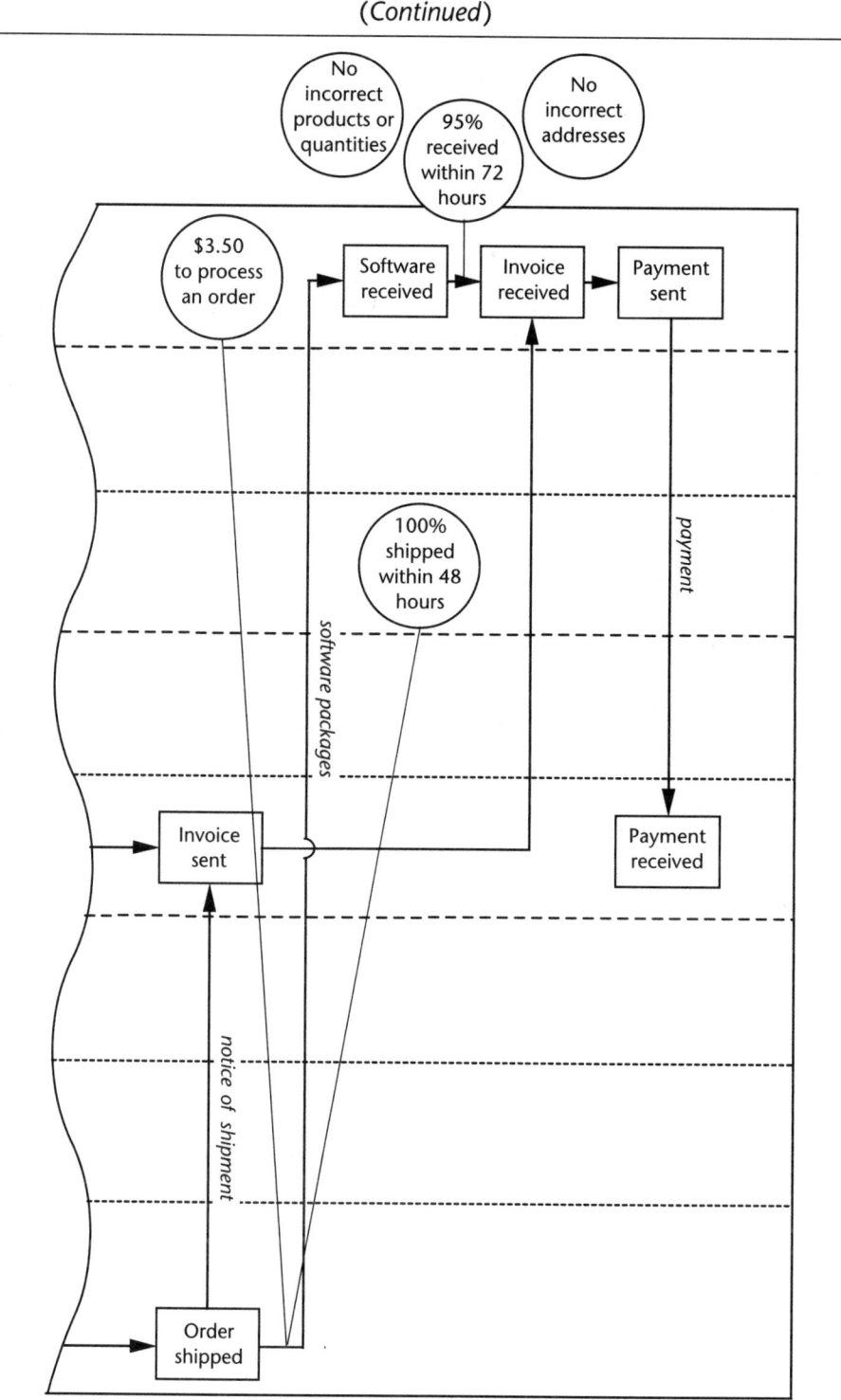

One way to summarize this contribution is through a Role/ Responsibility Matrix, an example of which is included in Chapter Twelve.

On the basis of these contributions, and on the basis of the process subgoals displayed in Figure 4.3, Computec should establish functional goals, such as those that appear in Table 4.2.

2. *Performance Management:* After Computec has established a workable order-filling process (Figure 4.2) and a set of goals and subgoals for its performance (Process Goals and Figure 4.3), its managers should establish systems for obtaining internal and external customer feedback on the process outputs, tracking process performance against the goals and subgoals, feeding back process performance information to the functions that play a role, establishing mechanisms to solve process problems and continuously improve process performance, and adjusting goals to meet new customer requirements. (In Chapter Twelve, we provide an example of a Performance Tracker that could be used to capture process performance information.)

During the last few years, we have learned a lot about managing process performance (which is, in effect, managing the horizontal organization). We have learned that if processes are to be managed on an ongoing basis (and not just fixed when they break), then managers must establish an infrastructure, which many organizations are beginning to call *Process Management.*

Computec senior managers could take several Process Management actions to ensure that the order-filling process is continuously managed:

- *Rate the performance of the process, giving it a grade in such areas as customer satisfaction, cost, clarity and thoroughness of documentation, and quality and quantity of measures. Each function's contribution to the process could also be rated.*
- *Designate a Process Owner to oversee the entire process. (The criteria for selecting Process Owners and a description of their possible roles are included in Chapter Thirteen.)*
- *Identify a permanent Process Team, which would meet monthly to review and improve process performance.*
- *Hold monthly operations reviews, in which process performance would be reviewed first and function performance would be reviewed second.*
- *Reward people within a function only if Process Goals were met and if the function's contribution goals were met.*

Process Management is such a pivotal theme within the Three Levels of Performance that we have devoted all of Chapter Thirteen to that subject.

TABLE 4.2. SELECTED FUNCTIONAL GOALS BASED ON COMPUTEC ORDER-FILLING PROCESS GOALS

Functional Goals Summary (Measures and Goals)

Function	Timeliness Measures	Goals	Quality Measures	Goals	Budget Measures	Goals	Other Measures	Goals
Total Process	Percent of orders received by customer within 72 hours of Computec receipt	95%	Percent of accurate orders	100%	Average handling cost per order	$3.50	Percent of bad debt	1%
Sales	Percent of orders entered within 10 hours of receipt	100%	Percent of accurate orders	100%	Inventory turns	12/yr		
Sales Administration								
Credit and Invoicing	Percent of credit checks done within 24 hours of order receipt	100%			Processing cost per order	$.50	Percent of bad debt	1%
Production Control					Processing cost per order	$.50	Inventory turns	12/yr
Copying			Number of scheduling errors per quarter	2				
Assembly and Shipping	Percent of orders shipped within 4 hours of receipt	100%	Percent of accurate orders	100%	Processing cost per order	$2.50		

3. *Resource Management:* Managers have always understood that resource allocation is a major part of their responsibility. However, process-focused resource allocation tends to be different from the usual function-oriented approach. Functional resource allocation usually results from a series of one-to-one meetings between a senior manager and his or her departmental or subdepartmental managers. In these meetings, each manager makes a case for a bigger slice of the pie, and the most persuasive presentations are rewarded with the largest budgets and headcount allocations.

Process-driven resource allocation is the result of a determination of the dollars and people required for the process to achieve its goals. After that is done, each function is allocated its share of the resources, according to its contribution to the process. If Process Management is institutionalized throughout an organization, each function's budget is the sum total of its portion of each process budget.

In Computec, for example, resources should be allocated to each step in the order-filling process, according to the quality, timeliness, and cost goals established for that process. Then the various functions should receive the resources they require to make their contributions to that process. For example, the process budget may be divided into order entry, credit checking, scheduling, picking, and shipping. Each of these process segments should receive an appropriate chunk of the process budget. The functions responsible for these process segments should therefore receive budgets that will enable them to make their process contributions. Activity-based costing is a tool that can help appropriately allocate budgets and costs across a process.

4. *Interface Management:* A Process Map (Figure 4.2) clearly displays the points at which one function (horizontal band on the map) provides a product or service to another function. At each of these points, there is a customer-supplier interface. As we discussed in Chapter One, these interfaces often represent the greatest opportunity for performance improvement. A process-oriented manager closely monitors interfaces and removes any barriers to effectiveness and efficiency.

As the Computec Process Map shows, the interfaces between sales and production control and between production control and assembly are particularly critical to the success of the order-filling process. Senior management and the Process Owner should pay particular attention to this "white space." To ensure proper attention, they should establish and monitor measures that indicate the quality and efficiency of these interfaces.

The Process Management questions are:

- Have appropriate process subgoals been set?
- Is process performance managed?
- Are sufficient resources allocated to each process?
- Are the interfaces between process steps being managed?

Summary

Work gets done in an organization through its primary, support, and management processes. If you want to understand the way work gets done, to improve the way work gets done, and to manage the way work gets done, processes should be the focus of your attention and actions. Viewing business issues from a process perspective often reveals a need to make radical changes in goals, in the design of business systems, and in management practices. The Process Level of Performance has significant implications for:

- *Executives,* who can use the process perspective and tools to link Organization Goals to individual performance, measure what's really going on in the business, benchmark performance against other companies, establish competitive advantages, assess the impact of mergers and acquisitions, and evaluate alternative organization structures
- *Managers,* who can use the process perspective and tools to identify and close quality, cost, and cycle time gaps; manage the interfaces with other departments and the interfaces within their own departments; implement change; and effectively allocate resources
- *Analysts,* who can use the process perspective and tools to diagnose business needs and recommend improvements that will have a significant impact on organization performance, to evaluate actions they are asked to take, and to facilitate improvement teams

If we had to pick one of the Three Levels as the area of greatest opportunity for most organizations, it would be the Process Level. Perhaps that is because it tends to be the least understood and therefore the least managed level of performance. Perhaps it is because work gets done through processes. Perhaps it is because it is the middle level and, as such, serves as the linking pin between the goals, the design, and the management at the Organization Level and at the Job/Performer Level. Or perhaps it is because application of the process tools can address some of the most fundamental needs facing organizations—building a customer-focused organization, quickly and intelligently adapting to new situations, implementing change, and breaking down barriers between departments.

Regardless of the reasons, the Process Level represents a wealth of largely untapped potential. We are learning that it is not enough to manage results. The way in which those results are achieved (the process) is also important. If we are achieving the results, we need to know why. If we are not achieving the results, we need to know why. In both cases, to a great degree, the answer lies in the process. Once we have processes that are designed and managed to meet Organization Goals efficiently, we can address the needs of the Job/Performer Level, which is covered in the next chapter.

THE JOB/PERFORMER LEVEL
OF PERFORMANCE

What is the city but the people?

—William Shakespeare

We could replace Shakespeare's *city* with the word *organization*. Perhaps as a result of its efforts at Levels I and II, Computec, Inc., may now have clear Organization and Process Goals. Its organization structure and its process flows may be logical, and its organization and process subgoals, resources, and interfaces may be effectively managed. However, that's not enough. By addressing the needs at the Organization and Process Levels, Computec has established a firm performance foundation. It now needs to construct a building on that foundation. That building is the performance of its people.

In Chapters Three and Four, we focused on systems, not because effective systems compensate for ineffective people but because ineffective systems hinder potentially effective people. Our experience has led us to a bias: most people want to do a good job. However, if you pit a good performer against a bad system, the system will win almost every time.

What Is the Job/Performer Level?

The Job/Performer Level is so named because it looks at jobs at all levels and at the people (performers) who serve in those jobs. At this Performance Level, we take the same systems view that we take at the Organization and Process Levels. We believe that performance can be improved only if jobs and performers are analyzed in an overall performance context. The need for a systems perspective is best illustrated by an examination of managers' typical responses to people problems. Aside from the all-too-frequent response of ignoring the problem, the actions we see most often are:

- Train them
- Transfer them
- Coach and counsel them
- Threaten them
- Discipline them
- Replace them

The common theme through all of these responses is *them*. Each action assumes that "them" is what's broken, and therefore "them" is what needs to be fixed.

Assuming that defective people are at the root of all performance problems is as illogical as assuming that a bad battery is at the root of all automobile malfunctions. While the battery may be at fault, a good mechanic realizes that it is part of an engine system. A number of components of that system may harbor the cause of the problem. Even if the battery is performing inadequately, it may be because of another component; the root cause may lie elsewhere in the engine. Similarly, we believe that people are one part of a "performance engine"—the Human Performance System—which has a number of components that influence performance.

The goals, design, and management at the Organization and Process Levels are part of the system that affects human performance. The Human Performance System builds on those levels by providing a more "micro" picture of people and of the immediate environment that surrounds them. The Human Performance System is displayed in Figure 5.1. As the figure shows, our view of the Job/Performer Level reflects the input-process-output-feedback perspective that also underpins the Organization and Process Levels.

Inputs are those raw materials, forms, assignments, and customer requests that cause people to perform. The input package also includes

FIGURE 5.1. THE HUMAN PERFORMANCE SYSTEM

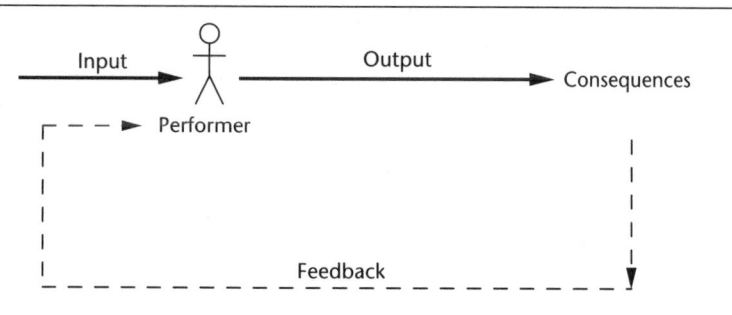

the performers' resources and the systems and procedures that represent the performers' link to the Process Level. For salespeople, the inputs may include leads, territory assignments, and market research information. Their resource inputs may include brochures, presentation aids, and product specifications. Lastly, the salespeople are expected to follow the steps in the sales process.

Performers are the individuals or groups who convert inputs to outputs. Salespeople, sales managers, market researchers, and customers are all performers.

Outputs are the products produced by the performers as their contribution to Organization and Process Goals. People's traits, skills, knowledge, and behaviors are all important performance variables. However, they are all means to the end that justifies the performers' existence in the organization—the outputs. The key output of salespeople is the sales volume they produce.

Consequences are the positive and negative effects that performers experience when they produce an output. Positive consequences may include bonuses, recognition, and more challenging work. Negative consequences include complaints, disciplinary action, and less interesting work. A consequence is determined to be positive or negative according to the unique perspective of each performer. The salespeople who bring in a lot of business may receive healthy commissions and public recognition, which they probably perceive to be positive consequences. Salespeople who fail to meet their quotas may receive the negative consequences of lower income, reassignment to undesirable back-office jobs, or seeing their names near the bottom of a sales performance chart.

Feedback is information that tells performers what and how well they are doing. Feedback can come from error reports, statistical compilations, rejects, oral or written comments, surveys, and performance appraisals. Salespeople get feedback from customers (who buy or don't buy), from sales managers (who may compile sales-performance information), and from the people who produce or deliver the product or service (who may comment on the quality of the sale).

The quality of outputs is a function of the quality of inputs, performers, consequences, and feedback. At the Job/Performer Level, we systematically analyze and improve each of the five Human Performance System components. We believe that comprehensive performance improvement results only from addressing each of the components.

Taking Action at the Job/Performer Level

In Chapters Three, Four, and Five, we discussed the consequences of taking action at the Job/Performer Level without addressing the

Performance Variables at the Organization and Process Levels. The risk of failing to address the Job/Performer Level is just as serious: organization and process improvements will not take root if they are not built into jobs. *If jobs are not designed to support process steps, and if job environments are not structured to enable people to make their maximum contributions to process effectiveness and efficiency, then Organization and Process Goals will not be met.*

For example, managers in an electronics manufacturing company identified order-to-delivery cycle time as a major competitive disadvantage (Organization Level). To address this disadvantage, they designed a far superior forecasting system for sales and production (Process Level). So far, so good. However, in their enthusiasm for the new process and its potential benefits, they announced and launched it as soon as the ink was dry. They did not identify the changes that were needed in the jobs affected by the new process, nor did they identify the resources and management practices required to support the new process. As a result, the launch of the new system was lengthy, painful, and more costly than necessary.

These managers failed to realize that the *Job/Performer Level does not automatically fall in line with changes at the Organization and Process Levels.* The only way to ensure that people make their maximum possible contributions to Organization and Process Goals is to address each of the three Job/Performer Level Performance Variables—Job Goals, Job Design, and Job Management.

The Performance Variables at the Job/Performer Level

Job Goals. Since the role of people is to make processes work, we need to make sure that their goals reflect process contributions. Figure 5.2 shows the links between Job Goals and goals at the other levels.

FIGURE 5.2. HIERARCHY OF PERFORMANCE GOAL SETTING

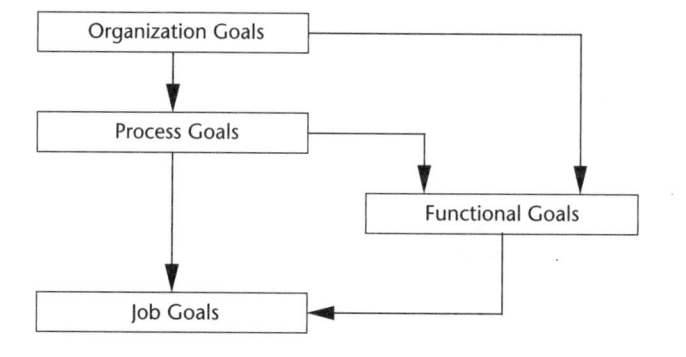

The major distinction between this goal "flow-down" and traditional approaches is the process (rather than functional) orientation. While Job Goals should be directly linked to functional goals, both should be derived from the processes they support. To continue our software company example, Computec identified order filling as a strategically significant cross-functional process. A critical step in that process involves checking the credit of a new customer. A Process Goal (shared by the finance department) is to accurately perform a credit check within twenty-four hours of receipt of the order. That goal translates into a set of goals for finance clerks:

- *100 percent of credit checks should be conducted within twenty-four hours of order receipt.*
- *100 percent of bad credit reports should be returned to a sales representative for resolution.*
- *No more than 1 percent of approved customers turn out to have insufficient credit.*

These goals communicate to performers what they are expected to do and *how well* they are expected to do it. These two ingredients specify the output component of the Human Performance System. For many performers, the "how well" (performance standard) dimension is missing. Without standards, performers cannot fully understand the level of performance they are expected to attain. We have found that the best way to build understanding of and commitment to Job Goals is to involve people in the process of establishing the goals for their jobs.

The purpose of Job Goal setting is to arrive at an affirmative answer to this question:

- Are job outputs and standards linked to process requirements, which are in turn linked to customer and organization requirements?

Job Design. Having established the Job Goals, we need to ensure that each job is structured to enable its incumbents to achieve these goals. Job Design is a function of:

- Allocation of responsibilities among jobs
- Sequence of job activities
- Job policies and procedures
- Ergonomics

When we establish Job Goals based on process requirements, we frequently find that jobs are cluttered with responsibilities that hamper incumbents' ability to support processes. For example, we studied the buyer position in an oil company. We found that the buyers' contribution to the purchasing process was diminished by administrative tasks, which took up a significant amount of their time. These responsibilities were transferred to a newly created position, assistant buyer. This reallocation of responsibilities freed the buyers to do what they do best—buy. In addition to establishing a new career path, the creation of this job enabled the process to function more efficiently, without compromising quality.

To help describe Job Goals and to ensure that responsibilities are allocated to appropriate jobs, we recommend constructing a Role/Responsibility Matrix. An example (using Computec) appears in Table 5.1.

The second dimension of Job Design is the sequence of job activities—the *process*—that performers go through to produce their outputs. For example, if buyers are expected to justify the expenditure of a certain amount of money *before* they can talk to potential vendors and obtain competitive bids, they may not be able to make their maximum contribution to the purchasing process.

Because they are closely linked to the sequence of job activities, job policies and procedures can significantly help or hinder process effectiveness. For example, if the sole-source policy and the capital expenditure request form are convoluted, buyers' performance will not reach its potential.

Lastly, the job's ergonomics must support optimum performance. The design of the workstation and the physical environment should present few if any barriers to meeting Job Goals. The buyers, for example, spend quite a bit of time working with their computers. Chair and table height, screen angle, and lighting should be designed for ease of computer use.

To continue our Computec example, we want to make sure that it makes sense for finance clerks to do credit checks, that they have a logical process for credit checking, that they have a set of policies and guidelines for credit checking, and that their workstations are conducive to optimum credit-checking performance.

These are the questions for the variable of Job Design:

- Are process requirements reflected in the appropriate jobs?
- Are job steps in a logical sequence?
- Have supportive policies and procedures been developed?
- Is the job environment ergonomically sound?

TABLE 5.1. ROLE/RESPONSIBILITY MATRIX FOR FINANCE FUNCTION AND CUSTOMER ORDER PROCESS

MAJOR PROCESS STEP	FINANCE FUNCTION ACCOMPLISHMENTS	FINANCE JOBS, RESPONSIBILITIES, AND GOALS					
		CLERK A		CLERK B		CREDIT SUPERVISOR	
		Accomplishments	Goals	Accomplishments	Goals	Accomplishments	Goals
2. Order entered	Order received	Order checked for completeness	Ø undetected errors 90% of omissions returned to sales within 8 hours of receipt				
	Customer status determined	Customer status checked in file	Ø errors in customer status info				
	Credit checked (new customer)			Customer credit checked	0.1% "OKs" have bad credit		
				If OK, order updated	100% checked within 24 hours of receipt		
					100% of orders updated within 24 hours of receipt		
				If not OK, sales representative informed	100% of "not OKs" returned to sales for resolution		
6. Order shipped and invoiced	Order invoiced						

Job Management. Managing the Job/Performer Level is managing the five components of the Human Performance System depicted in Figure 5.1. We have found that six factors affect the effectiveness and efficiency of the Human Performance System. These factors are depicted in Figure 5.3.

The purpose of Job Management is to put capable people in an environment that supports their accomplishment of Job Goals. Factors 5 and 6 in Figure 5.3 address the capability of the performers. Factors 1 through 4 list the factors in a supportive environment.

1. *Performance Specifications* are the outputs and standards that comprise the Job Goals. A manager who participatively establishes process-driven Job Goals is taking steps to ensure that the questions behind this factor are answered affirmatively. By contrast, the answers are *no* for salespeople who

FIGURE 5.3. FACTORS AFFECTING THE HUMAN PERFORMANCE SYSTEM

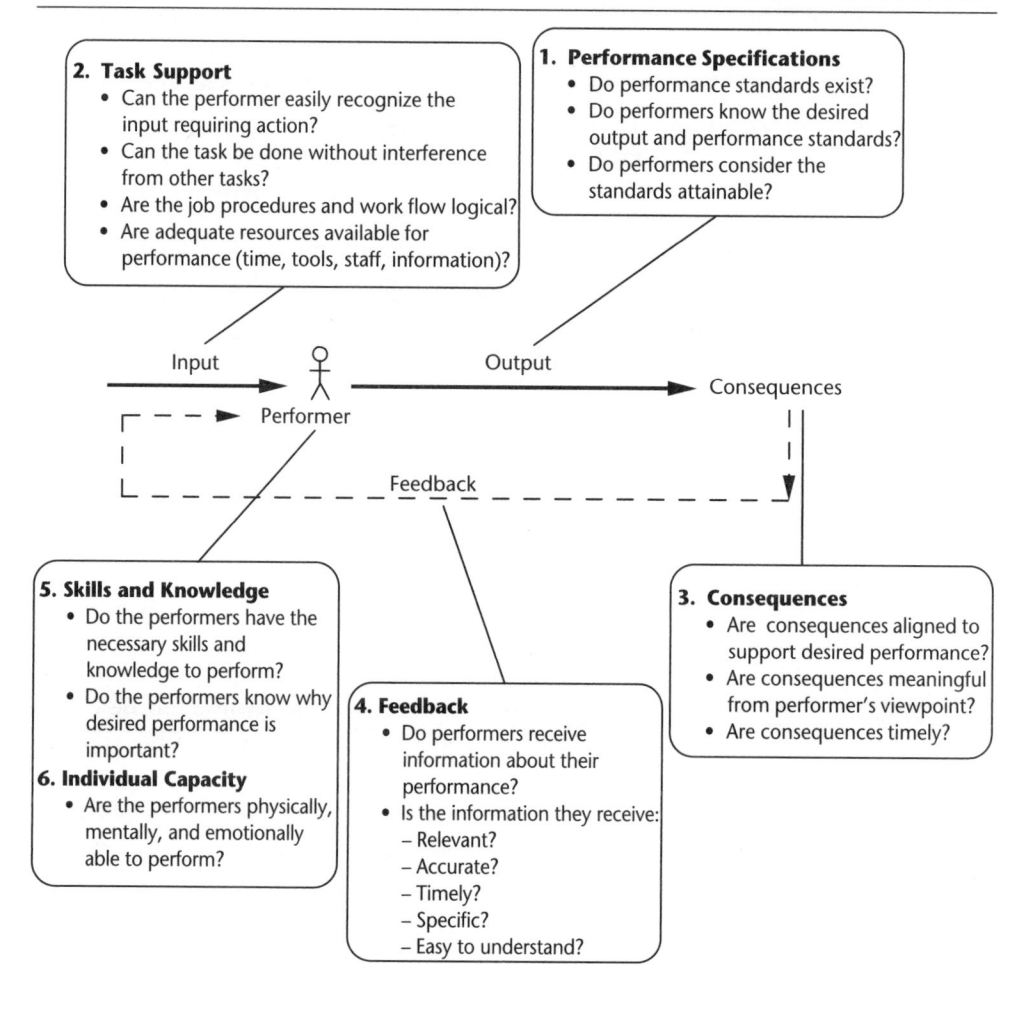

are not clear on the mix of products they are expected to sell. They have a Performance Specification deficiency.

2. *Task Support* is partially addressed by Job Design. A well-structured job (in a well-structured process) contains easily recognized high-quality inputs, minimal interference, and logical procedures. Managers who want to minimize Task Interference take one additional step. They provide their people with adequate resources to do the job. For example, the volume of paperwork may take a significant amount of salespeople's time away from their primary responsibility—selling. If so, their selling performance is impeded by Task Interference.

3. *Consequences* must support efficient achievement of Job Goals. Because of a strategic (Organization Level) thrust, one of a salesperson's Job Goals may be to sell a certain volume of new products. If the commission system supports selling the old products, the salesperson's consequences are not aligned to support desired performance. The consequences must also be meaningful to the performer. A given salesperson might not perceive a promotion to sales manager as a positive consequence. Lastly, consequences must occur quickly enough to provide an ongoing incentive. A salesperson who does want to be a sales manager is unlikely to find that consequence sufficiently motivating if he or she cannot reasonably expect it to be delivered in the next five years. The promotion is aligned to support desired performance, but does not come quickly enough to serve as the sole incentive.

4. *Feedback* tells a performer to change performance or to keep on performing the same way. *Without feedback, good performance can fall off track, and poor performance can remain unimproved.* Effective feedback meets the criteria listed in Figure 5.3. If feedback is delivered only to the sales force as a whole, individual salespeople may not perceive it as relevant or be able to use it to guide their performance. If feedback is provided only during an annual performance review, it is probably not timely enough to be effective. If feedback is not specific ("Good job" or "Please strengthen that forecast next time"), it will fail to make its contribution to the effectiveness of the Human Performance System.

5. *Skills and Knowledge* are required in any job. If they are missing, job performance is impaired and training may be required. Included in this category is not only the official way of doing the job but also hints and shortcuts ("tribal knowledge") that enable some performers to be exemplary. Salespeople need to know their product or service lines and be skilled in the techniques of selling.

6. *Individual Capacity* involves performers' internal capabilities. No matter how supportive their environment (Factors 1–4) or effective their training (Factor 5), they will not be able to do their jobs if they lack the physical, mental, or emotional capacity to achieve the goals. A salesperson who cannot take rejection may have an Individual Capacity deficiency.

People occasionally tell us that we've missed a factor. They indicate that the key performance variable is motivation (or desire, or drive, or attitude, or morale). We agree that motivation is key; however, it's a symptom. When we look behind weak (or strong) motivation, we find our six factors. *If capable (Factor 6), well-trained (Factor 5) people are placed in a setting with clear expectations (Factor 1), task support (Factor 2), reinforcing consequences (Factor 3), and appropriate feedback (Factor 4), then they will be motivated.*

As the examples illustrate, one powerful use of the questions in Figure 5.3 is as a troubleshooting checklist. Each *no* answer represents some "dirt in the performance engine" and an opportunity for performance improvement. In our experience, the highest percentage of performance opportunities can be found in the environment (Factors 1–4) in which performers work. While the figure varies somewhat in different jobs, industries, and countries, *we have found that about 80 percent of performance improvement opportunities reside in the environment.* Usually, 15 to 20 percent of the opportunities are in the Skills and Knowledge area. We have found that fewer than 1 percent of performance problems result from Individual Capacity deficiencies.

Our experience is consistent with that of W. Edwards Deming, who maintained that only 15 percent of performance problems are worker problems and 85 percent are management problems. Since the odds are against the performer being the broken component of the Human Performance System, the typical management responses to performance problems (listed at the beginning of this chapter) are not likely to address the need.

We have presented the Human Performance System and its related questions as a diagnostic tool. The bad news is that diagnosing a situation does not in itself bring about performance improvement. The good news is that each diagnosed deficiency within the six factors (each *no* answer) suggests an action.

To address the need for clear *Performance Specifications,* we recommend creating a *Job Model,* which specifies the outputs and standards that are linked to process requirements. (The Job Model format is presented in Chapter Twelve.)

To ensure *Task Support,* restructure the job so that it has clear inputs, a logical sequence of activities, minimal interference among tasks, and sufficient resources. While Job Design can be difficult, most large organizations have specialists in this area. If these skills are not available, a work team of incumbents, supervisors, and analysts can usually, without any sophisticated technology, make the changes necessary to remove the most significant Task Support barriers.

Consequence deficiencies can be eliminated by adding positive consequences and removing negative consequences for desired responses. While this may sound like it requires one or two degrees in psychology, it doesn't. Performers are very willing to tell anyone who will listen what they find punishing and what incentives work for them. Again, an organization that does not have resident expertise in this area can draw on the collective wisdom of a team of incumbents and supervisors and, perhaps, an analyst.

Designing an effective *Feedback* system tends to require a bit more specialized background. However, an informal system may be all that is needed. The objective is to develop an efficient means of regularly and frequently providing specific performance information to people. The sole feedback mechanism in many organizations is the annual performance appraisal process. However, most appraisal systems are weak in two key feedback areas: frequency and specificity. A manager or analyst who is not able to change the formal performance appraisal form or process must develop other ways to get people the feedback they need when they need it.

To overcome deficiencies in *Skills and Knowledge*, provide classroom training, on-the-job training, and/or a job aid. While training and job-aid design require a body of expertise, those skills usually reside within an organization's human resource development department.

The action to address an *Individual Capacity* deficiency depends on the nature of the deficiency. One of three responses is appropriate: change the job to fit the person (for example, redesign the workstation to accommodate a wheelchair), develop the person to fit the job (for example, arrange for counseling in coping with stress), or remove the person from the job (for example, transfer him or her to a job that doesn't require mathematics).

There are lots of great medications out there. Training, for example, is an effective cure. However, it treats only the disease known as a Skills and Knowledge deficiency. It probably won't ease the pain of the other five afflictions. Another popular treatment is reorganization. An effective reorganization can remove some barriers to Task Support, but will do little to address other needs. *The net message is that one should diagnose the need before implementing a solution.*

Diagnosing and overcoming deficiencies represents only one of three uses of the Human Performance System. *The six factors can also be used to improve performance that is already meeting expectations.* Any improvement in Feedback or Consequences, for example, will make good performance even better. *Managers and analysts can also use the questions as a checklist, which can help them create a supportive environment around a **new or changed** job.* For example, they can design clear Performance Specifications and structure reinforcing Consequences before the job is created and filled.

There's yet another benefit. While each enhancement of the Human Performance System improves the quality and efficiency of performance, it also enriches the quality of work life. As a result, performers are willing partners in all three applications of the tool.

At Computec, finance clerks need to:

- *Understand their three credit-checking goals.*
- *Have manuals, phones, credit-history information, calculators, and other resources required to check credit.*
- *Be rewarded for reaching or exceeding their Job Goals.*
- *Receive frequent, specific feedback on their credit-checking performance.*
- *Know the what, why, and how of effective and efficient credit checking.*
- *Be mentally and emotionally able to conduct credit checks in the environment of the finance department.*

At a high level, these are the questions for Job Management:

- Do the performers understand the Job Goals (the outputs they are expected to produce and the standards they are expected to meet)?
- Do the performers have sufficient resources, clear signals and priorities, and a logical Job Design?
- Are the performers rewarded for achieving the Job Goals?
- Do the performers know if they are meeting the Job Goals?
- Do the performers have the necessary skills and knowledge to achieve the Job Goals?
- If the performers were in an environment in which the five questions listed above were answered yes, would they have the physical, mental, and emotional capacity to achieve the Job Goals?

Summary

Organization and Process Goals can be achieved only through performance at the Job/Performer Level. Managing people is not easy, but it's less mystical than it may seem. Rather than hiring good people and hoping for efficient, high-quality performance, effective managers use the Human Performance System to manage the factors that enable those good people to perform at an exemplary level. Managers recognize that everyone is in a Human Performance System, and they recognize the six factors that influence the effectiveness of that system. Furthermore, they realize that the four environmental factors (which are largely within their control) tend to harbor the greatest opportunities for performance improvement. We have found that:

- *Executives* can use the Job/Performer Level's outlook and tools to clarify the responsibilities and measure the performance of their direct reports; to ensure that the Human Performance System will and can support the policies that they are considering issuing; to create Human Performance Systems that maximize the quality of outputs, productivity, and work life of their direct reports; to diagnose and improve *their own* Human Performance Systems; and to ensure that organization-wide changes are supported by the environments in which they will be carried out.
- *Managers* can use the Job/Performer Level's outlook in the same ways as executives for their direct reports, themselves, and the changes they manage.
- *Analysts* (especially human resource specialists, industrial engineers, and systems analysts) can use the Job/Performer Level's outlook and tools to diagnose and address performance needs; to ensure that the changes they recommend or are asked to make are supported by the Human Performance System; to manage their bosses and others with whom they have to work; and to diagnose and improve their own performance and enhance the quality of their own work life.

The concepts and tools in this chapter are used throughout the "application" chapters that follow.

PART THREE

APPLYING THE THREE LEVELS OF PERFORMANCE

CHAPTER SIX

LINKING PERFORMANCE TO STRATEGY

*The bravest are surely those who have the clearest vision of
what is before them, glory and danger alike, and yet
notwithstanding go out to meet it.*

—THUCYDIDES

Before performance at any level can be managed, the expectations for
that performance need to be clearly established and communicated.
This need is particularly strong at the Organization Level. If we have
not clearly defined the business we are in, we certainly cannot effectively
design and manage the Organization Level of Performance or establish
goals, structure, and management practices at the Process and Job/
Performer Levels. Without the guiding hand of a clear strategy, we cannot
be sure that we are allocating our resources appropriately, managing our
critical business processes, and rewarding the right job performance. To
slightly alter the old Chinese proverb, "If we don't know where we are
going, any processes and jobs will get us there."

We will not add to the vast number of models, theories, and methodologies for strategic planning. Our objective is to identify those questions
that need to be answered if an organization's strategy is going to effectively
guide the Three Levels of Performance. A clear strategy leads to a set of
superordinate Organization Goals, which should drive the Nine Performance Variables depicted in Table 6.1.

What Is Strategy?

Organization strategy is made up of two parts: strategy development and
strategy implementation. At the core of strategy development are four
elements:

Performance Levels

TABLE 6.1. STRATEGY'S POSITION IN THE NINE PERFORMANCE VARIABLES

Performance Needs

	GOALS	DESIGN	MANAGEMENT
ORGANIZATION LEVEL	**ORGANIZATION GOALS** • Has the organization's strategy or direction been articulated and communicated? • Does this strategy make sense, in terms of the external threats and opportunities and the internal strengths and weaknesses? • Given this strategy, have the required outputs of the organization and the level of performance expected from each output been determined and communicated?	**ORGANIZATION DESIGN** • Are all relevant functions in place? • Are all functions necessary? • Is the current flow of inputs and outputs between functions appropriate? • Does the formal organization structure support the strategy and enhance the efficiency of the system?	**ORGANIZATION MANAGEMENT** • Have appropriate function goals been set? • Is relevant performance measured? • Are resources appropriately allocated? • Are the interfaces between functions being managed?
PROCESS LEVEL	**PROCESS GOALS** • Are goals for key processes linked to customer and organization requirements?	**PROCESS DESIGN** • Is this the most efficient and effective process for accomplishing the Process Goals?	**PROCESS MANAGEMENT** • Have appropriate process subgoals been set? • Is process performance managed? • Are sufficient resources allocated to each process? • Are the interfaces between process steps being managed?
JOB/PERFORMER LEVEL	**JOB GOALS** • Are job outputs and standards linked to process requirements (which are in turn linked to customer and organization requirements)?	**JOB DESIGN** • Are process requirements reflected in the appropriate jobs? • Are job steps in a logical sequence? • Have supportive policies and procedures been developed? • Is the job environment ergonomically sound?	**JOB MANAGEMENT** • Do the performers understand the Job Goals (outputs they are expected to produce and standards they are expected to meet)? • Do the performers have sufficient resources, clear signals and priorities, and a logical Job Design? • Are the performers rewarded for achieving the Job Goals? • Do the performers know if they are meeting the Job Goals? • Do the performers have the necessary knowledge and skill to achieve the Job Goals? • If the performers were in an environment in which the five questions listed above were answered "yes," would they have the physical, mental, and emotional capacity to achieve the Job Goals?

1. Products and services we will offer (*what* we are going to do)
2. Customers and markets we will serve (*whom* we will do it for)
3. Competitive advantages (*why* the customers will buy from us)
4. Product and market priorities (*where* we will place our emphasis)

At the core of strategy implementation is a fifth, multifaceted element:

5. *Systems and structures (how* we are going to bring about the *what, who, why,* and *where)*

We are not implying that these five elements are all there is to strategy. However, we believe that all other strategic analysis, decisions, and actions are either:

- Inputs to the first four elements (market research, industry analysis, competitive analysis, environmental monitoring, portfolio planning)
- Ways of measuring the effectiveness of the first four elements (financial results, market share, nonfinancial critical success factors)
- Philosophical guides to all five elements (values, culture)
- Subparts of the fifth element (budgets, marketing plans, human resource plans, technology plans)
- Problem solving and action planning to remove barriers to the fifth element

What are the questions that top managers (of an entire organization or of any component within an organization) need to answer before they can design and manage organization performance?

Questions that precede strategic decision making:

1. What values are going to guide our business?
2. How far down the road are we going to look?
3. What assumptions about the external environment (regulation, the economy, resource availability, technology, competition, the market) underpin our strategy?

Questions that address products and services (Element 1):

4. What existing and new products and services will we be offering (and not offering)?
5. What criteria will we use to evaluate a new product or service opportunity?

Questions that address customers and markets (Element 2):

6. What existing and new customer groups will we be serving (and not serving)?
7. What criteria will we use to evaluate a new market opportunity?

Questions that address competitive advantages (Element 3):

8. What factors (price and/or the various dimensions of quality) are meaningful to our customers?
9. Which of these factors will represent our competitive advantages?

Questions that address product and market emphasis (Element 4):

10. In which of our current product or market areas will we be placing the greatest emphasis (resources and attention)?
11. In what new product or market areas will we be placing the greatest emphasis?

Figure 6.1 shows how the answers to these questions help us effectively define each part of the systems view of performance, which we introduced in Chapter One.

FIGURE 6.1. THE IMPACT OF STRATEGY ON THE COMPONENTS OF AN ORGANIZATION SYSTEM

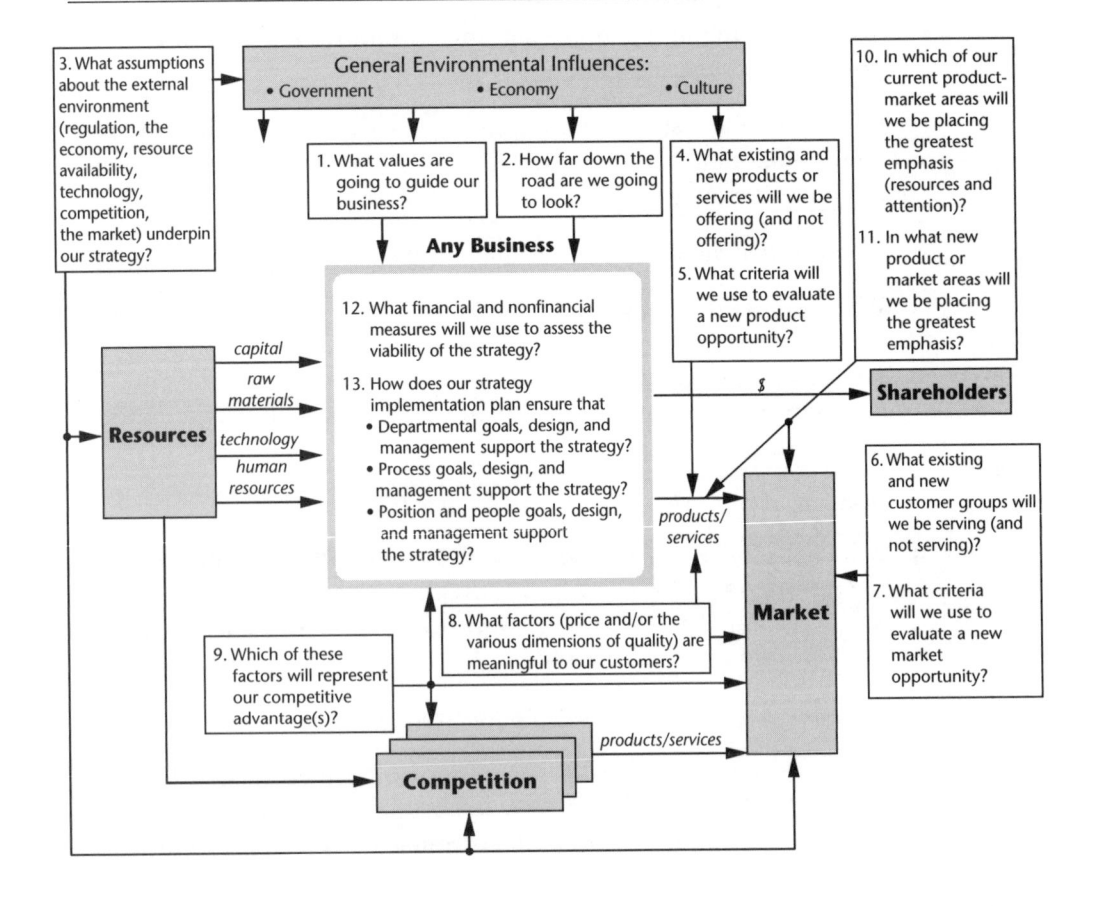

Without answers to questions 1 through 11, the organizational ship has no rudder. Without strategic definition and goals, which position an organization in its environment, performance management is at best a guessing game. We subscribe to the old saw that says an organization needs not only to do things right but also to do the right things. The right things are those activities that are in concert with a viable, comprehensive, and clearly articulated strategy.

Why Do Strategies Fail?

A solid strategy is only half the battle. In our experience, the majority of the strategies that have never come to successful fruition have failed not because they lack a clear, viable vision; rather, they are gathering dust because they have been poorly implemented. Unfortunately, even the best strategies do not spontaneously guide performance. Comprehensive actions to implement a strategy must be planned, carried out, and monitored. Moreover, no matter how talented and hardworking they may be, top managers cannot implement a strategy by themselves. A key implementation contribution must be made by middle managers and by those others who manage the systems and people who will make or break the strategy.

An early implementation step should be widespread communication of the strategy. The downside of communication (a possible leak to competitors of information that they probably know anyway, just by observation in the marketplace) is far less serious than the downside of noncommunication (failure to implement the strategy).

Once people understand the strategy, management should establish an infrastructure that supports strategy implementation. That infrastructure needs to be established at the Organization, Process, and Job/Performer Levels. To our eleven questions, therefore, let us add two more:

Questions that address strategy implementation (Element 5):

12. What financial and nonfinancial measures will we use to assess the viability of the strategy?
13. How does our strategy implementation plan ensure that:

- Departmental goals, design, and management support the strategy?
- Process goals, design, and management support the strategy?
- Position or people goals, design, and management support the strategy?

The "dollars to shareholders" component of the system is a measure of how well the organization has addressed these thirteen questions.

The Three Levels of Strategy Implementation

In Chapter Three, we discussed the need to develop Organization Goals that are driven by strategy. Among our examples was the strategic goal of introducing three new software products and two new system integration services within two years. That goal is unlikely to be achieved if it is not reflected in the goals of product development, operations, and marketing (Organization Level), supported by an efficient product development and introduction process (Process Level), and reinforced by the reward systems for research engineers and the sales organization (Job/Performer Level).

The most powerful strategy implementation tools we have found are those that help us effectively design and manage performance at the Organization, Process, and Job/Performer Levels. Once we have formulated a strategy by answering the first eleven questions listed in Figure 6.1, we can focus our implementation planning by answering the questions that lie behind question 13:

Organization Level

- *Goals:* What specific customer and financial goals will we set and track against?
- *Design:* What internal customer-supplier links do we need to achieve our competitive advantage?
- *Management:* How many and what kinds of resources need to be allocated to the various functions?

Process Level

- *Goals:* What are the goals for the processes that are critical to our competitive advantage?
- *Design:* What are we doing to make sure that our strategically critical processes are working efficiently and effectively?
- *Management:* How are we making sure that our critical processes are being managed on an ongoing basis?

Job/Performer Level

- *Goals:* What are the goals for the jobs that are most critical to process (and, in turn, strategic) success?
- *Design:* What are we doing to design each of these key jobs so that it best contributes to strategic success?
- *Management:* What are we doing (feedback, training, incentives) to create an environment that supports each job's strategic contribution?

The responses to these questions represent the core of a strategy implementation plan. Throughout this book, we present tools—

organization mapping, process management, human performance management, measurement—designed to help develop these responses.

Linking Performance to Strategy: An Example

Baldwin Drug Stores, Inc. (a fictional company) is a retail pharmacy and sundries chain. To succeed in its highly competitive industry, Baldwin's executives realize that they need to establish a strategy that clearly guides day-to-day performance. They use the eleven questions to be sure that all of the bases are covered. We can summarize the results of top management's strategy formulation decisions:

1. They establish a list of value statements. Among them are:

- *Baldwin will sell only the highest-quality products.*
- *Baldwin employees will go the extra mile to provide service that meets or exceeds customers' expectations.*
- *Because employees are the best source of ideas, the business will be run in a participative, open-door style.*

2. They decide that in their highly turbulent industry a three-year strategy is appropriate.

3. They use market research information and their own understanding of the industry to document a list of assumptions about the environment in which Baldwin will be doing business three years from now. Some of these assumptions are:

- *Easing of pharmaceutical industry regulation will increase the quantity of new drugs and dramatically increase the number of generic drugs.*
- *The economy in Baldwin's geographical territory will continue to grow.*
- *Inexpensive full- and part-time cashiers and stockpeople will be increasingly difficult to find.*
- *Discount drug outlets and superstores will continue to represent the most formidable competition.*
- *Customers will continue to be willing to pay a bit more if they perceive that they are receiving value beyond that provided by the basic product.*

4. The executives, after much debate, decide that they will resist the temptation to offer groceries, automotive products, and toys. They also decide not to manufacture any products. They will continue to offer prescription and patent medicines, health care products, cosmetics, camera supplies, and office supplies. In short, they decide that Baldwin can succeed by continuing to be a chain of old-fashioned corner drugstores. They develop a complete list of categories of products they will and will not offer during the next three years.

5. When evaluating a new product line, the executive team will use these criteria:

- *Has the potential to meet profitability goals*
- *Fits with the "corner drugstore" image and the current Baldwin product categories*
- *Is able to meet an enduring need*
- *Requires no new forms of display or significantly new employee skills*

6. They decide that Baldwin will target three primary markets (customer groups): elderly people, disabled people, and young affluent families. While these niches clearly exclude a large percentage of the population, the top team believes that this focus will enable Baldwin to develop a significant competitive advantage and a thriving business.

7. When evaluating a new market opportunity (be it a new geographical area or a new customer type), the primary "go–no go" criteria will be concerned with whether the area or group of customers has a documented need for the current product line, whether the new venture is able to establish Baldwin's competitive advantages, and whether it requires new investment that can be recouped within two years.

8. To ensure that their strategy is customer-focused, the executives use survey and focus-group information to identify the requirements of customers in the elderly, disabled, and affluent-family markets. They decide that these groups are primarily driven by convenience, product availability, and service. While price is a factor (particularly for Medicare patients), the top team believes that Baldwin customers will be willing to pay a bit more for convenience, availability, and service.

9. Baldwin's competitive advantage will be in the three areas just identified. Baldwin will establish an advantage in convenience through store locations, business hours, and home delivery. Baldwin will ensure that a full line of products for elderly and disabled people and affluent families is always available. In addition to home delivery, Baldwin's services will include knowledgeable photographic and cosmetics personnel, a medication hotline, and the kind of personal attention that comes from strong relationships with the doctors used by Baldwin's customers. The executives firmly believe that these factors will differentiate Baldwin from the low-service, low-price discount stores, grocery stores, and drug warehouses.

10. During the next three years, Baldwin will place a disproportionate marketing and sourcing emphasis on the patent medications that it currently provides to elderly and disabled people.

11. Given the competitive advantages Baldwin plans to establish, its management will emphasize new products (such as supplies for disabled people) that will enable it to be a "one-stop shopping" store for its target markets.

These eleven points represent only a high-level strategy, but they establish a clear sense of direction and reflect an analysis of all the components of the systems view of performance. To make sure that their vision is implemented, Baldwin's top managers take two more actions:

12. They select three measures that will enable them to evaluate the success of the strategy: return on net assets, market share, and customer satisfaction ratings.

13. They establish a set of organizationwide and departmental goals that reflect their strategic thrusts. First, they establish specific goals for service quality for all departments that have contact with customers. Second, they ensure that all departments are structured and linked in a way that enables Baldwin to provide differentiated customer service. Third, they make sure that resources are appropriately allocated. For example, market researchers receive the money and staff they need to gather comprehensive information on the three target markets.

They make sure that key processes (customer service, market research, and supplier selection) are documented and have goals that support the strategic goals. They make sure that these strategic processes are efficiently accomplishing their goals, and they install a Process Management infrastructure to monitor and continuously improve these strategic processes.

Within each strategic process, they identify a number of jobs that are particularly critical to organization success. In Baldwin's customer service process, all customer contact jobs are critical. For these jobs, goals (derived from process goals) are established and communicated. The jobs are designed to enhance customer service. Most important, the management team creates an environment (through training, feedback, and rewards) that supports outstanding customer service.

Summary

The Three Levels framework makes two contributions to organization strategy. To strategy *formulation,* it offers the systems framework (see Table 6.1), which ensures that an organization's direction is based on an analysis of all the strategic variables. The systems components suggest eleven questions that an effective strategy should answer.

To strategy *implementation,* the Three Levels framework offers the Nine Performance Variables, which must be addressed to ensure that the strategic vision becomes organizational reality. A management team that cascades its strategy through the Organization, Process, and Job/Performer Levels dramatically increases the odds of that strategy taking root. At each level, the strategy is implemented through Goals, Design, and Management.

Chapters Seven through Fourteen delve more deeply into a variety of dimensions of strategy implementation.

CHAPTER SEVEN

MOVING FROM ANNUAL PROGRAMS TO SUSTAINED PERFORMANCE IMPROVEMENT

Beware, lest you lose the substance by grasping at the shadow.

—AESOP

At most large and medium-sized organizations, top managers like to embark on performance improvement programs. These programs tend to have a focal slogan, which includes terms like *quality, customer service, reengineering,* and *teamwork.* They tend to be launched with a great deal of publicity. They are initially supported by a large expenditure of resources (often cited as a symbol of significant support from top management).

Unfortunately, betterment programs frequently end up grasping at the shadow, rather than establishing an infrastructure for substantive, sustained performance improvement. To wit, here is an excerpt from an issue of a Fortune 100 company newsletter:

> With the presentations recently of two quality teams, the program closed its ledger and ended. From the five pilot teams, the program grew to 327 teams. Ninety-three presentations included cost savings. During its existence, the program became an integral part of the philosophy of participative management. It provided both tangible and intangible results, such as developing problem-solving, leadership, and communication skills.

When it initially became clear that U.S. involvement in the Vietnam war was a no-win proposition, Vermont's Senator Aiken proposed that America declare victory and withdraw. Similarly, this company counted up the number of teams and recommendations, declared the quality program a success, and shut it down.

A human resource development professional in this organization (displaying rare commodities—memory and perspective) developed a family tree that positions the quality team program as one of thirty-six productivity, quality, participative management, and culture change programs his company has embarked on in the last ten years. Each of them began with impressive fanfare, lofty expectations, and large budgets. Most are now dead or comatose. It is no surprise that, in this organization, the prevailing employee reaction to any new management initiative was BOHICA—Bend Over, Here It Comes Again. After ten years of programs, employees perceived the organization, with only a few pockets of exception, as the same old place.

The short-term financial perspective of U.S. business has been thoroughly documented and castigated (with little effect) in a number of books and articles over the years. This shortness of attention span extends to organization improvement as well. Perhaps American management's impatient search for the magic bullet is at the root of its impressive record in entrepreneurship and product innovation. However, when it comes to substantive, sustained gains in performance, there is no magic bullet.

In our experience, even the most effective training programs and organization development interventions tend to offer only one or two of the many pieces of the performance puzzle. We have found that any improvement effort—whether it is driven by quality, customer focus, productivity, cycle time, cost reduction, or even culture change—is effective only to the degree that it encompasses the Three Levels of Performance.

Four Examples of Flawed Performance Improvement Efforts

How would you grade these performance improvement programs?

Example 1. The president of ABC Electronics, Inc., has been exposed to the "quality" religion and becomes a true believer. Realizing that quality is getting insufficient attention in his company, he:

- Arranges for a "fire and brimstone" quality speaker to deliver a one- or two-day session for all managers
- Directs the human resource development department to prepare each supervisor to conduct video-plus-discussion sessions with his or her subordinates
- Appoints a full-time quality director, who will report directly to him
- Asks the quality director to produce a one-paragraph quality statement and circulate it to all employees
- Directs the employee communications department to manage a poster contest, with an award going to the winning design
- Tells the personnel department to arrange for all employees to wear badge inserts that say "Quality—It's as Basic as ABC"

- Provides additional funds to the human resource development department for the purchase or development of workshops on quality
  techniques

Assessment. The ABC Electronics president has embraced much of the
form and little of the substance of an effective quality effort. While his
actions are nobly motivated and not necessarily dangerous, he gets an
overall grade of F for doing nothing of lasting significance at the
Organization, Process, or Job/Performer Level.

There is no evidence that he has articulated a quality strategy for the
organization or designed the functional relationships through which he will
carry it out. He hasn't initiated any efforts to build quality into any strategically critical business *processes,* and the company doesn't appear to have
built quality into the measurement, training, feedback, and reward systems
of individual *jobs.* This scenario has all the trappings of a short-lived,
minimum-impact program.

Example 2. The corporate quality director of the Sleep Inns hotel chain
hires, at great expense, a top-notch consulting firm to reengineer the
guest check-in and checkout systems. The consultants involve representatives of supervisory and nonsupervisory front-desk staff in the analysis and
development of proposed changes. The recommended improvements are
blessed, with only minor modifications, by the quality director. The
improvements are implemented, along with a measurement and reward
system that reinforces accurate and speedy check-in and checkout
performance.

Assessment. Sleep Inns has done a bit better than ABC Electronics. It has
taken action to improve the performance of a business process (check-in
and checkout). The people closest to the action have been involved in the
analysis. The quality director gets high marks for seeing that the results
of the Process Improvement effort are built into the support systems at
the Job/Performer Level. What's missing is attention to the Organization
Level. Is check-in/checkout the most strategically significant process?
Where is speedy checkout in customers' priorities? Is the chain attempting
to match the competition or establish a competitive edge? Having selected
that process, why limit the involvement in the project to the front-desk
function? (Doesn't the check-in/checkout process involve the reserva-
tions, bell, and accounting staffs as well?) And where is top management?
With all due respect to the quality director, what signal does top management's absence in this project send to the organization?

Example 3. After extensive market research and competitive assessment,
the top management team at the Cars R Us automotive parts company

decides that it is going to build a competitive advantage by shortening order processing cycle time—the time that elapses between the customer's placement of an order and the customer's receipt of the correct part. A group of analysts is assigned to examine and recommend ways of reducing the time it takes to execute each of the three processes that affect order processing cycle time and order entry, manufacturing and assembly, and distribution. In three weeks, the analysts have developed systems that, without sacrificing quality or increasing cost, can shorten the cycle time from the current twenty-eight days to eleven days, the best time in the industry. The systems are implemented as recommended.

Assessment. Cars R Us has addressed the strategic dimension of the Organization Level. Order processing cycle time has been designated as a potential competitive advantage. Our question at the Organization Level is this: Have the functions been aligned (in terms of customer-supplier relationships) to achieve the strategic goal? A critical process has been selected and studied. Unfortunately, we can't give this company more than a C at the Process Level because the process analysis was carried out by analysts, rather than by key players in the order process. Involving them would have strengthened their cross-functional relationships and increased their commitment to the changes.

The major shortcoming, however, is at the Job/Performer Level. Here, we have a sin of omission. A clear strategy and a well-structured process are worthless if they do not drive the performance of people.

Nothing appears to have been done to incorporate the cycle-time strategy and process improvements into the jobs of people who work in the order processing system.

Example 4. As part of its planning for an increasingly deregulated (competitive) environment, the Universal Telephone Company establishes a strategic objective: to improve, by 10 percent, the ratings on the repair questions that are part of the quarterly customer satisfaction surveys. The policy committee clearly communicates this strategic goal and increases the repair department's headcount ceiling and budget allocation for trucks and tools. The human resource development department is told to extend and enhance repairers' and repair supervisors' training programs. In each section within the repair department, quality teams are formed. Under the guidance of a skilled facilitator, the teams meet once a week to solve problems in their areas.

Assessment. Universal Telephone has established an Organization Level objective to improve performance. The objective is strategic because it addresses customer and competitive concerns. Furthermore, the company has ensured that organizationwide communication and sufficient resource allocation support the objective. The only fly in the Organization Level ointment is the top team's apparent failure to see repair as an area that most likely involves more than just the repair department. Training and team problem solving are ensuring that the Job/Performer Level is adequately addressed. (Perhaps it is being addressed *too* adequately; there's no evidence of a Skills and Knowledge deficiency that warrants the investment in training.) The policy committee wisely realizes that the men and women closest to repair are best equipped to develop the most effective improvements. However, the repair process undoubtedly involves handoffs (interfaces) among functions inside and outside repair. As a result, the functional (section-by-section) approach to the quality team's structure is a bit troublesome. We also wonder whether the improvements that come out of the teams will be adequately supported by the measurement and reward systems.

The major flaw in Universal Telephone's approach is the absence of the link we most frequently find missing—the Process Level. There is no indication that the repair process is being systematically and holistically addressed. The potential shortcomings in measurement and the likely survival of "white space" issues (see Chapter One) considerably lower the odds of success in this effort. The Organization Level goal is unlikely to be achieved without the creation of an effective repair process. The team recommendations at the Job/Performer Level are liable to be constrained by any weaknesses in the repair process as a whole, which is beyond the charter of any one sectional team.

Organizationwide Performance Improvement

Our critique of the four attempted performance improvement programs underscores our belief that any effort that does not address all Three Levels of Performance is liable to produce only piecemeal results. If the president of ABC Electronics were to follow the Three Levels approach, he would take nine steps, which mirror the Nine Performance Variables discussed in Chapters Two through Five:

Organization Level

1. *Goals:* Develop a set of companywide, customer-driven performance improvement goals linked to the competitive advantages and/or gaps outlined in the company strategy.
2. *Design:* Design an organization in which functional customer-supplier relationships support the strategy.
3. *Management:* Allocate resources so that the goals can be achieved and establish a system for tracking and improving performance.

Process Level

4. *Goals:* Identify the processes that are most critical to the strategy and establish goals that describe the performance required of those processes.
5. *Design:* Charter cross-functional teams to find the disconnects in the current processes and to design processes to eliminate the disconnects.
6. *Management:* Establish goals at critical junctures in the process and continuously monitor and improve process performance.

Job/Performer Level

7. *Goals:* Identify the jobs that are critical to the success of the process and establish goals for the outputs of those jobs.
8. *Design:* Design and organize the jobs so that they can efficiently and effectively achieve the goals.
9. *Management:* Create a job environment in which capable, adequately trained people have clear statements of, regular feedback on, positive consequences for, and few barriers to goal achievement.

The president might still want to provide awareness training, appoint a quality director, and blanket the organization with posters and badge inserts. However, by addressing the Nine Variables outlined in the Three Levels approach, he would be moving from program-of-the-month symbols to an infrastructure for substantive, long-term performance improvement.

As flawed as it is, the ABC quality program has one major strength—the involvement of the president. We have found few examples of successful and sustained efforts in which senior management is not actively involved. In exemplary programs, top managers do more than give their blessing and some money. Figure 7.1 describes the five responsibilities assumed by top managers who are actively involved in a performance improvement effort.

Two Case Studies

Douglas Aircraft Company. We had the opportunity to help the Douglas Aircraft Company (a division of McDonnell Douglas Corporation) design and implement a companywide performance improvement effort. The top management team was determined to fight the "just another program" (BOHICA) attitude and to implement a quality and productivity effort with teeth.

FIGURE 7.1. TOP MANAGEMENT'S ROLE IN A PERFORMANCE IMPROVEMENT EFFORT

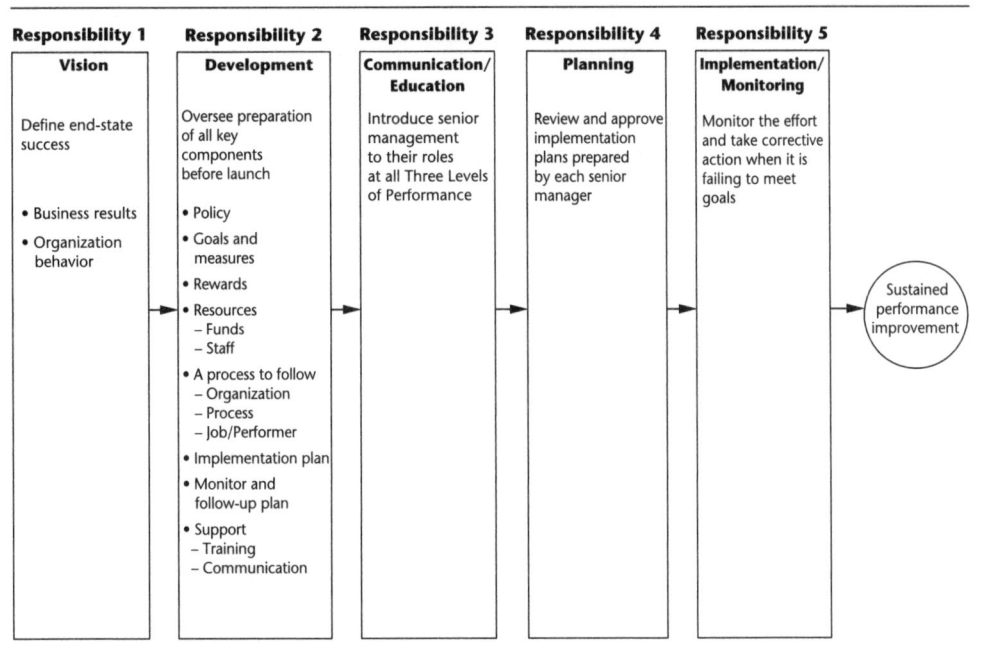

They began by identifying what they called the company's Significant Business Issue: "Satisfy Your Customer Through First-Time Quality." They set up a structure in which natural work groups, which are either vertical (work-unit groups) or horizontal (cross-functional groups), meet regularly, assisted by line people who are trained as full-time facilitators. The teams went through a five-phase process:

1.   The leader presented to the team the competitive reasons for the Significant Business Issue effort and described the purpose and mechanics of the process.

2.   On the basis of objectives that originated with the organization strategy and flowed down to them through the program offices (representing each product line), the team members used a Relationship Map (see Chapter Three) to document their customers, products and services, inputs, and suppliers. They then selected the product or service and customer that they believe can have the greatest impact on the objectives. Focused on the key product and customer, they set a tentative goal, which described the team's contribution to the objective. (Phases 1 and 2 address the *Organization Level* of both the company and the team.)

3.   The team selected one or more representatives to interview individuals from the customer organization (which, more often than not, was

an internal unit). Through a set of structured questions, the team learned the customer's requirements for the product or service and got feedback on current performance. The tentative goal from Phase 2 was refined and finalized based on these requirements.

4. The team members used a Process Map (see Chapter Four) to design a process that enabled them to satisfy the customer's requirements with first-time quality (which includes efficiency and cost as well as traditional quality considerations). The team documented any gaps between the current process and this customer-driven "SHOULD" process. After the Process Map was completed, the team developed a proposed numerical measure and standard for each customer requirement. These standards were then negotiated with the customer in a second meeting.

5. In the final phase, the team members planned and implemented actions to move from the "IS" to the "SHOULD" process, resolving any problems they identified during the first four phases. They converted the customer-approved standards into a measurement system, which the unit used to track performance on an ongoing basis. They then established a mechanism for regularly gathering data on the customer's needs and feedback. (Phases 3, 4, and this portion of Phase 5 address the *Process Level* of performance.) Last, they committed to actions that drove the measures, the improved process, and a customer-focused mind-set into the jobs of individuals who work within the process. (This part of Phase 5 addresses the *Job/Performer Level.*)

It was not a flawless effort. There were some pockets of BOHICA, in which people treated it as a "this, too, shall pass" program. The formal process is a bit light on the Job/Performer Level. Some of the floweddown objectives did not give specific guidance to the teams. Too few of the teams were cross-functional. However, it was probably as successful as a thirty-thousand-person effort can be. It addressed all Three Levels of Performance. It was sustainable. It was customer-driven. It placed a great deal of emphasis on measurement, and it was implemented by individuals within the natural structure of the organization.

Our use of the past tense here may make this effort look suspiciously like a short-lived program. However, while few teams formally follow the Significant Business Issue process today, it spawned subsequent improvement efforts and widespread use of the tools introduced during the five phases.

GTE. The GTE approach to performance improvement is also based on the Three Levels of Performance, but it is quite different from the approach taken by Douglas Aircraft. Rather than establishing teams, the GTE effort uses management team training as the catalyst for performance improvement.

The effort began with the corporate policy committee's identification of quality as the primary competitive issue in all of GTE's businesses. The committee members (the top seven executives in the company) returned from their annual strategic-planning retreat with a mandate for executive-level quality training. While the company had taken and was continuing to take a variety of formal steps to enhance quality, most of the programs did not have heavy top-management involvement. The committee saw this involvement as critical to the success of any quality effort.

Independently, the vice president for quality services and the director of executive education had also concluded that the next step in the quality journey was senior management's education. They had been working on a quality training and education program, and the policy committee's mandate was all they needed to launch it. The vice president and the director broke the mold by developing a training program that met these criteria:

- It was a hands-on workshop, rather than a quality-awareness program.
- It was driven by the need for quality to be a strategic weapon, rather than merely a set of quality tools.
- It was attended by teams from each business unit. The teams were made up of the business-unit president or general manager and his or her direct reports.
- The work sessions continued after the formal classroom training. The teams submitted their action plans to a policy committee member, who held them accountable for taking the actions and achieving the promised results.

The first group of participants in the workshop, called Quality: The Competitive Edge (QCE), was the policy committee itself. The members recognized that they needed to learn about quality and commit to specific actions that would enable them to lead the quality effort. Following this session, the presidents of GTE's thirty-five business units, along with their vice presidents, attended one of twelve QCE sessions.

According to the primary architect of QCE, "The course itself, and the action plans of the SBU [strategic business unit] teams, was built on a structure we call 'The Three Levels of Quality':

Level 1: The Organization Level: Development of a customer-driven quality strategy which supports the SBU business plan

Level 2: The Process Level: The cross-functional work flows which produce outputs for internal and external customers

Level 3: Individuals and Teams: Creating an environment which supports the natural desire of employees to do quality work."

In the three-day sessions, the teams learned about quality at each of the three levels and spent a significant amount of time in team planning sessions. During these workshop activities, the teams committed to a series of actions at each of the Three Levels of quality.

The 550 executives who attended QCE developed quality strategies for their business units or staff departments, selected tools for implementing those strategies, and planned to engage in specific leadership behaviors to support that implementation. Not surprisingly, the majority of their implementation plans included workshops for the next two or three levels of management. QCE-II was developed to meet this need.

The two-day QCE-II workshop was offered at the business-unit locations to managers (and occasionally to nonmanagers). QCE-II was a vehicle for these employees to understand the quality strategy developed by their top management and to commit to making the most direct possible contribution to that strategy through the implementation of their own action plans at each of the Three Levels of quality. These action plans are based on the business-unit executives' list of "killer gaps" that currently or potentially represent competitive quality disadvantages. To ensure that QCE-II was not "just another program," the instructors were the business-unit presidents and vice presidents, assisted by videotapes of the faculty presentations.

The QCE and QCE-II sessions served their purpose. In addition to generating actions that led to measurable improvements in quality (including customer survey ratings), they spawned the next phase of the improvement effort, which includes benchmarking and, most significant, massive reengineering of the core processes in telephone operations.

The GTE QCE effort is a rare example of a training-driven program achieving significant hard (quantitative quality improvement) and soft (culture change) results. Certainly, the commitment from the top of the house and the unflagging efforts of the vice president for quality services and the director of executive education are key factors in its success. However, a significant amount of the credit also goes to the comprehensive tools and actions taken at each of the Three Levels of Performance.

Summary

Beware of programs. By definition, programs end. Performance improvement, by contrast, should never end. Successful performance improvement efforts tend to meet four criteria:

- They establish an infrastructure, which enables them to be sustained without "special program" mechanisms.

- They are goal driven. They begin with a set of goals and include a mechanism for reestablishing goals over time.
- They involve substantive actions at the Organization, Process, and Job/ Performer Levels.
- They are driven by the active involvement of the top management in the organization.

The Nine Performance Variables provide a checklist of substantive actions that can be taken at each of the Three Levels. However, this performance improvement technology is just the start. An organization's top managers must take responsibility for sticking with the effort and carving out a significant role for themselves.

CHAPTER EIGHT

DIAGNOSING AND IMPROVING PERFORMANCE: A CASE STUDY

Medicine, to produce health, has to examine disease.

—PLUTARCH

The pharmaceutical industry has developed a host of effective medicines. Penicillin, for example, is a drug of demonstrated effectiveness. However, it probably won't help a cataract. There's no evidence that cortisone will do anything for a fever. Aspirin has been called a wonder drug, but it is actually harmful to someone suffering from an ulcer. Unfortunately, every effective medicine addresses only a limited number of ailments. Professional diagnosticians, called doctors, are paid to match medications with patients' illnesses.

Similarly, there are lots of proven performance improvement "medicines" out there. Training is one form of medication. Reorganization is another. A management information system is another. An incentive compensation plan is yet another. The question is, Who are the "doctors" being paid to match these (and other) medications with our organizations' illnesses?

Typically, the professionals who are paid to solve organization performance problems and to help capitalize on performance opportunities are in staff functions, such as human resource development (HRD), data processing (DP), and industrial engineering (IE). That's fine. We cannot expect line managers to be masters of all of the possible performance improvement interventions. However, we have not, in general, carved out the appropriate roles for our staff people. They tend to be perceived (and, often, to perceive themselves) as providers of specific solutions. For example, the HRD folks provide training solutions, the DP people provide computer-systems solutions, and the IE mission is to provide work flow streamlining and ergonomic solutions.

Unlike diagnostically focused doctors, however, our staffers are frequently purveyors of their functions' unique brands of patent medicine, claiming that their potions will cure what ails you. We believe that every staff analyst or consultant, regardless of the breadth of his or her "product line," should be first of all a diagnostician. A dose of performance medication that does not address the disease is at best a waste of money. At worst, it causes side effects more serious than the original affliction.

Ideally, a line manager with a need would conduct a diagnosis and call in representatives of all the staff functions that can contribute to a comprehensive solution. However, we have found that a line manager generally does not have these skills, any more than a sick person has the ability to diagnose his or her own illness before calling in the appropriate specialist. Line managers have a feeling of pain or opportunity, and they know they need to take some action. However, in our experience, *line managers rarely know what action they need to take to address a performance improvement opportunity*. This reality puts the burden on staff people to diagnose situations before implementing solutions.

The Three Levels Approach to Performance Diagnosis and Improvement

We have found that the Three Levels Performance Improvement Process is an effective way for any staff person to diagnose a situation before recommending action. At the least, it enables the analyst to tailor his or her solution to the organization unit's unique situation. At the most, it may indicate that a solution involving his or her elixir does not address the highest-priority need.

A Situation Requiring Diagnosis

The vice president of operations for the partially fictionalized Property Casualty, Inc. (PCI) has requested that Larry Monahan, one of his procedures analysts, develop an updated, clearer, and more comprehensive claims manual for the organization's claims representatives.

Larry will be using the fourteen-step Three Levels approach, which appears in Figure 8.1. As we discuss the application of each step to this situation, we will display some of the forms he may use. However, the process should not be forms driven and need not be as formal as it's depicted here. The heart of the process is the sequence of steps, the questions that need to be answered at each step, the organization of the information obtained in response to the questions, and the link between actions and diagnosis.

FIGURE 8.1. THE THREE LEVELS PERFORMANCE IMPROVEMENT PROCESS

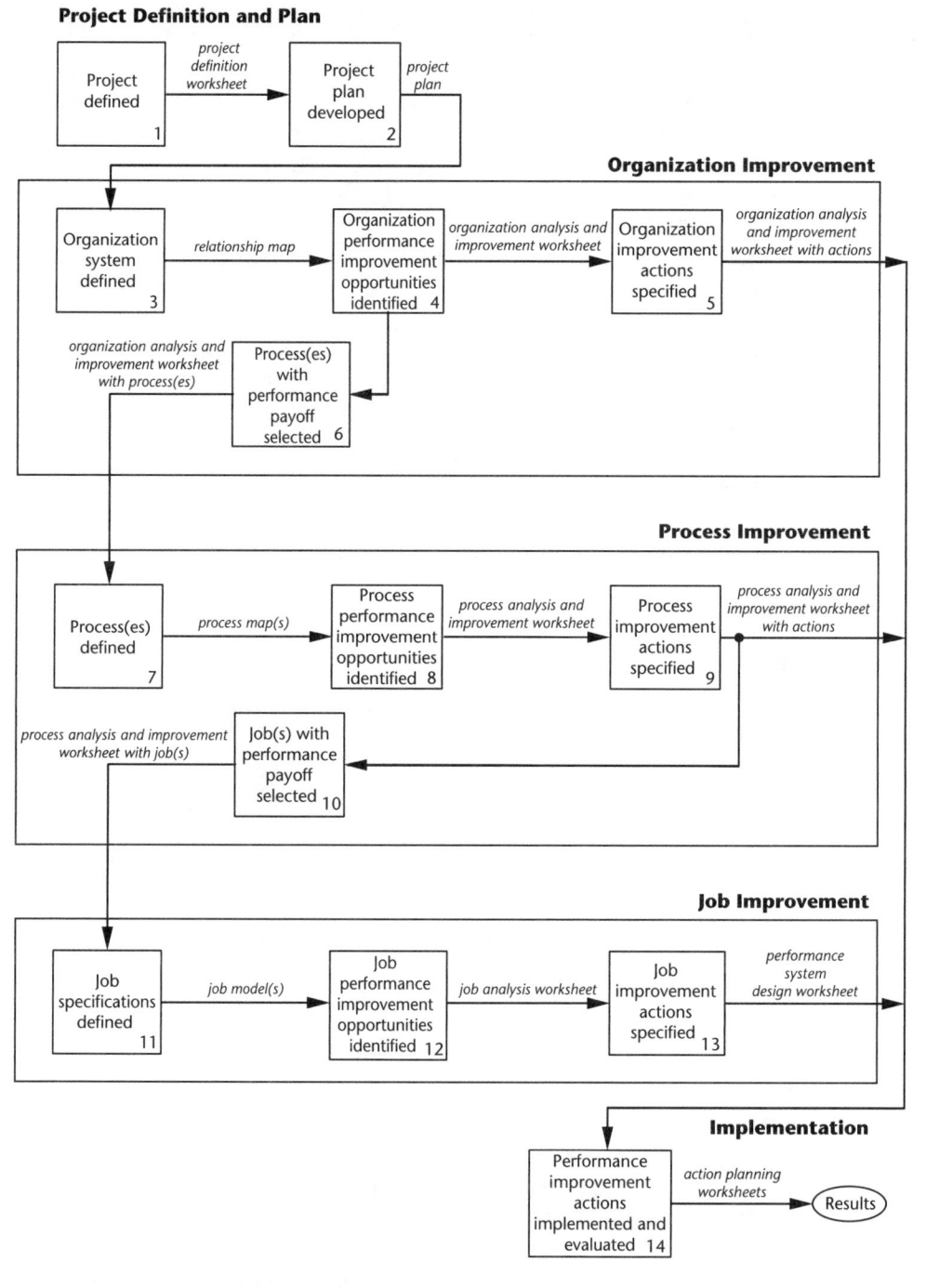

NOTE: **THE PERFORMANCE IMPROVEMENT PROCESS CAN BE USED TO:**
- Enhance performance that is at or above standard
- Correct performance that is below standard

Project Definition and Plan

Step 1: Project Defined. In this step, Larry interviews the vice president of operations. His goal is specifically to define the Critical Business Issue (CBI) that stimulated Larry's assignment. Updating the claims manual is clearly the vice president's preferred solution to some problem. If Larry is to be an effective diagnostician, he will need to understand that problem. During the interview, he learns that the vice president's concern is *excessive claim payouts.* The average amount that PCI is paying per claim is too high and is negatively affecting the company's margins.

During Project Definition, Larry will also take these actions:

- Learn the specific financial effect the problem is having on the organization.
- Establish project goals based on the desired payout amount.
- Define the scope of the project.
- Identify his client and define the roles he and other key persons will play in the analysis.
- Reach some conclusions regarding the constraints, odds of success, and value of the project.

Assuming that the project makes sense, and that the Three Levels approach is acceptable to his client, Larry proceeds to Step 2.

Step 2: Project Plan Developed. In this step, Larry plans the events and dates for the project. He is careful to indicate the data and data sources he needs at each of the three levels of analysis.

Organization Improvement

Step 3: Organization System Defined. To be sure that the vice president's proposed "fix" will solve the problem, and to identify other factors that may affect claim payouts, Larry begins his analysis at the Organization Level. His first step is to develop a Relationship Map of PCI. He knows that this map of functions, inputs, and outputs will help him see how his project fits into the big picture and ensure that he has identified all of the areas he should probe during his analysis. Figure 8.2 is Larry's map.

Step 4: Organization Performance Improvement Opportunities Identified. In Step 4, Larry wants specifically to identify high-impact gaps at the Organization Level. He begins with the focus provided to him by the vice president but is alert to other opportunities. During his analysis, he unearths claims-processing cost as a second high-impact opportunity.

FIGURE 8.2. PCI RELATIONSHIP MAP

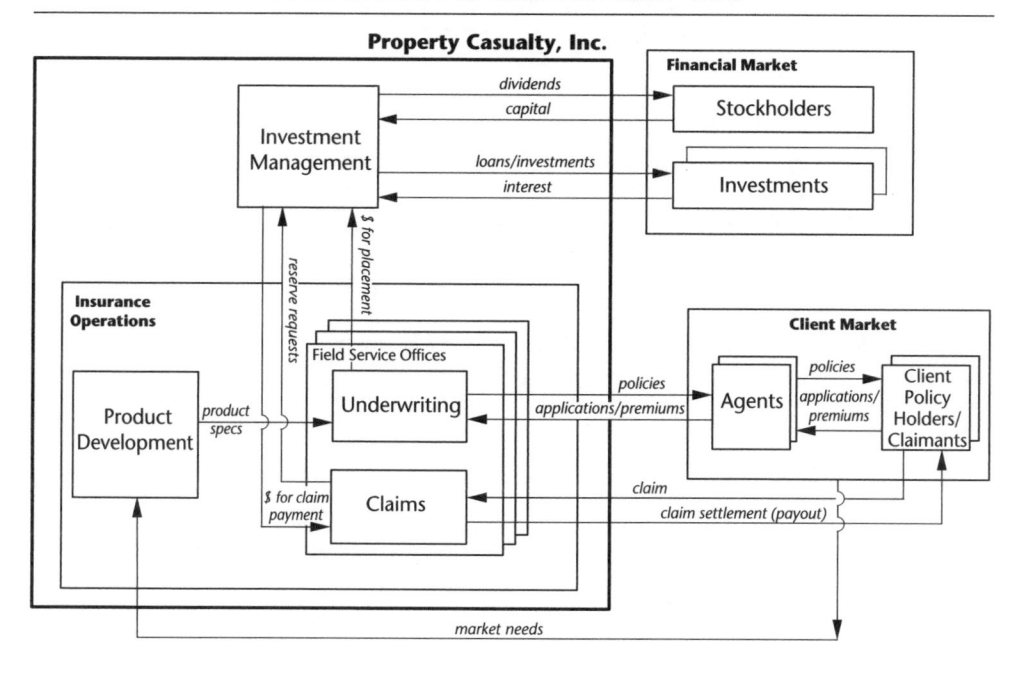

Step 5: Organization Improvement Actions Specified. While he is gathering his data, Larry identifies some of the Organization Level causes of the high-impact gaps. Since he realizes that these causes can be addressed at the Organization Level, without exhaustive analysis at the Process and Job/Performer Levels, he develops a set of recommended actions to address these causes on the basis of the Three Performance Needs at the Organization Level: Organization Goals, Design, and Management. For example, Larry sees no problem with Organization Goals and Design, but in the area of Organization Management, he learns that the underwriting and claims departments often don't understand the insurance products that come out of Product Development. He recommends vehicles for providing this feedback to product development and for establishing a stronger link between the customer and product development. These Organization Level recommendations will be added to those Larry develops at the Process and Job/Performer Levels.

Step 6: Processes with Performance Payoff Identified. To bridge to the Process Level, Larry analyzes the three PCI processes that have impacts on payout amount. He investigates the underwriting and new-product development processes. While he has no doubt that those processes could be improved, Larry identifies the claim-handling process as the one with the greatest impact on the goals of his project. At this point, Larry updates his plan, specifying the steps he will take at the Process Level. Table 8.1 presents a summary of Larry's work in Steps 4, 5, and 6.

TABLE 8.1. PCI ORGANIZATION ANALYSIS AND IMPROVEMENT WORKSHEET

CRITICAL BUSINESS ISSUE: Settlements
ORGANIZATION: Insurance operations and claims

ORGANIZATION OUTPUTS (PRODUCTS)	DESIRED PERFORMANCE (STANDARDS)	ACTUAL PERFORMANCE	GAP (IF ANY)	IMPACT OF GAP	CAUSE OF GAP	ORGANIZATION IMPROVEMENT ACTION	PROCESS THAT INFLUENCES GAP
Claim settlements	A. Payout/claim $1500	$1700	$200	$1.8 million	Bad specs on new policies Policies misrated Poor measurement of payout performance	• Feedback to product development on claim performance • Better input on customer needs • Feedback to underwriting • Change underwriting objectives • Better tracking of payout performance	Claim handling
	B. Time/claim 60 days	60 days	None				
	C. Handling cost/ claim $215	$375	$160	$1.4 million ⎦→	Claims misrouted through agents	• Clarify proper rate for claims and/or • Develop procedures for how agents should process misrouted claims	

Process Improvement

Step 7: Processes Defined. In this step, Larry works with a group of claims representatives and claims supervisors to construct a Process Map, which depicts the claim-handling process as it should flow. (In most instances, this type of group first needs to document the "IS" process as a backdrop for the creation of the "SHOULD.") Their Process Map appears in Figure 8.3.

Step 8: Process Performance Improvement Opportunities Identified. Having documented the claim-handling process, Larry identifies the desired performance for each process step, the actual performance, any gaps between desired and actual performance, and the impact of those gaps. He identifies significant gaps in the "claim qualified" and "claim assigned" process steps.

Step 9: Process Improvement Actions Specified. In Step 9, Larry identifies the causes of gaps revealed in Step 8 and the Process Improvement actions that will remove the gaps. He limits his list of recommended actions to those that can be taken at the Process Level, without analysis at the Job/Performer Level. Larry finds causes that require clarifying performance expectations and providing feedback.

Step 10: Job(s) with Performance Payoff Identified. As the last step in Process Improvement and as a bridge to Job Improvement, Larry identifies the jobs that contribute to the process steps in which there are gaps. His analysis indicates that the claims supervisor job—*not the claims representative job*—requires the most attention during the Job Improvement phase. Table 8.2 summarizes Larry's work in Steps 8, 9, and 10.

FIGURE 8.3. PCI CLAIM-HANDLING PROCESS

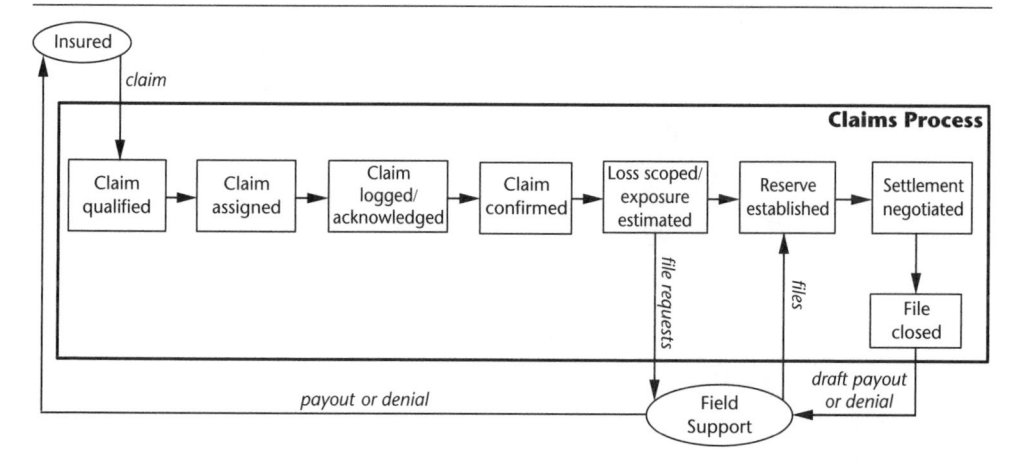

TABLE 8.2. PCI PROCESS ANALYSIS AND IMPROVEMENT WORKSHEET

CRITICAL BUSINESS ISSUE: Settlements
PROCESS: Claims Handling

PROCESS STEPS/ OUTPUTS	DESIRED PERFORMANCE (STANDARDS)	ACTUAL PERFORMANCE	GAP (IF ANY)	IMPACT OF GAP	CAUSE OF GAP	PROCESS IMPROVEMENT ACTIONS	JOBS THAT INFLUENCE GAP
Claim qualified	Recovery potential identified on all claims	Not done on 82% of cases on post audit	82%	Cost per claim	No feedback to permit improvement of identification skills	Provide feedback on the outcome of identified cases of potential recovery	Claims supervisor
	Missing or inaccurate information identified and obtained from agent	Identified in 65% of all cases so requiring	35%	Timeliness	No consequences or feedback to support continued performance where skills are in place		
				Cost per claim	Expectations inconsistently communicated	Clarify and communicate expectations	Claims supervisor
Claim assigned	Claim-processing method selected minimizes processing cost and payout variation potential	Economic assignment not occurring	No economic basis for assignment	Payout high and increasing			

Job Improvement

Step 11: Job Specification Defined. In Step 11, Larry and a group of claims supervisors and managers define the outputs and standards that the "SHOULD" process requires of the claims supervisor job. Table 8.3 displays a portion of the Job Model that the group creates for the claims supervisor.

Step 12: Job Performance Improvement Opportunities Identified. The Job Model produced in Step 11 describes the performance that the claims supervisor needs to produce. In Step 12, Larry compares the current performance to the Job Model's standards and identifies gaps, the impact of the gaps, and the causes of the gaps. He uses the Human Performance System (see Chapter Five) to help him identify the causes of gaps. One of his more significant findings is that the claims supervisors, when qualifying claims, should identify the recovery potential 75 percent of the time. They are doing this in only 18 percent of the cases. Larry's analysis reveals that supervisors are not measured, evaluated, or trained in recovery-potential identification. Table 8.4 summarizes some of his analysis for the supervisor job.

Step 13: Job Improvement Actions Specified. For each gap, Larry develops a recommended gap-closing action. Cognizant of the fact that an effective medicine is one that fits the disease, his action development is focused on the causes of the gaps. A partial picture of Larry's Step 13 is in Table 8.5.

Implementation

Step 14: Performance Improvement Actions Implemented and Evaluated. In this final step in the process, Larry summarizes the recommendations from all three levels of his analysis. He uses the questions associated with the Nine Performance Variables (Chapter Two, Table 2.2) as a checklist to make sure his recommendations address the performance needs at all three levels. He conducts a cost-benefit analysis on the recommendations and develops a proposed high-level implementation plan. Last, he takes his recommendation package through the process that he and the vice president of operations agreed on during the project definition and planning phase.

TABLE 8.3. PCI CLAIMS SUPERVISOR JOB MODEL

JOB: Claims Supervisor
JOB PURPOSE: Claims Processing

ACCOMPLISHMENTS/SUBACCOMPLISHMENTS	CRITICAL DIMENSIONS	MEASURES	STANDARDS
CLAIMS QUALIFIED			
Loss notice received	Accuracy	Percentage of cases of recovery potential identified	75% of cases of recovery potential identified
Claim type identified		Percentage of coverage issues identified later	Additional or corrected coverage issues identified in less than 5% of cases
Coverage determined – Recovery potential identified – Legal trends identified and considered			
Missing/inaccurate information identified	Timeliness	Percentage of loss notices entered in correct claim category	All loss notices entered. Loss notice entries reported by claim category
Claims progress tracked		Average loss notice processing/confirmation time	15 minutes per loss notice
CLAIMS ASSIGNED			
Economic assignment determined – $ exposure estimated – Settlement variance potential estimated – Method option availability determined	Accuracy	Percentage of adequate justification of method mix variances greater than 5%	All method mix variances greater than 5% adequately justified
		Average size of outside assigned claims	Outside assigned claims $1000 or more
		Percentage of cases coinspected/reinspected	10% of cases coinspected/reinspected
REP PROCESS SUPERVISED			
Claim progress log reviewed	Volume	Number of cases in caseload	Average caseload: 25 cases
Files reviewed as diaried	Timeliness	Average settlement time	Average settlement time: 20 working days
Coinspections/reinspections conducted as scheduled	Accuracy	Percentage of payout variance	Payout variance on postaudit of 10% or less in no more than 2% of audited cases
Representative performance opportunities identified			*Any representatives performing below standards identified and appropriate corrective action implemented*

TABLE 8.4. PCI JOB ANALYSIS WORKSHEET

JOB: Claims Supervisor

STANDARDS	ACTUAL PERFORMANCE	GAP	IMPACT OF GAP	CAUSE OF GAP (X)*					
				PS	TS	FB	CONS	K/S	CAP
75% of cases of recovery potential identified	Recovery potential identified in 18% of cases	57%	Cost per claim goes up	X	X	X	X		
Additional or corrected issues identified in less than 5% of cases	Additional or corrected issues identified in less than 3% of cases	None							
15 minutes per loss notice	15 minutes per loss notice, average	None							
All loss notices entered; loss notice entries reported by claim category	Not done	No loss data in claim office	Payout increases						
All method mix variances greater than 5% adequately justified	Method mix variances greater than 5% and not justified 8 out of 12 months	Economic assignment not achieved (or not verified) 75% of processing year	Cost per claim goes up		X	X	X	X	
Outside assigned claims $1000 or more	20% of outside claims $500 or less	20% of claims misassigned	Cost per claim goes up				X	X	
10% of cases coinspected/reinspected	Coinspection/reinspection in 3% of cases	Quality control sample 7% below requirement	Payout increases						
All representatives performing to the following levels: – Average caseload: 25 cases – Average settlement time: 20 working days – Payout variance on postaudit of 10% or less in no more than 2% of audited cases	55% of reps performing to standard	45% substandard	Payout increases and cost per claim goes up			X			
	Corrective action plans implemented for 50% of substandard performers	50% of substandard not addressed or supported							

* PS: performance specifications
TS: task support
FB: feedback
CONS: consequences
K/S: knowledge or skill
CAP: capacity

TABLE 8.5. PCI PERFORMANCE SYSTEM DESIGN WORKSHEET

Job: Claims Supervisor

PERFORMANCE SPECIFICATIONS						
ACCOMPLISHMENTS	STANDARDS	TASK SUPPORT	FEEDBACK	CONSEQUENCE	KNOWLEDGE AND SKILL	CAPACITY
(See Job Model Worksheet and Job Analysis Worksheet)						
Claim qualified	75% of cases of recovery potential identified	Ensure sufficient time for claim qualification	Provide data on recovery $ from all cases	Evaluate supervision on this aspect of their performance	Develop job aid for claim qualification	
	All loss notices entered	Analyze field support processes		Return notices with errors or incomplete data to agent to fix	Provide training on notice preparation	
Claim assigned	All method mix variance >5% adequately justified		Determine measurement system and use consistently to verify economic assignment			
	Assign outside claims $1000 or more		Manager evaluation criteria to be based on claim-processing cost versus sales representative activity level	Evaluation criteria on performance appraisal		
	10% of cases coinspected				Initiate skill training	

Summary

At first blush, this process may appear to overkill the assignment. After all, Larry was just asked to update a manual. However, he took it upon himself to get at the problem that had stimulated the request. Through the Three Levels Performance Improvement Process, he identified actions that will result in a far more significant payback than what would have been realized from a better claims manual.

This entire process could certainly occupy twenty days of Larry's time. However, we have to examine the output of that twenty-day analysis and compare it to the output of twenty days of manual rewriting. We also need to acknowledge that Larry could have used shortcuts that retained the integrity of the Three Levels approach and significantly reduced the number of work hours and amount of elapsed time.

Larry is an effective "performance doctor." He specifically pinpointed the illness. He thoroughly diagnosed the patient at the Organization, Process, and Job/Performer Levels, and he recommended a treatment that was based on his diagnosis. He has provided an exemplary staff service: the analysis and improvement of line performance.

CHAPTER NINE

PROJECT DEFINITION: THE TEN ESSENTIAL STEPS

*Processes are the windows into the way the organization
operates. If we look there, we will find many hidden
opportunities, new passages that promise more powerful
performance.*

—PRICE PRITCHETT

One of the great strengths of the Rummler-Brache Group's (RBG's) methodology is that you can scale it to your needs and it will still yield robust results. From our experience, creating *only* the *minimum* Rummler-Brache deliverables will still deliver significant performance improvements in a critical process. For most organizations, this amount represents large financial gains. What are the critical deliverables in a process improvement project? If you were to boil Phases 1 and 2 of the RBG methodology down to their cores, what would be the most important things to know?

Chapters Nine and Ten cover the mission-critical steps and tools in the project definition, analysis, and design phases of the RBG methodology. The tools will help you produce the minimum outputs for a Rummler-Brache "Quick PIP" (Process Improvement Project). This is all practical, real-world stuff. No fluff or academic theory. For each tool, we explain how and when to use it, how long it will take to use it, and the materials required. Plus, we provide an example of an actual deliverable that each tool creates. The bare-bones essentials of Rummler-Brache's Phase 1 ("DEFINE") involve ten steps, as shown in Figure 9.1.

Phase 1: Project Definition

Phase Ø, Performance Improvement Planning, should be completed before Phase 1. Phase Ø is designed to ensure that the process

FIGURE 9.1. PHASE 1 STEPS

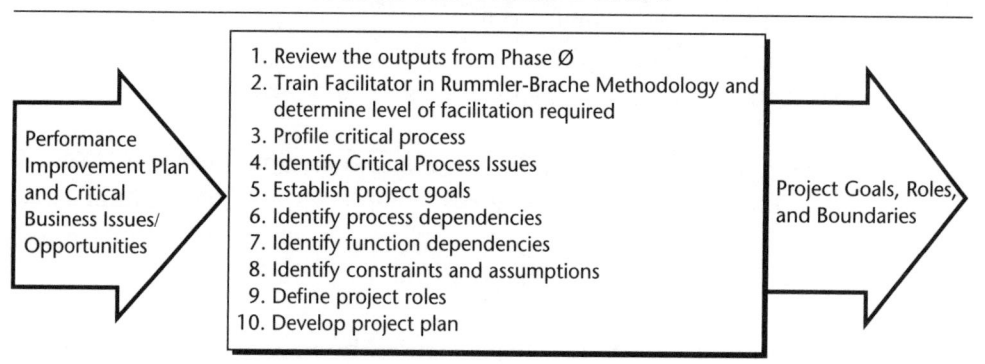

Performance Improvement Plan and Critical Business Issues/ Opportunities

1. Review the outputs from Phase Ø
2. Train Facilitator in Rummler-Brache Methodology and determine level of facilitation required
3. Profile critical process
4. Identify Critical Process Issues
5. Establish project goals
6. Identify process dependencies
7. Identify function dependencies
8. Identify constraints and assumptions
9. Define project roles
10. Develop project plan

Project Goals, Roles, and Boundaries

improvement and management effort is driven by strategic and operational priorities.

Step 1: Review the Outputs from Phase Ø—Performance Improvement Planning

The Phase Ø outputs include:

- The Critical Business Issues (CBIs), which are the threats or opportunities that are most pivotal to the success of the strategy. Because it has organizationwide implications, a CBI often is not process-specific. CBIs usually relate to revenue, profit, or market share.
- The Critical Success Factors (CSFs)—those variables essential to world-class performance in the environment (super-system) in which the organization does business—serve as the guide to the identification of the core processes.
- The core (or other) processes that, if improved, will have the greatest impact on the CBIs. A powerful input to this determination is the current cost of each process.
- A Process Improvement Management plan that includes the actions to be taken to address the CBIs through Process Improvement Projects (PIPs).

Step 2: Train Facilitator and Determine the Level of Facilitation Required

We recommend that a Facilitator receive a minimum of two weeks of training in project definition, process analysis and design, and metric chains. Rummler-Brache certifies Facilitators in our methodology if they have attended training and worked side by side with a Rummler-Brache consultant on at least one significant project.

The Facilitator's role is critical to project success, so making sure this person is properly trained, well experienced, and up to date on the Rummler-Brache methodology is an important step.

During the "DEFINE" Phase (Phase 1), the Facilitator:

- Leads the Project Sponsor, Process Owner, and Executive Team in defining the project scope, goals, boundaries, staffing, and timetable

During the "IS" Phase (Phase 2), the Facilitator:

- Helps keep the Design Team focused by providing structure for its work and documentation
- Prepares a draft map of the "IS" Process based on interviews with those knowledgeable about the process
- Plans and conducts the "IS" Sessions with the Design Team and is responsible for collecting, recording, and summarizing information on process performance

During the "SHOULD" Phase (Phase 2), the Facilitator:

- Continues to provide assistance to the Design Team by helping them prepare for their meeting with the Steering Team
- Prepares draft maps to assist in designing the new process(es)
- Facilitates "SHOULD" sessions
- Updates the map between "SHOULD" sessions and prepares documentation
- Guides the Design Team as it prepares its recommendations and implementation plans for presentation to management

The Facilitator of the project should have strong planning and organizing skills and the skills to influence senior executives. The Facilitator will be the methodology expert on the Design Team.

We recommend all Design Team members attend at least two days of training to learn the basics on how to:

- Define critical business issues
- Scope improvement projects
- Create maps that document the "IS" state
- Identify areas for improvement
- Construct maps to document the "SHOULD" process

Training in the Rummler-Brache methodology gives Design Team members a greater appreciation for the critical, central role that processes play in the execution of the organization's strategy.

The level of facilitation support that Design Teams receive during a project can vary according to your answers to the questions shown in Figure 9.2.

Full Facilitation

Full facilitation means that a trained Rummler-Brache Facilitator assumes an active role in all phases of the project, attends all team meetings, and generally takes the lead in interviewing, Process Map development, and team meetings.

Full facilitation is recommended for:

- Projects aimed at resolving high-profile business issues
- Projects involving complex, cross-functional processes
- Projects initiated by organizations new to the Rummler-Brache Process Improvement methodology

Following are success factors associated with full facilitation:

- A certified Rummler-Brache Facilitator (Rummler-Brache suggests that at least two Facilitators work together on large-scale projects involving full facilitation)

FIGURE 9.2. DETERMINANTS OF FULL, PARTIAL, OR NO FACILITATION

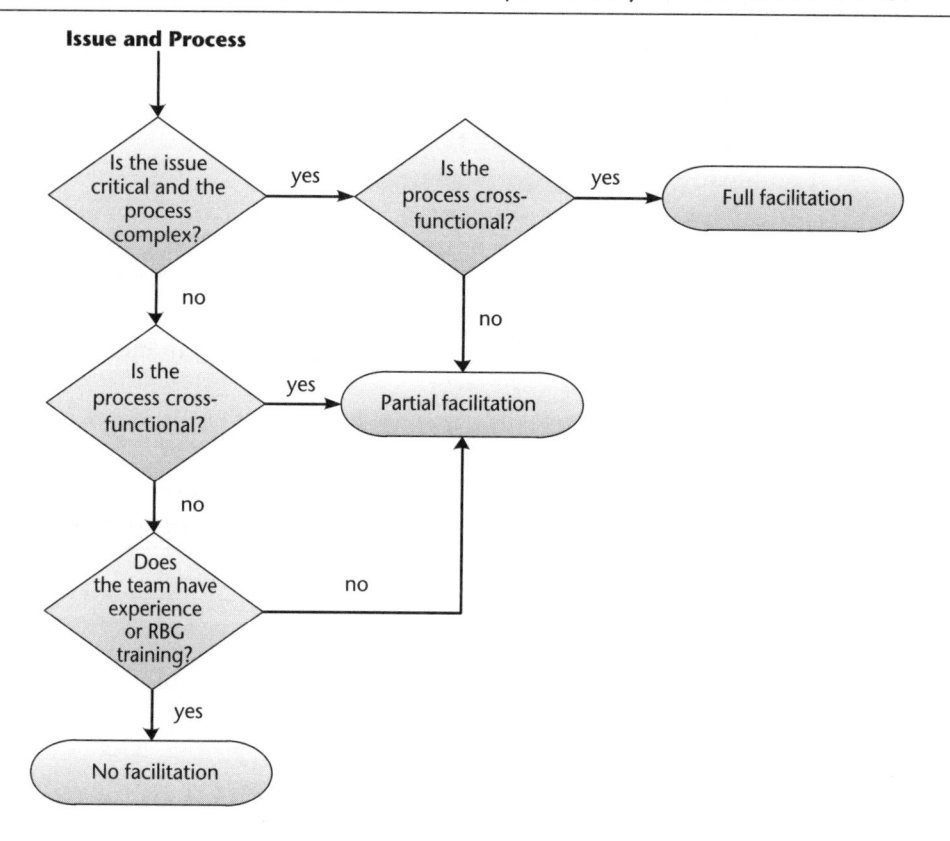

- Clear understanding of, and agreement on, the roles and responsibilities of the Facilitator, the Sponsor, Steering Team members, and Design Team members
- Written documentation at all phases of the project
- Formal progress reviews with senior management at major milestones in a project

Rummler-Brache's methodology software is designed to support full facilitation of a Process Improvement Project.

Partial Facilitation

In partial facilitation, the Rummler-Brache Facilitator supports the Steering Team and the Design Team at key points in the project, but may not be present at all meetings and may not necessarily lead or participate in all phases of the project.

The Design Team typically does much or all of the process mapping and conducts its own meetings.

Partial facilitation can be appropriate when:

- The business issue associated with the project is relatively low-profile
- The business is not overly complex (for example, it is contained within a small number of functions)
- The organization and the Design Team members have had experience with Rummler-Brache Process Improvement methodology

Such support could include:

- Helping the Sponsor define the project
- Conducting or supporting team training
- Participating in the Project Startup Meeting
- Responding to requests for assistance from Design Team members as they develop the "IS" map
- Attending the "IS" session
- Reviewing the results of the "IS" session prior to presentation of results to the Steering Team
- Assisting the Sponsor and Design Team Leader in developing a "SHOULD" design strategy
- Attending all or selected parts of the "SHOULD" sessions
- Reviewing the results of the "SHOULD" sessions prior to their being presented to the Steering Team
- Assisting in development of an implementation and high-level implementation plan

Some success factors associated with partial facilitation are:

- An experienced Sponsor and/or Design Team Leader
- Experienced Design Team members

- Thorough project definition
- Specification of critical points for facilitation support
- Clear expectations about the level of facilitation support
- Dependable access to a certified Rummler-Brache Facilitator

No Facilitation

No facilitation means that the Design Team conducts its project without a Rummler-Brache Facilitator. This approach may be feasible when:

- The project is associated with a low-visibility issue
- The process to be improved is relatively simple (for example, it is contained within one function)
- The organization (including the Design Team) has been trained and has considerable experience in the Rummler-Brache Process Improvement methodology

Success factors associated with no facilitation:

- A highly experienced Sponsor and/or Design Team Leader
- Experienced and trained Design Team members
- A Sponsor or Team Leader willing and able to perform facilitation tasks, as necessary, during the course of the project
- A reliable source of Rummler-Brache facilitation help, if needed

Step 3: Profile Critical Processes

Tool: Critical Process Profile

The Critical Process Profile helps you understand each key process at a high level. It provides information about:

- Where the process starts (trigger) and ends (outputs)
- What other processes provide input or receive output from the process
- The supplier and customer of the process
- Major portions of work or subprocesses included in the process

When to Use

The questions you use to profile a critical process are typically asked early in your data-gathering interviews. Usually you will gather this information from individuals identified by the Executive Team rather than from Executive Team members themselves, because senior managers generally cannot provide the level of detail you need to profile a critical process.

How to Use

Answer the questions in the Critical Process Profile that follows to ensure you understand the process to be improved and its boundaries. The

Critical Process Profiles will also be used to develop a series of linked measures for the critical processes.

Time Required
Expect to spend at least fifteen to thirty minutes profiling each process. The actual amount of time will depend on the complexity of the process and how much thinking the organization has given to the process in the past.

Materials Required
• Critical Process Profile (see the following example)

Example: Critical Process Profile

1. What is the critical process name?
   Customer order process
2. What is the process output?
   Course materials
3. For the purpose of this project, what is the last step in the process?
   Course materials received by the customer
4. Who is/are the receiver(s) of the output of this process?
   User companies (typically $100M annual sales and larger)
5. For the purpose of this project, what is the first step in the process?
   Salesperson receives the order from the customer
6. What is/are the input(s) or trigger(s) that initiate the process?
   Customer request for course materials
7. What are the major portions of work or subprocesses included in the process?
   Order entry subprocess, order preparation subprocess, order shipping subprocess
8. Are there other types of inputs the process must accommodate that may cause the process to operate differently?
   No—the process handles any order for any product, standard, or custom
9. Who is/are the supplier(s) of the process input(s)?
   The customer
10. What other process(es) "touch" this process? What significance do those related processes have to improvement of the selected process? (See Table 9.1.)
11. What does the process look like? (See Figure 9.3.)

TABLE 9.1. SIGNIFICANCE OF RELATED PROCESSES

Other Processes	Significance
Sales process	No significance—will assume proper sale has been made
Sales forecasting process	Affects inventory levels in customer order process—may require a separate Process Improvement Project
Procurement process	No significance
New product development process	No significance

FIGURE 9.3. SAMPLE PROCESS

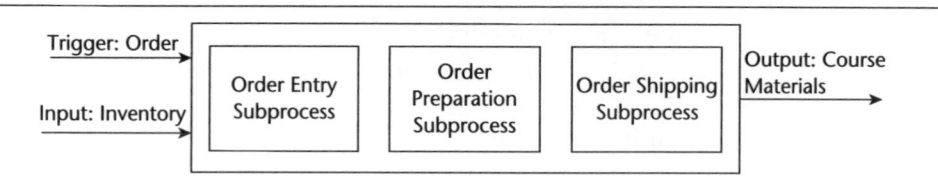

Step 4: Identify Critical Process Issues

Tool: Critical Process Issues
Critical Process Issues (CPIs) are the link between the target process and the Critical Business Issue (CBI).

CPIs:

- Describe the specific aspect(s) of process performance that must be addressed in a Process Improvement Project (PIP)
- Serve as a focus for a PIP and are a major factor in determining Project Goals
- Can guide the Design Team in deciding how to improve the process and in developing appropriate measures for managing the improved process
- Answer the question, "What is it about the process that must be improved to have a positive effect on the Critical Business Issue?"

When to Use
You will identify the CPIs after the CBI has been identified. The CPIs need to link the target processes to the CBI.

How to Use

1. Review the CBI and your interview notes.
2. Identify the process(es) that need to be improved.
3. Describe what it is about the process(es) that must be improved to positively affect the CBI.

Time Required
Information gathered in your interviews with the Steering Team and others will inform you of the CPIs.

Materials Required

- CBI
- Interview notes

Example: Critical Process Issues

Following are a few examples of CPIs:

- Frequently we are unable to deliver orders on the dates promised to the customer.
- It takes us three years to get a new product to market—twice as long as our major competitor.
- Approximately 20 percent of the orders submitted by the sales reps are inaccurate or incomplete. This results in added cost and time to fill those orders.
- We perform poorly in delivering specials to customers:
  - Orders frequently are late
  - Often what customers receive is not what they ordered
  - Customers are frequently invoiced incorrectly (wrong invoice for product received)
- Order fulfillment:
  - Overall management process for inventory is limited
  - Delivery costs are not first quartile
  - Inventory turns are low
- Financial reporting and budgeting through expenditure to payment and corporate reporting:
  - Financial information is not assembled for decision making
  - Accountability is not aligned with responsibility
- Preventive maintenance:
  - Plant uptime is approximately 65 percent
  - Maintenance costs are not first quartile
- Renewal:
  - Products are introduced that do not meet customers' and business profitability needs
  - Product quality is not consistent and not to specs

Step 5: Establish Project Goals

Tool: Project Goals

Process Improvement Project Goals are based on how the organization wants the process to perform. You must know how the process is currently performing so you can determine the gap between current and desired performance. This will also help you conduct a cost-benefit analysis.

When to Use

Identify Project Goals prior to launching a Process Improvement Project and after the Critical Process Issues (CPIs) have been identified.

How to Use

1. To develop the Project Goals, you must determine the required level of performance as well as the current, or baseline, level of performance. This is essential, because the gap between how the process "is" performing and how it "should" be performing influences both design and implementation.

2. When determining the required level of performance, be sure to write quantitative goals that are:

   - Specific
   - Measurable
   - Ambitious, but achievable
   - Understandable

3. Recognize that performance improvements will be achieved over a period of time, so you will need to establish interim targets to measure progress toward the overall goal. See the two examples of Project Goals with interim targets presented in Tables 9.2 and 9.3.

4. Follow these guidelines to determine baseline performance:

   - Ideally, performance data are collected by your organization on an ongoing basis. "Cost per unit" or "average days from order received to order shipped" are both examples. These data help provide the baseline needed to demonstrate the success of the project.
   - If ongoing data are not available, conduct a brief study of historical performance data. For example, a review of project files for the past three years may enable you to determine an average cycle time to get new products to market.

TABLE 9.2.   PROJECT GOALS EXAMPLE 1

Process Performance Measures	Baseline Performance	Interim Targets: Q1	Interim Targets: Q2	Interim Targets: Q3	Interim Targets: Q4	Process Goals
Order cycle time	Approximately 30 days	≥28 days	≥25 days	≥20 days	≥15 days	≥10 days
Handling cost/ order	Averages $200.00 per order	≥$180.00 per order	≥$150.00 per order	≥$125.00 per order	≥$100.00 per order	≥$70.00 per order
Unit inventory	5,292 units	4,500 to 5,000 units	4,000 to 4,500 units	3,500 to 4,000 units	3,000 to 3,500 units	2,000 to 3,000 units

Additional project goals: *This Process Improvement Project will become a model for the New Product Development project that will follow.*

TABLE 9.3. PROJECT GOALS EXAMPLE 2

Process Performance Measures	Baseline Performance	Interim Targets: Q1	Interim Targets: Q2	Interim Targets: Q3	Interim Targets: Q4	Required Level of Performance
Performance to electrical and mechanical specifications	100% to specification	100% to specification	100% to specification	100% to specification	100% to specification	100% to specification
Unit cost to manufacture	12% over cost for standard product	10% over cost for standard product	8% over cost for standard product	6% over cost for standard product	4% over cost for standard product	Same cost as for standard product
Percent on-time shipment	83%	85%	87%	89%	95%	100%
Percent accurate shipments	89%	91%	93%	95%	97%	100%
Percent billing errors	12%	10%	8%	5%	2%	Zero

Additional project goals: *Develop module on Process Improvement for Management Training Program.*

- If no data exist, determine how to gather data starting now, so that you have several months of baseline data by the time implementation begins. If you are unable to determine how to gather the data, you may need to change the Project Goal.

5. Identify all applicable nonquantitative or intangible goals. Examples of nonquantitative goals include:

- Create a customer-focused culture.
- Standardize the look and feel of process documentation.
- Create a common language within the organization for the target process.
- Increase empowerment of frontline employees.

Time Required

The time required to establish Project Goals depends on the type of current performance data you must gather. If current data exist, it is a matter of quickly establishing and validating goals with the Executive Team. If current data do not exist, considerable time could be required to determine:

- What measures to track
- The tracking frequency
- Where to place the "meters" so data are collected and formatted

Materials Required

- Critical Business Issue
- Critical Process Issues
- Baseline performance data, if available

Step 6: Identify Process Dependencies

Tools: Process Inventory

A Process Inventory is a list of the major processes in the organization. It is a useful input to profiling processes and developing a Process Relationship Map (PRM).

When to Use

Use the Process Inventory when summarizing your "DEFINE" interview notes and prior to developing a PRM.

How to Use

Using the Process Inventory Template

1. List all of the organization's processes in the Process column (as shown in Table 9.4).
2. Categorize each process by type: customer, management, primary, support, or supplier (see descriptions in the example).

TABLE 9.4. EXAMPLE OF A PARTIAL PROCESS INVENTORY

Process	Type	Key Output	Receiving Process
Planning and budgeting process	Management	Operational plans/budgets	All processes
Raw materials purchasing process	Supplier	Paper	Manufacturing process
Staffing process	Support	Staff/policy	All processes
Manufacturing process	Primary	Product	Customer's training process
Customer's ordering process	Customer	Order	Selling process

3. Identify the key process outputs of each process and list them in the Key Output column.
4. Identify the receiving processes of each process and list them in the Receiving Process column.
5. You now have all the information needed to draft your PRM.

Example: Process Inventory

Tool: Process Relationship Map

The Process Relationship Map (PRM) is a picture of the input-output relationships between the major work processes in an organization (see Figure 9.4). It will help you understand and display the network of processes required to run the business. It will also identify how other processes affect or are affected by a specific process selected for improvement.

FIGURE 9.4. COMPONENTS OF A STANDARD PRM

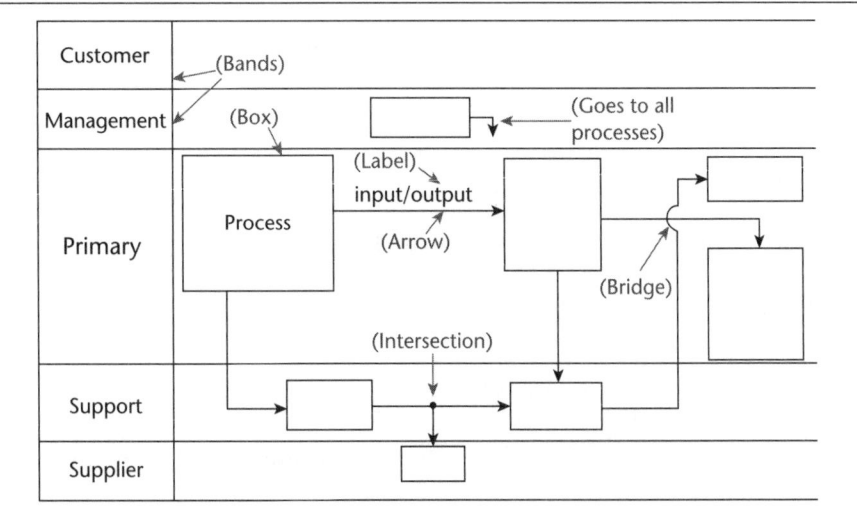

When to Use

Use the PRM:

- Any time the business's operating context needs to be understood
- During any analytical, definition, or design work where it is important to understand the big picture
- During any project where it is important to understand how processes affect each other

How to Use

First, develop a Process Inventory using the Process Inventory Tool. Then follow these steps to build a PRM:

1. Lay out a chart with bands for the process types, as shown in Figure 9.5.

    - The customer band represents the processes that occur in the client's customers' organizations that interface with the client's processes.
    - The management band represents the processes that provide direction and guidance to the organization, such as strategic planning process, budgeting process, and business planning process.
    - The primary band represents the processes that produce the product or service that the client organization produces. The value chain is another name for these key or core processes, such as selling process, order fulfillment process, customer support process.
    - The support band represents the processes that enable the other processes to work effectively, such as staffing process, IS or IT process, accounts payable process, capital appropriation process.
    - The supplier band represents the processes that occur in the client's suppliers' organizations that interface with the client's processes.

2. Place the first process box from your Process Inventory in the appropriate band, leaving space for other processes that occur chronologically before this process. On the PRM, a box represents an entire process (see Figure 9.6). If it is important to show subprocesses, put them inside the process box.

3. Add "upstream" and "downstream" processes that provide input or receive output (see Figure 9.7 and refer to your Process Inventory). Time moves from left to right.

FIGURE 9.5. SAMPLE CHART

Customer	
Management	
Primary	
Support	
Supplier	

4. Connect the process boxes with labeled arrows representing the inputs and outputs for each process. Typically, you should focus on the most important two or three outputs for each process (see Figure 9.8 and refer to your Process Inventory).
5. Number the boxes from top to bottom and from left to right as identifiers, not to indicate specific sequence.
6. Validate the map and revise again.

Time Required

The information you need to build a PRM is the process profile data gathered in your interviews with either the Executive Team or other designated specialists. Once that information is collected, it may take you several hours to build the map, depending on its complexity.

Materials Required

You will need the following materials to construct your PRM:

- Process Profile information
- Process Inventory

Tips

Give each process box a title that indicates the name of the process and not the name of the department with most responsibility for the process.

FIGURE 9.6. SAMPLE CHART WITH PROCESS BOX

Customer	
Management	
Primary	
Support	
Supplier	

FIGURE 9.7. SAMPLE CHART WITH "UPSTREAM" AND "DOWNSTREAM" PROCESSES

Customer	
Management	
Primary	
Support	
Supplier	

FIGURE 9.8. SAMPLE CHART WITH INPUT AND OUTPUT ARROWS

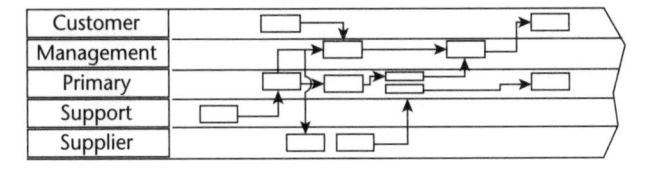

It is easy to misinterpret the map if the boxes "sound" like departments. For example, it is better to call a process "Product Design" than "Engineering" or "New Product Development" instead of "R&D." If necessary, add the word "Process" to each title to ensure the user reads the map as processes, and not as departments. See the example maps in Figures 9.9 and 9.10.

Step 7: Identify Functional Dependencies

Tool: Function Relationship Map

The Function Relationship Map (FRM) depicts the functions (departments) in the organization and their input-output relationships. The purpose of this map is to help analyze, improve, and design the organization's functional relationships. The map can be developed so that it depicts the general relationships of all functions or specific relationships that exist within a process.

General FRM (see Figure 9.11 for a sample General FRM):

- The general FRM is a picture of the organization that helps relationship managers and consultants understand how the business operates.
- The general FRM is often depicted as the center of the Supersystem Map. It shows the inputs and outputs of the organization to the rest of

FIGURE 9.9. PRM EXAMPLE 1

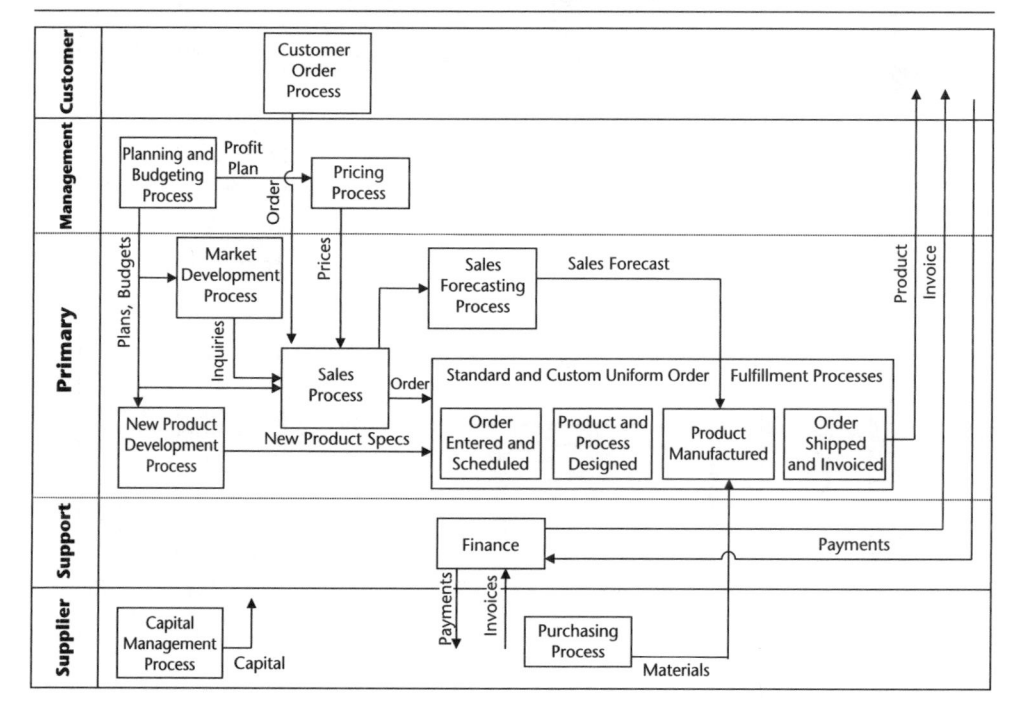

FIGURE 9.10. PRM EXAMPLE 2

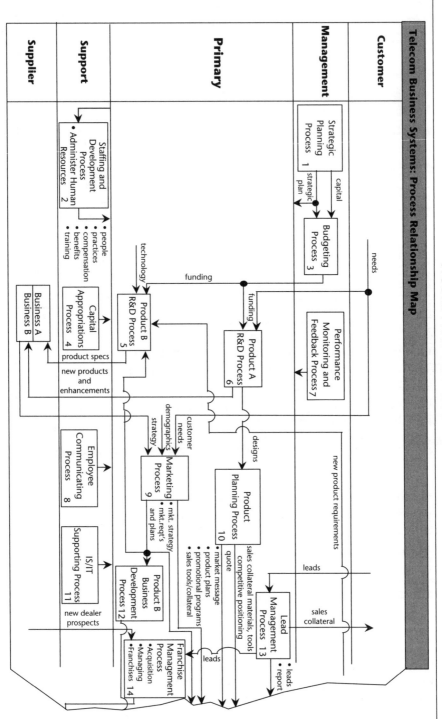

FIGURE 9.11. SAMPLE GENERAL FRM TEMPLATE

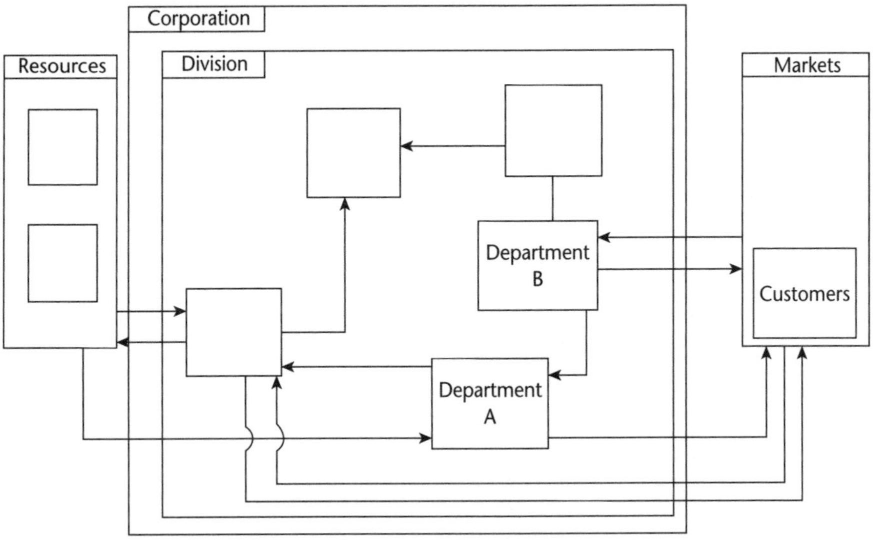

the system. The arrows between the functions identify the outputs of the functions and which functions receive the outputs. It is possible to "trace" the high-level path of the organization's value chain using the general FRM.

Specific FRM (see Figure 9.12 for a sample Specific FRM):

- The specific FRM is a tool analysts use to see more detail about how the business or part of the business operates.
- Specific FRMs are usually built to depict the functions (departments) that are involved in a specific process or system of processes.

As a Process Improvement Project progresses, the FRM can become a critical map. It can be used for organization or process redesign and for testing the impact of various changes.

When to Use
Use the FRM when:

- The business's value chain needs to be understood
- Functions involved in one or more processes need to be identified
- Functional relationships need to be understood

How to Use
Follow these steps to create a *general* FRM:

1. Identify the organizational entity.

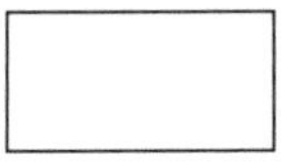

2. Identify the major outputs and where they go. Label the arrows.

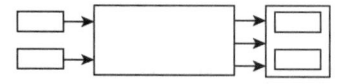

3. Identify the key inputs that are converted to outputs and where they come from. Label the arrows.

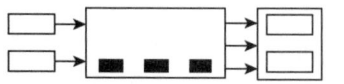

4. Identify the major functional entities (divisions, departments) within the organization.

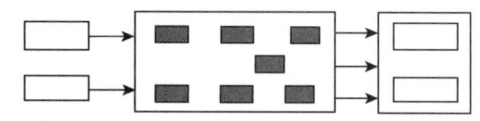

5. Note all other relevant functions.

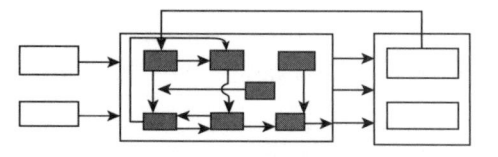

6. Note the one or two key inputs and outputs flowing between the functions. Label the arrows.

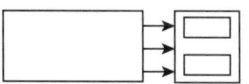

FIGURE 9.12. SAMPLE SPECIFIC FRM TEMPLATE

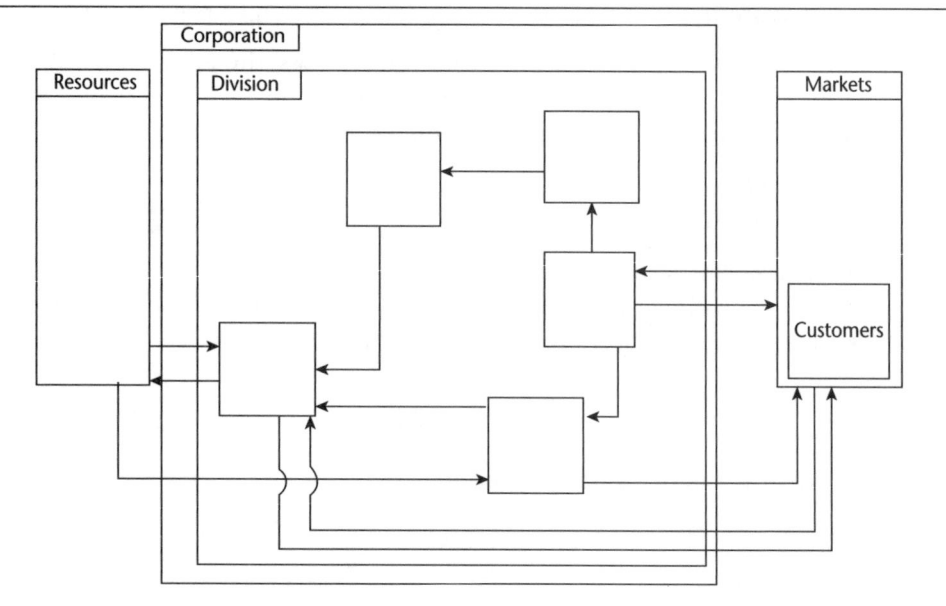

Follow these steps to create a *specific* FRM:

1. Build the *general* FRM.

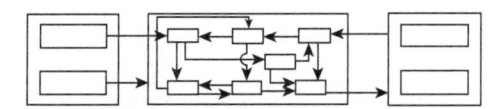

2. Trace the flow of the selected process through the functions, adding input-output detail where needed.

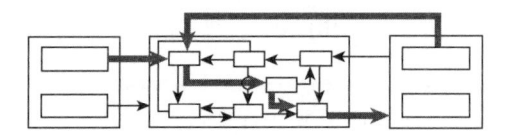

OR

3. Identify the first input to the first function for the selected process.

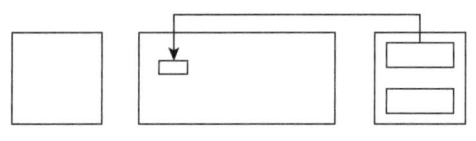

4. Note that function's output and where (to which other functions) it goes.

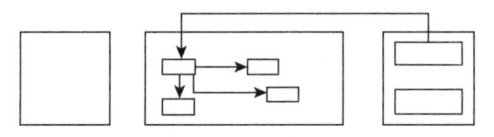

5. Note the next function's output and where it goes. Continue through the organization as needed to complete the map.

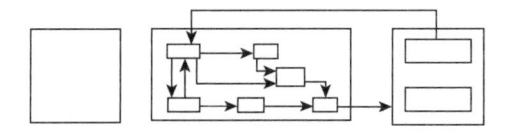

Time Required
After interview information is collected, it may take you several hours to build the map.

Materials Required
You will need the following materials to construct your FRM:

- Information gathered from your "DEFINE" interviews
- Organization chart(s)
- 11" × 17" grid paper and flip chart paper
- Sticky notes and pens
- Business-diagramming software

Examples: Function Relationship Map

Figures 9.13, 9.14, and 9.15 are three examples of Function Relationship Maps (FRMs) from two different projects. (The second two are the same FRM, but one is a *general* FRM and the other is a *specific* FRM.)

Step 8: Identify Constraints and Assumptions

These include the limitations placed on resources available for the project and organizational boundaries within which the project is confined.

Some examples of project constraints are:

- Capital availability is very limited. Recommendations should be for solutions requiring limited capital. Any recommendations for capital should have a detailed cost-benefit analysis including alternatives considered.
- The organization has recently undergone massive restructuring. Proposed process improvements must not involve changes to organization structure.

FIGURE 9.13. FRM EXAMPLE 1

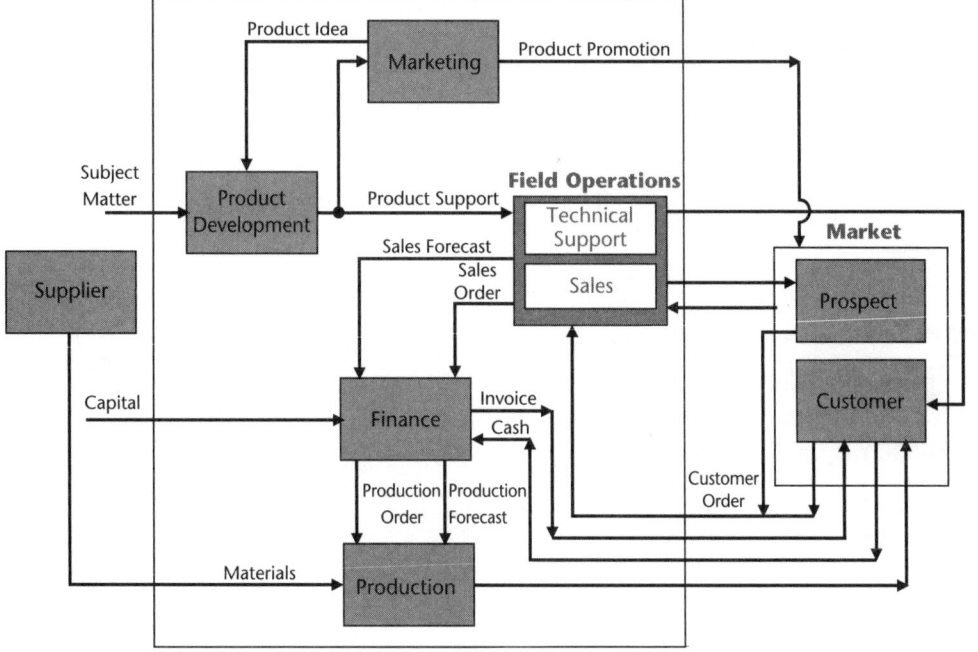

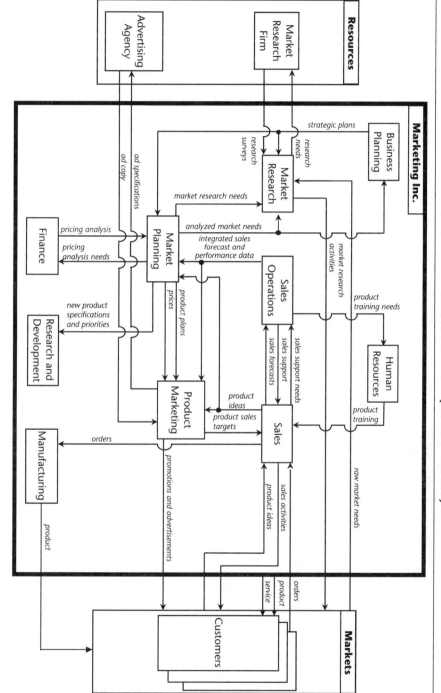

FIGURE 9.14. FRM EXAMPLE 2 (GENERAL FRM)

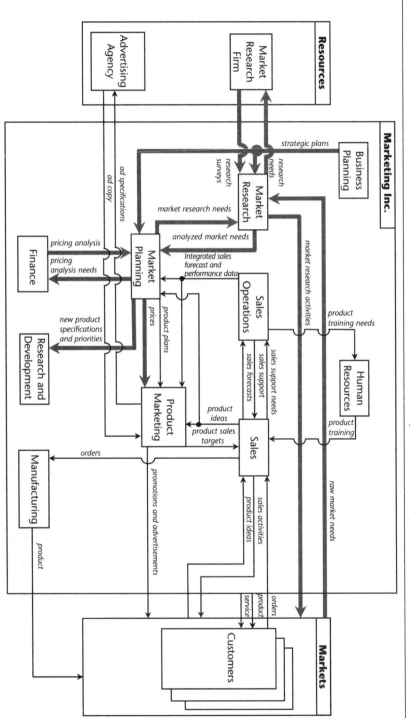

FIGURE 9.15. FRM EXAMPLE 3 (SPECIFIC FRM)

- We never outsource work.
- The recommendations must be linked with other key efforts underway, such as the implementation of the new ERP system such as SAP.
- You cannot change anyone's compensation.

Some examples of project assumptions are:

- The CEO never supports projects that involve investments in new technology.
- Process changes cause a significant dip in productivity.
- Frontline staff cannot participate on project teams because we can't afford for them to be taken away from their jobs for any period of time.

Constraints and assumptions typically fall into one or more of these categories:

- Availability of the appropriate people to:
    Work on the project
    Implement the process improvements
- Money for:
    Process analysis
    Process improvements
- Time by which the team must:
    Get the project started
    Make recommendations
    Resolve the Critical Business Issue
- Access to:
    Customers
    Suppliers
    Potentially sensitive information
- Authority of:
    The Design Team
    The Project Sponsor and Process Owner
- Extent of the changes that can be made to:
    Policy
    Organization structure
    Measures or goals
    Job design
    Compensation and other rewards
    Computer systems
    Other hardware or equipment
    Roles and power
    Geography or physical layout of the work space

- Upcoming internal or external changes that may affect the process
- Communications requirements involving:
    Secrecy
    Cooperation with other efforts

Consider a company president who, when he formed a Design Team, personally gave team members authority to make all changes needed to improve process performance, with three constraints:

1. They could not change anyone's compensation.
2. They could not violate the collective bargaining agreement.
3. Any requests for capital spending had to go through normal approval channels.

Because the constraints involved considerable empowerment, they had no negative effects on the team's ability to achieve project goals (which were ambitious).

On the other hand, it is important to remember that there are times when constraints can and should be challenged. For example, consider a Design Team that challenges its constraints by: (1) redesigning the process within its specified constraints and recommending changes that would result in meeting project goals, and (2) presenting a second set of recommendations that ignored several of the constraints—but that would result in markedly greater savings. Many of the second set of recommendations would likely be accepted and implemented by management.

Step 9: Define Project Roles

Tool: Summary of Project Team Roles
This tool describes the teams and individuals involved in a typical Process Improvement Project (PIP).

Design Team
The Design Team is composed of eight to fifteen members who:

- Represent the functions involved in the process being analyzed and improved.
- Represent all geographic areas affected (if the process crosses regional or national boundaries).
- Are stakeholders in the process (selected if necessary to assure their commitment to implementation).
- Are *not* assigned just because they have the least amount of work to do at a particular time or are otherwise "available."

The Design Team may include individual contributors and supervisors if:

- There are no direct reports included on the team.
- The supervisor(s) are intimately familiar with the day-to-day workings of the "IS" Process.

The Design Team begins its work in the "IS" Phase by adhering to the interview schedule and handling "front-end" interview logistics. During the "IS" Sessions, the Design Team confirms and identifies relationships, inputs, outputs, problems or issues, and baseline measures. It also develops "SHOULD" design specifications and "COULD BE" alternatives. After the "IS" Sessions, the Design Team identifies linkages to other processes and reviews all "IS" documentation.

Continuing its work in the "SHOULD" Phase, the Design Team designs the new process, summarizes the recommended changes, and checks to be sure the new process addresses all the disconnects identified during "IS" Analysis. The team then develops its recommendations (including a strategy for implementing them) and presents them to management.

At the conclusion of "SHOULD" Design, Design Team members are recognized for their performance and are recommissioned to Implementation Teams, as appropriate. It is common to recommission Design Team members as Implementation Team Leaders.

The Design Team can profit from having one or more "catalysts" among its membership. These are people who can energize and challenge the whole team.

Design Team membership can be expected to change somewhat as the project progresses. People quit, get transferred, and so forth. It is also not unusual to add (temporarily) resource people during the "SHOULD" Phase or technical experts during the "IS" Phase.

Design Team Leader
The Design Team Leader takes the lead role, working closely with the Facilitator in all Design Team sessions. He or she leads the Design Team in doing the work.

Executive Team
If there is an Executive Team, its role during the "DEFINE" Phase is to be a primary resource for data gathering to define the project. They also raise any questions or concerns and select membership for the Steering Team. This team continues to review and monitor progress throughout the PIP and clarify objectives, when needed.

Facilitation Support Team
On large projects, the task of coordinating meetings, collecting information, creating maps, and facilitating sessions can become too much for

one person. To avoid burnout, it is a good idea to augment the primary Facilitator with additional support. Usually this can be accomplished by defining project support requirements. In some cases, however, it may be necessary to have another Facilitator.

Facilitator

See Step 2 of Phase 1 for a description of the Facilitator's role.

Implementation Team

After the new process has been designed, the Implementation Teams are organized around work to be done to implement the new process and are cross-functional in structure. For example, the recommendation to update or install a new information system that will support process automation will be implemented by experts from the systems department and others whose jobs or expertise are integral to the task. The recommendation to revise a policy would include those people whose expertise or specific job would help in developing the new policy.

Implementation Team Leader

After the new process has been designed, the Implementation Team Leader manages the activities of her or his Implementation Team as they implement the new process. She or he is responsible for communicating the status of the team's progress to the Project Manager on a regular basis.

Project Manager

During Implementation, the Project Manager coordinates the efforts of all the Implementation Teams to make sure the Implementation Plan is executed on time and within budget. He or she conducts regular status meetings with management to inform them of progress and escalate issues, as applicable. He or she typically reports to the Process Owner.

Project Sponsor

The Project Sponsor is the champion for the project—he or she is generally the person who initiated the PIP. The Facilitator is accountable to the Project Sponsor (and the Process Owner) for results. This person may be the same person as the Process Owner.

Process Owner

The Process Owner is the person who is on the line for the success of the process—this role may be equated to a Process Manager. The Process Owner's primary activities include:

- Establishing and clarifying the project scope
- Acquiring project resources
- Providing access to interviewees, as needed, to ensure their attendance at the interviews

- Providing access to key decision makers in the organization and ensuring their commitment
- Helping to plan Steering Team review meetings and attending those meetings personally, as much as possible
- Briefing the Steering Team and Executive Team and other key stakeholders on progress, issues, and recommendations

The Process Owner *must* be on the Steering Team. If the organization is in flux, there may be no logical Process Owner at the beginning of the project; however, in this situation, an interim or temporary Process Owner must be appointed. If the process is being fundamentally redefined, the logical owner of the process may change as the boundaries of the cross-functional process change. He or she may be the same person as the Project Sponsor; however, his or her key responsibility is process ownership.

Receiving Organization
The Receiving Organization(s) install the new process in their organizations with assistance from the Implementation Teams. These groups then take on responsibility for monitoring daily process performance to achieve performance targets.

Stakeholders
Stakeholders are persons or organizations that potentially will be affected by the changes. Determining who these people are, how the changes will affect them, and gaining their support is very important to the eventual installation of the new design. This group generally plays an advisory role, as opposed to a decision-making role throughout the PIP. Stakeholders are advised of progress throughout the project by the Process Owner.

Steering Team
The Steering Team is formed toward the end of the "DEFINE" Phase once the project is clearly scoped. This team reviews and monitors progress throughout the PIP and plays the role of decision-maker. Its members may also raise issues and resolve them.

Step 10: Develop Project Plan

Tool: Project Plan
The Project Plan lists the major activities and deliverables associated with a Process Improvement Project (PIP).

While there are many ways to represent a Project Plan (such as Gantt charts and PERT charts), this should be a high-level plan and kept as simple as possible.

When to Use
You should develop a Project Plan after the PIP has been fully defined and validated. (See Table 9.5 for an example.)

TABLE 9.5. EXAMPLE: PROJECT PLAN

Major Milestone and Deliverable(s)	Estimated Level of Effort	Dependencies	Due Date	Responsibility	Comments
Project Kickoff: DT trained and informed	DT: 1 day	Project identity created	Sept. 17	K. Potter, Facilitator	
"IS" Interviews: process steps identified by function; perceived disconnects and issues identified; draft "IS" Map developed	1-1/2 to 2 hours each	Interviewees identified and interviews scheduled	Sept. 18–21	G. Bell, DT Leader	One-on-one interviews for DT members and other key people
"IS" Session: "IS" Map confirmed; disconnects confirmed and prioritized	DT: 3 days	Interview findings	Sept. 26–28	G. Bell, DT Leader	
ST Review:"IS" analysis reviewed	DT: 1 day ST: 1 day	Confirmed "IS" Map and disconnects	Sept. 29	K. Potter, Facilitator	
"SHOULD" Session 1: Linear Process Map developed; measures identified	DT: 2 days	"SHOULD" Design specs	Oct. 4–5	G. Bell, DT Leader	
"SHOULD" Session 2: Cross-Functional Role/Responsibility Map developed	DT: 2 days	"SHOULD" Linear Process Map and measures	Oct. 11–12	G. Bell, DT Leader	

DT = Design Team; ST = Steering Team

How to Use

Review the steps involved in a PIP to determine:

- The major milestones applicable to the PIP
- The estimated level of effort required to accomplish each milestone
- The dependencies between milestones
- The due date for each milestone
- The person responsible for each milestone

Time Required

The time required to complete a high-level Project Plan will depend on the complexity of the project and whether you will be including communications and change management–related milestones. Although this plan will be your road map going forward, it will be a working document. Therefore, do not spend too much time thinking about any one milestone. Make your best estimate and move on.

Materials Required

- Project planning software
- Generic milestones for a Project Plan

Tips

- Although dependencies and level of effort may be helpful in determining due dates or sequence, it is not always necessary to document them in the Project Plan.
- Add a "Notes" column to your Project Plan to capture any important information that does not fit into the other sections of the plan.

CHAPTER TEN

PROCESS ANALYSIS AND DESIGN: THE TEN ESSENTIAL STEPS

How can an organization cover the ground it needs to as fast as it should? Get rid of all that wasted motion spent on non-value-adding work. Eliminate the delays in hand-off zones. Most process improvement opportunities lie at the boundary lines, both vertical and horizontal. You find them in the white space.

—PRICE PRITCHETT

As soon as Phase 1 has produced a project that is properly scoped and defined, begin Phase 2 of the Rummler-Brache methodology—process analysis and design.

The objective of Phase 2 is to design a new ("SHOULD") process that will:

- Meet the specifications established by the Steering Team
- Accomplish the project goals
- Address the Critical Business Issue

Phase 2: Process Analysis and Design

In Phase 2, the existing "IS" process and opportunities for improving it are documented. Then a new or improved "SHOULD" process is designed that meets the Project Goals and resolves disconnects. The ten core steps of process analysis and design are shown in Figure 10.1.

Step 1: Document "IS" Process

Tool: Cross-Functional Process Map
A Cross-Functional Process Map is a picture of the sequenced steps across functions that depict how input(s) are converted to output(s). It shows the flow of inputs and outputs across a process and the applicable functions in the organization.

FIGURE 10.1. THE TEN CORE STEPS OF PHASE 2

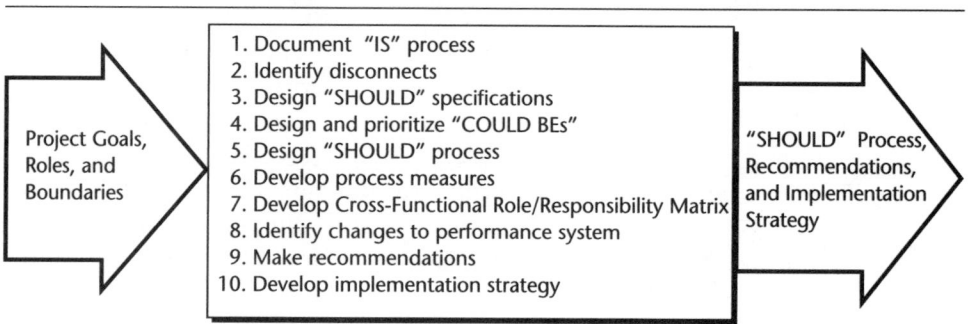

Project Goals, Roles, and Boundaries

1. Document "IS" process
2. Identify disconnects
3. Design "SHOULD" specifications
4. Design and prioritize "COULD BEs"
5. Design "SHOULD" process
6. Develop process measures
7. Develop Cross-Functional Role/Responsibility Matrix
8. Identify changes to performance system
9. Make recommendations
10. Develop implementation strategy

"SHOULD" Process, Recommendations, and Implementation Strategy

When to Use

Use the map to:

- Document the "IS" process for understanding and analysis.
- Document the "SHOULD" process for implementation and continuous improvement.
- Show cross-functional workflows.

How to Use

1. Lay out the horizontal bands that represent the functions on the chart, as shown in Figure 10.2.
2. Place the Customer or Markets band on top and the Suppliers band on the bottom. Label the other bands accordingly, as shown in Figure 10.3.

FIGURE 10.2. CROSS-FUNCTIONAL PROCESS MAP TEMPLATE

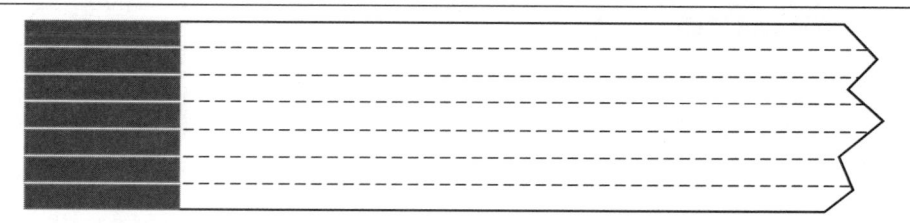

FIGURE 10.3. CROSS-FUNCTIONAL PROCESS MAP LABELED

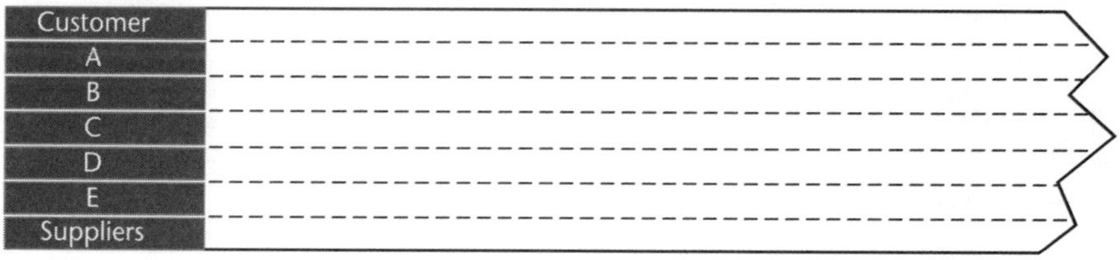

Customer
A
B
C
D
E
Suppliers

3. You may want to include a "Miscellaneous" band at the bottom, where you can include such items as remarks, times, costs, quality components, and comments. If systems are involved in the process, you may want to place a systems band near the middle.

4. Identify the subprocesses involved in the process, as shown in Figure 10.4.

5. Place the first step in the process in the appropriate band, as shown in Figure 10.5. Indicate the step's activity with a noun and a verb in the past tense (such as Needs Evaluated, Quotes Requested, or Product Concept Tested).

6. Identify the output and where it goes. Place another step in the appropriate band and label the step, as shown in Figure 10.6. Draw an arrow from the output side of the previous step to this step and label the arrow with the output.

FIGURE 10.4. CROSS-FUNCTIONAL PROCESS MAP WITH SUBPROCESSES

FIGURE 10.5. CROSS-FUNCTIONAL PROCESS MAP: STEPS

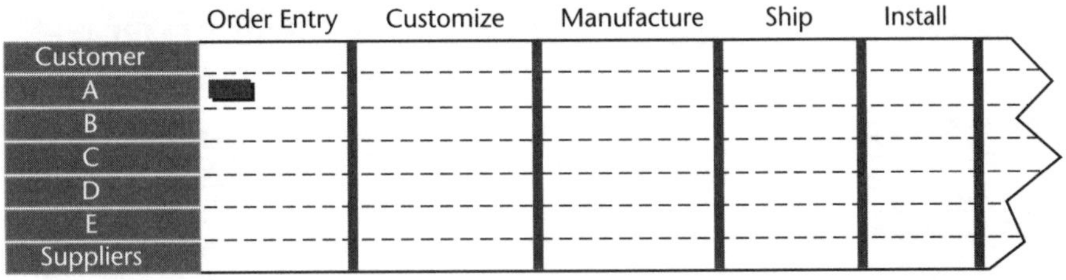

FIGURE 10.6. CROSS-FUNCTIONAL PROCESS MAP: OUTPUT

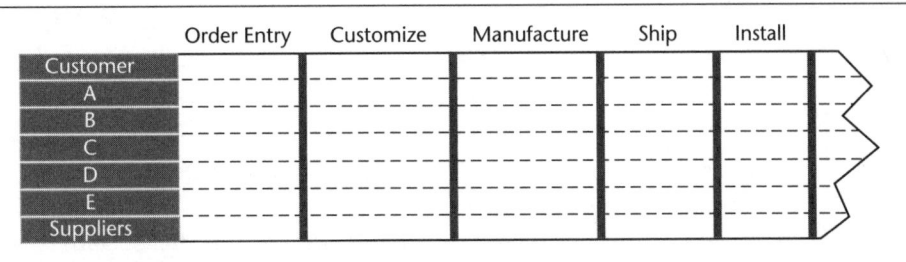

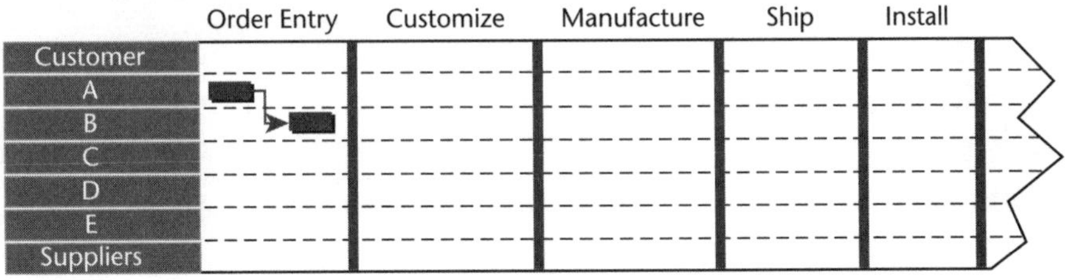

7. Continue by asking yourself, "What is accomplished or completed in this step? What is the output and where does it go?" Place additional steps in their appropriate bands, as shown in Figure 10.7.
8. Refer to the mapping conventions shown in Figure 10.8.
9. Revise the map as needed and number the boxes from top to bottom (left to right for reference purposes only).
10. When creating the draft Cross-Functional "IS" Process Map, *do not* label the potential disconnects perceived by the interviewees on the map at this point. You do not want to predispose the Design Team to potential disconnects. Instead, you will walk through the map step-by-step, allowing them to identify and discuss the disconnects. The idea is to create ownership of the process by Design Team members so that they are vested in the improvement.

Time Required

The time required to complete a Cross-Functional Process Map will vary based on the complexity of the process. Plan to spend at least a few hours.

FIGURE 10.7. CROSS-FUNCTIONAL PROCESS MAP: OUTPUT, CONT.

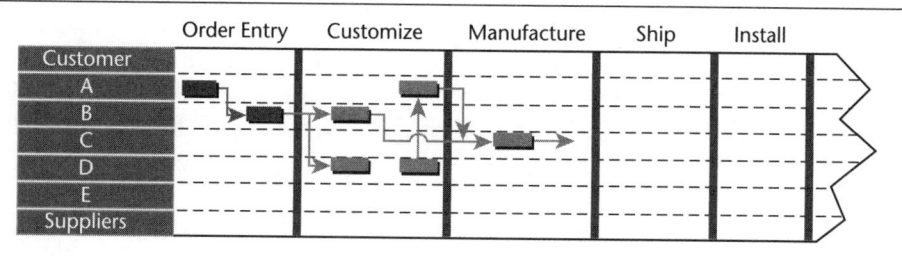

FIGURE 10.8. MAPPING CONVENTIONS

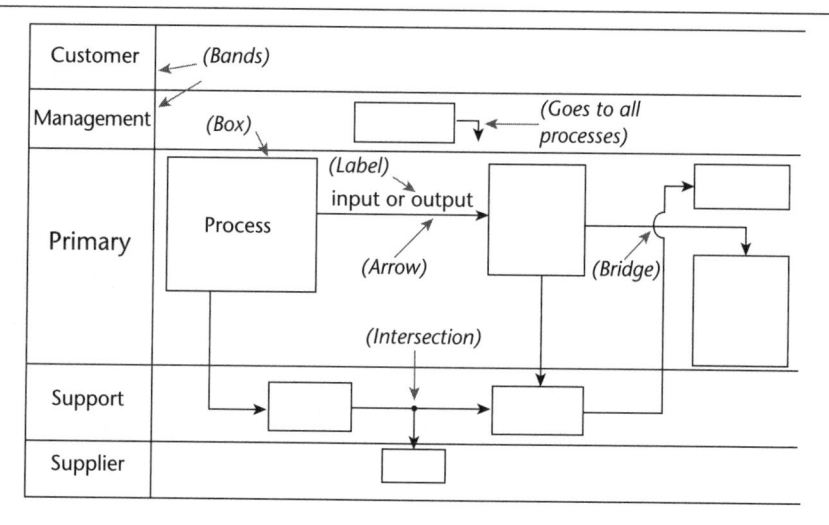

Step 2: Identify Disconnects

Tool: Disconnects

A disconnect is defined as anything that negatively impacts the effectiveness or efficiency of a process.

When to Use

Disconnects, both real and perceived, are first identified during the "IS" interviews with the Steering Team and Design Team, then further documented by the Design Team during the "IS" process validation session.

How to Use

- The Facilitator should note all perceived disconnects that surface during the "IS" interviews.
- While the Design Team is reviewing and validating the Cross-Functional "IS" Process Map, disconnects and issues should be noted as follows:

  Draw a number with a circle around it on a sticky note and place it on the map at the point where the disconnect or issue occurs. Using sticky notes rather than writing directly on the map will make it easier to move the disconnects around as group members change their minds.

  On a flip chart, write the number and a description of the disconnect next to it.

  After the "IS" map has been validated, the team will revisit the disconnects and develop a disconnect list using a template that includes a description of the impact of each disconnect. The impacts will be useful when it comes to prioritizing the disconnects.

Time Required

The time required will depend on the number of disconnects identified and the extent of discussion needed to clarify and describe the impact of each one.

Materials Required

- Cross-Functional "IS" Process Map
- Flip chart, paper, and markers
- Hard or soft copy of the disconnect list
- Sticky notes

Example: Disconnect List

Table 10.1 is an example of a disconnect list that resulted from a review of the order fulfillment process at Eagle Education Products. The "Full" and "Partial" columns will be completed after the "SHOULD" process is designed and recommendations are developed.

Note: The Category column is used to identify the disconnects by systems, policy, roles and responsibilities, or specific bands on the "IS" map. In other words, they are descriptors that add an additional perspec-

TABLE 10.1. EXAMPLE: ORDER FULFILLMENT PROCESS DISCONNECT LIST

No.	Priority H: High M: Med L: Low	Type	Category	Addressed Full	Partial	"IS" Step No.	Disconnect Description	Disconnect Impact
1	M	Org	Resource			14	Lack of available resources from Engineering group to support Sales	Potential for lost sales because we cannot respond to customer in timely manner
2	H	Proc	Roles and Responsibilities			12	ABCs are processing orders for CDE customers and vice versa; confusion as to who should handle the customer	Duplication of effort leading to multiple dispatches
3	H (very)	Org	Policy			12	The organization's way of splitting responsibilities for handling customers has created a lot of problems	See item 2
4	H (very)	Proc	Policy			11	The rationale used to determine how customers are assigned to ABC or branch is not correct	Multiple definitions cause confusion as to who should handle the customer
5	H (very)	Proc	System		3		There is no electronic repository where a complete, accurate customer profile is accessible	Wasted time and ineffective marketing; proposals based on inaccurate information—need to check multiple systems
6	L	Proc	Executive			14	DEFs are priced manually and not loaded into systems on a timely basis	Billing delays

tive and headline so you don't have to read the entire disconnect to understand where it fits.

Step 3: Design "SHOULD" Specifications

Tool: "SHOULD" Design Specifications

This tool will assist the Design Team in developing a set of "SHOULD" design specifications that will meet Project Goals and have a positive effect on the Critical Business Issue. They consist of three components:

1. Output specifications (requirements)
2. Input specifications (requirements)
3. Process specifications (characteristics or features)

When to Use

"SHOULD" design specifications are developed by the Design Team, then reviewed and approved by the Steering Team *prior* to designing the "SHOULD" process.

How to Use

1. Develop the output specifications *first* by asking Design Team members:

   What should be the outputs of the redesigned process?
   What should be the critical dimensions for each output?
   What should be the goal(s) of each output?

2. Next, develop the input specifications by asking Design Team members:

   What should be the inputs to the redesigned process?
   What should be the critical dimensions for each input?
   What should be the goal(s) of each input?

3. The process specifications are derived from the input and output specifications and tend to fall into distinct dimensions as shown next.

Process Performance

- Cost (materials, labor, assets)
- Timeliness (cycle time, responsiveness, on-time delivery)
- Regulatory (health, safety, environment, financial, human resources management)
- Process quality (error rate, scrap rate, repeated work/cost, cost/ease of performance)
- Process capability (throughput, technology, resource consumption)

Adaptiveness or Flexibility

Interaction of the process with:

- Other processes
- Customers
- Performers

Manageability of the Process

- Monitoring
- Troubleshooting

A full set of process specifications will be developed *after* the "SHOULD" process has been fully designed. Until that point, it is only necessary to identify those process specifications that are obvious from input or output specifications.

Time Required

Plan on spending at least half a day. The additional time required will depend on the complexity of the process.

Materials Required

- Sources of data for output specifications are:
    The Critical Business Issue and Project Goals
    Business strategy
    Customer satisfaction data
    Competitive analysis/benchmarking data
    Organizational competitive requirements (to gain competitive advantage, preserve competitive advantage, and so forth)
- Sources of data for input specifications are:
    The Critical Business Issue and Project Goals
    Customer needs and requirements data
    Supplier needs and requirements data
    Input disconnects

Figure 10.9 shows an example of "SHOULD" design specifications in a tabular format. The process specifications shown represent a complete set that you would develop *after* the "SHOULD" process has been fully designed and the input and output specifications have been confirmed.

This is a conceptual model depicting the design specification components as they "flow" through a process. Below the model are specific examples for each component.

Specific examples of output, input, and process specifications appear in Tables 10.2, 10.3, and 10.4. As with Figure 10.9, the process specifications in Table 10.4 should likewise be completed *after* the "SHOULD" process is fully designed.

Tips

- Process characteristics may not line up with critical dimensions and goals as neatly as the above example suggests, but it is always reasonable to question the inclusion of a process characteristic if it can't be related to any major process specification.

FIGURE 10.9. EXAMPLE: "SHOULD" DESIGN SPECIFICATIONS

Trigger or Input (Requirements)	→	Process (Characteristics or Features)	→	Output (Requirements)

Any order:
- Any quantity
- Order for standard or custom product
- Order form completed and signed
- New and existing customers

- Handling cost / order of $70.00
- Maximum of three functional handoffs
- Ten-day cycle time
- Zero defects
- Capable of handling standard or custom product

Orders:
- Received by customer within ten days
- 100% accurate

Invoices:
- Received at time of order
- 100% accurate

Assumptions and Constraints:
- No money available for automation
- No reorganization
- Forecasts will be accurate

TABLE 10.2.   OUTPUT SPECIFICATIONS

Outputs	Critical Dimensions	Goals
Product	On-time delivery	Within 24 hours of promised delivery date
	Completeness	Orders complete 100% of the time
	Cost	Price not to exceed quote
Invoice	Accuracy	100% accurate
	Timeliness	Sent within 24 hours of product shipment

TABLE 10.3.   INPUT SPECIFICATIONS

Inputs	Critical Dimensions	Goals
Customer order	Completeness	100% complete Includes delivery date Includes price quote
	Accuracy	Data 100% accurate
Customer specifications	Completeness	All performance dimensions specified
	Accuracy	Zero revisions or corrections

TABLE 10.4.   PROCESS SPECIFICATIONS

Process Characteristics	Critical Dimensions	Goals
Automated inventory planning system	Cost: materials	Within standards
Build from stock Standard bill of materials (BOM)	Timeliness: cycle time	10 days or less
In-line QA Machine-adjusted operating parameters	Quality: conforms to specs	Parts within .0001 tolerance
Environmental specs built into BOM	Regulations: environment	Meets federal EPA specs
No exceeding of process limits	Safety	No accidents
Database of product orders, specs On-line BOM On-line access via PC	Manageability: performance monitoring	Archived data available 24 hours a day

- The goals and critical dimensions are established here. The process characteristics are subject to change pending development of the "SHOULD" design.

Step 4: Design and Prioritize "COULD BE"

Tools: "COULD BE" Designs

This tool provides several examples of "COULD BE" designs that can be shared with Design Team members.

When to Use

The Design Team should create some "COULD BE" designs *after* they have developed the "SHOULD" design specifications.

How to Use

1. You may want to precede this activity with some creative-thinking exercises.
2. Emphasize that this is a brainstorming type of activity:

    There are no "wrong" or "bad" ideas.
    Make no judgments.
    Accept all ideas.
    Build on each other's ideas.

3. Provide the Design Team with some general guidelines:

    Each "COULD BE" should be an attempt to meet or exceed "SHOULD" design specifications (some or all of them).

"COULD BE" designs are how you think the "SHOULD" process "could" operate and how various problems "could" be solved; they are not "should" until you design them in "SHOULD."

A single "COULD BE" might address only part of a process, but if it has promise, it can later be combined with other alternatives.

A "COULD BE" often resembles a relationship map, displaying at a macro level how a process flows across an organization; the details are usually sketchy.

4. Divide the Design Team into several small teams of roughly equal size. Groups of four to six members work well.

5. Provide each team with an area to work in, a blank flip chart pad, and mapping kit supplies.

6. If possible, each "COULD BE" design should include:

A drawing of the "COULD BE"
A name
A brief description, if necessary
A list of process characteristics and operating style characteristics
A list of benefits
A list of inherent risks
A list of assumptions underlying the design

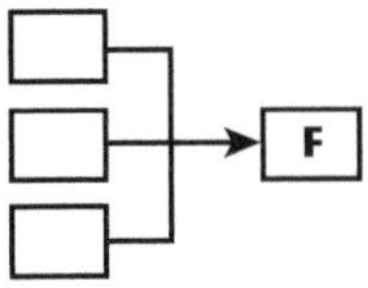

Example: "COULD BE" Designs

Figures 10.10, 10.11, and 10.12 show examples of "COULD BE" designs that may help Design Team members think "outside the box." These

FIGURE 10.10. REMOTE JOB ENTRY

Process Characteristics	Benefits of Adopting This Design	Risks Inherent in This Design	Assumptions Implied by This Design
None applicable	• Improved accuracy • Increased speed of response	• High cost of decentralized sites • Dependence on electronic data processing • How to staff?	• Responsiveness is important to customers • Quick service to major customers is paramount to our survival • Nearness to customer is a competitive advantage • Electronic data entry is feasible from major customer site

FIGURE 10.11. CENTRALIZED FRONT END

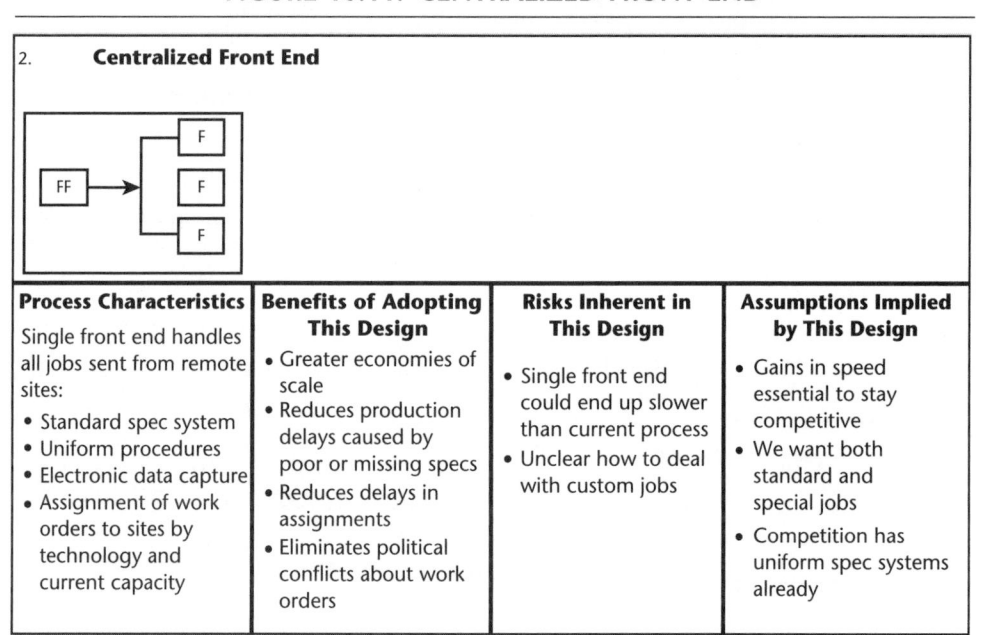

2. **Centralized Front End**

Process Characteristics	Benefits of Adopting This Design	Risks Inherent in This Design	Assumptions Implied by This Design
Single front end handles all jobs sent from remote sites: • Standard spec system • Uniform procedures • Electronic data capture • Assignment of work orders to sites by technology and current capacity	• Greater economies of scale • Reduces production delays caused by poor or missing specs • Reduces delays in assignments • Eliminates political conflicts about work orders	• Single front end could end up slower than current process • Unclear how to deal with custom jobs	• Gains in speed essential to stay competitive • We want both standard and special jobs • Competition has uniform spec systems already

FIGURE 10.12. VENDOR OPTION

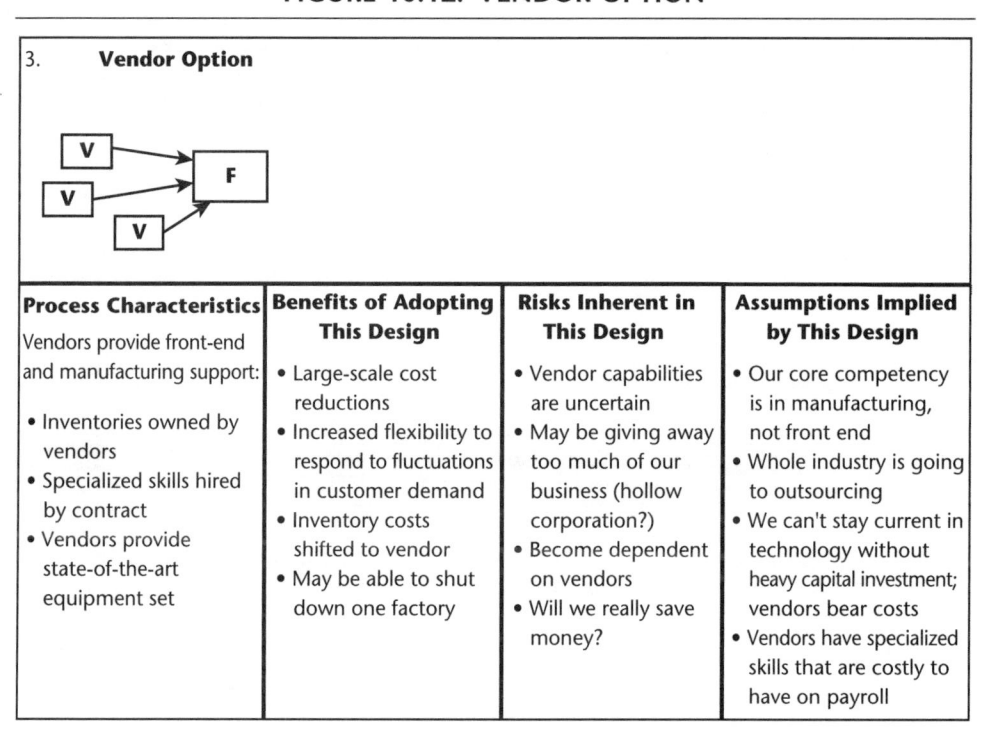

3. **Vendor Option**

Process Characteristics	Benefits of Adopting This Design	Risks Inherent in This Design	Assumptions Implied by This Design
Vendors provide front-end and manufacturing support: • Inventories owned by vendors • Specialized skills hired by contract • Vendors provide state-of-the-art equipment set	• Large-scale cost reductions • Increased flexibility to respond to fluctuations in customer demand • Inventory costs shifted to vendor • May be able to shut down one factory	• Vendor capabilities are uncertain • May be giving away too much of our business (hollow corporation?) • Become dependent on vendors • Will we really save money?	• Our core competency is in manufacturing, not front end • Whole industry is going to outsourcing • We can't stay current in technology without heavy capital investment; vendors bear costs • Vendors have specialized skills that are costly to have on payroll

examples reflect the organization's desire to reduce the cost of manufacturing across three plants. The Design Team was asked specifically to consider the option of closing one of the plants and consolidating operations—they came up with the three designs in Figures 10.10, 10.11, and 10.12.

Tool: "COULD BE" Prioritization Worksheet

Use this worksheet to guide the Steering Team in prioritizing the "COULD BE" Designs against Project Goals and other criteria.

When to Use

The Steering Team should complete the "COULD BE" Prioritization Worksheet (see Table 10.5) when prioritizing the "COULD BE" designs.

How to Use

1. Before the "IS" findings review session with the Steering Team, complete the following sections of the "COULD BE" Prioritization Worksheet (Table 10.5):

   Enter the Project Goals in the "Musts" section at the top of the template.

   Enter the output, input, and process specifications in the appropriate sections of the template.

2. Distribute the prepared worksheet to Steering Team members during the "IS" findings review session when discussing the "COULD BE" designs.

TABLE 10.5. "COULD BE" PRIORITIZATION WORKSHEET

Musts (Project Goals)	"COULD-BE" Alternatives			
	A	B	C	D
Outputs (list your output specifications below):				
Inputs (list your input specifications below):				
Process (list your process specifications below):				

Wants (list any "wants" expressed by the Steering Team here):

3. Ask each Steering Team member to check those "COULD BE" designs they think are most likely to achieve the Project Goals based on the output, input, and process specifications listed on the worksheet.
4. Ask them to also list any "Wants" they have relative to the new design in the bottom section of the worksheet.

Table 10.6 is a completed "COULD BE" Prioritization Worksheet from an "IS" findings review session.

TABLE 10.6. EXAMPLE: "COULD BE" PRIORITIZATION WORKSHEET

"COULD BE" Prioritization Worksheet

Musts (Project Goals)	"COULD BE" Alternatives			
	A	**B**	**C**	**D**
Order Cycle Time less than or equal to 10 days				
Handling cost/order less than or equal to $70.00 per order				

Outputs

	A	B	C	D
Product delivery within 24 hours of promised date				XX
Product orders complete 100% of the time	XX			XX
Product prices not to exceed quote	X			
Invoices 100% accurate	XX			
Invoices sent within 24 hours of product				XX

Inputs

	A	B	C	D
Customer order 100% complete	XX			
Customer order 100% accurate	XXX			
All performance dimensions specified per customer specifications	XX			
No revisions or corrections to customer specifications	XXXX	XXXX		

Process

	A	B	C	D
Materials within standard cost		XX		
Cycle time within 10 days		XX	XX	XX
Parts within .0001 tolerance		X		
Federal EPA specs met		XX		
No accidents		XX		

Wants

Step 5: Develop "SHOULD" Maps

Tool: "SHOULD" Process Design Approach

1. Review Rummler-Brache's Design Principles.
   Design for 80 percent and build separate paths for exceptions.
   Eliminate or reduce the impact of low-value steps.
   Simplify complex steps.
   Combine simple steps.
   Work to design quality into the work, rather than inspect step outputs after the fact.
   Use parallel paths wherever possible.
   Broaden job content and empower employees.
   Don't design things to the task level unless the risk of variation is unacceptable and you're willing to invest in testing prior to implementation.
2. Review and update "IS" analysis documentation, noting additional Disconnects as needed.
3. Review and update the "SHOULD" design specifications to include Steering Team additions and changes as needed.
4. Identify the subprocesses (four to ten macro process blocks) within the process, as shown in Figure 10.13.
5. For each subprocess, list outputs, output requirements, and assumptions. Also identify measures for the end-of-process and the end-of-subprocesses, as shown in Figure 10.14.
6. Determine the major process steps within each subprocess from trigger to completion.

FIGURE 10.13. SAMPLE MACRO PROCESS BLOCKS

Subprocess A   Subprocess B   Subprocess C   Subprocess D

FIGURE 10.14. MACRO PROCESS BLOCKS WITH OUTPUTS, OUTPUT REQUIREMENTS, AND ASSUMPTIONS

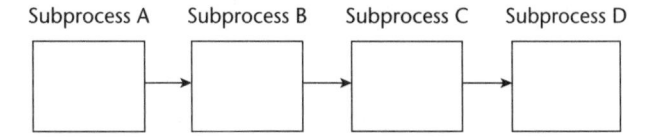

Subprocess A   Subprocess B   Subprocess C   Subprocess D

Subprocess Measure   Subprocess Measure   Subprocess Measure   Subprocess Measure   Process Measure

Outputs Requirements   Outputs Requirements   Outputs Requirements   Outputs Requirements

Assumptions

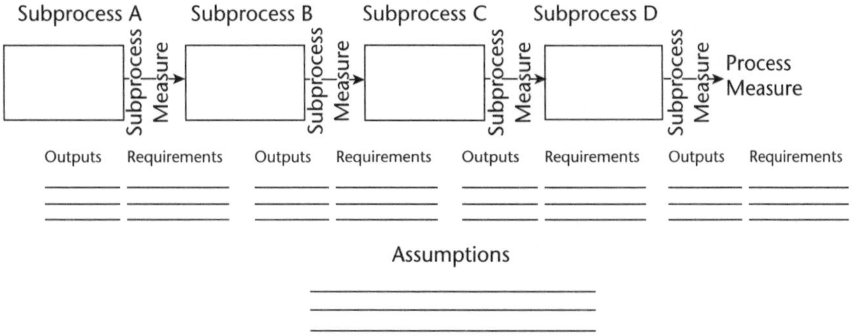

FIGURE 10.15. LINEAR PROCESS MAP WITH OUTPUTS, REQUIREMENTS, AND ASSUMPTIONS

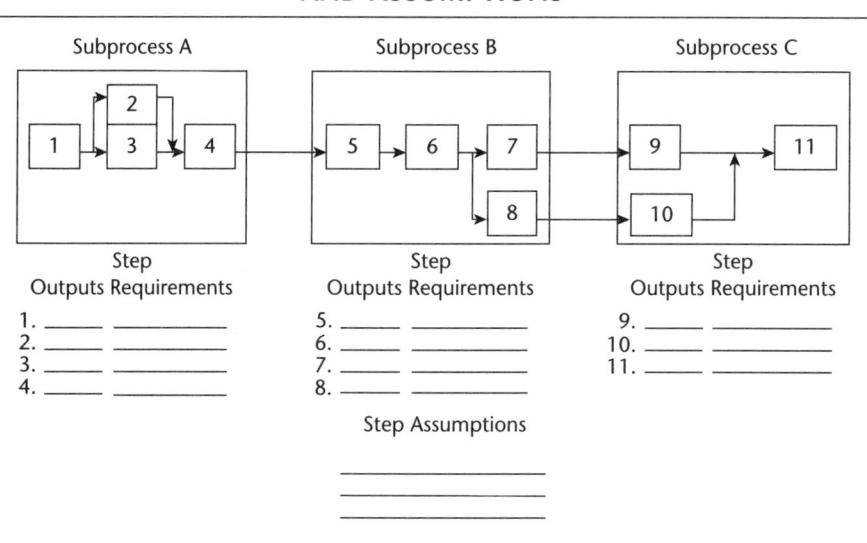

7. Develop a step-by-step linear map of the process with no reference to which functions own which step. This is to ensure the emphasis is on *what* rather than *who*. Below the linear process map, highlight outputs, requirements, and assumptions, as shown in Figure 10.15.

8. After the linear map is deemed complete, define new roles and create a new Cross-Functional Process Map, adding specific information about how certain steps may have changed (technology, procedures, and so on). This "SHOULD" Cross-Functional Process Map, as shown in Figure 10.16, will meet the "SHOULD" design specifications. The map will show the flow of inputs and outputs of the process across all applicable functions in the organization. See Step 1 for information on the Cross-Functional Process Map Tool.

FIGURE 10.16. HIGH-LEVEL VIEW, CROSS-FUNCTIONAL PROCESS MAP OF MAJOR PROCESS STEPS

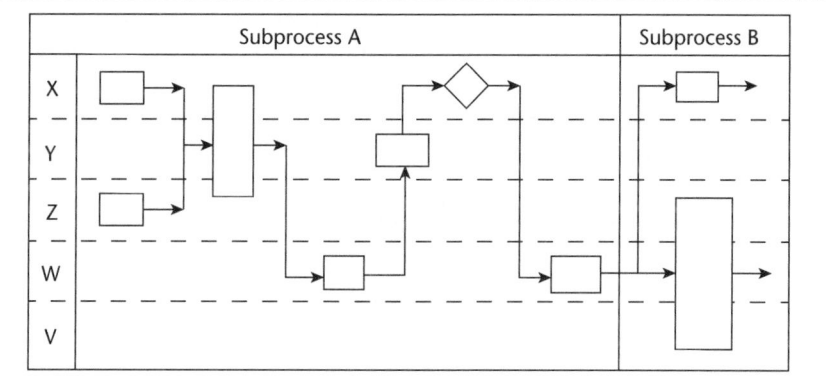

Step 6: Develop Process Measures

Tool: Measures Chain

M1s are end-of-process measures, and M2s are subprocess measures. By developing only those M2s that are linked to M1s, you reduce the number of measures.

The Measures Chain Worksheet is a tool for linking process and subprocess outputs. Also, the measures chain helps you build a measurement system that will meet your troubleshooting criteria.

When to Use

Use the Measures Chain Worksheet to define the project and set process performance goals. Use the worksheet again during the "SHOULD" design session, when you identify the *new* process measures.

How to Use

1. Beginning at the right side of the worksheet, for the process output, identify the aspects of process performance (critical dimensions) that the customer values. The worksheet shows the four basic categories of dimensions: quality, timeliness, financial, and volume. Not all of these categories may be relevant.
2. For each of the critical dimensions identified, identify the appropriate measures. (These are the M1-Es, or end-of-process measures from the customer's perspective.) The standards can be identified at this point, or you can return to them after you have finished the M2s.
3. Moving right to left across the worksheet, for each of the M1-Es that have been identified, identify an appropriate M1-I, or end-of-process measure from management's perspective. If there is an M1-E of interest to a customer, you need an end-of-process measure that allows management to track how well the process is performing to that critical dimension.
4. Determine if there are any critical dimensions of the process output that are important to company management but not necessarily important to the customer. For example, the customer seldom cares about the cost of producing an output, but management usually does. If so, add these as additional M1-I measures.
5. Document on the Measures Chain Worksheet the outputs from each subprocess that relate to the process output (at the bottom of the worksheet). Work from right to left as you do this, doing only one process output at a time. If you have more than one end-of-process output, you might want to build a separate worksheet and chain for that output.
6. For each M1-I that has been established, begin building an M2 measures chain, moving from right to left. M2s are the end-of-subprocess measures. Identify only M2s that are linked to M1s.
7. Not every subprocess will have an M2 for each M1-I.

8. In summary, the procedure for determining the M2s is to start with an M1-I and work backward (left) up the chain, identifying relevant M2s for that particular M1-I. Then select the next M1-I and do the same thing until all M1-Is have been considered.

Time Required

The time needed to complete the Measures Chain Worksheet will depend on the complexity of the process. Plan on spending at least a few hours.

Materials Required

- To develop the measures for Project Definition, you will need the Measures Chain Worksheet (see Figure 10.17) and the Critical Process Profile.

FIGURE 10.17. EXAMPLE: MEASURES CHAIN

M2a	M2b	M2c	M2d	M1-I	M1-E	
Number of requests for clarification of customer requirements	Number of redesigns	Number of defects per unit	Number of incorrect products shipped Number of incorrect invoices sent	Percent of orders sent to correct address	Percent of defective products returned Percent of customer complaints about invoice	Quality
Percent of orders scheduled within 24 hours of receipt	Percent to Manufacturing per schedule Number of material shortages	Percent to shipping per schedule Number of orders requiring rework	Percent shipped per schedule	Percent of time process performs to schedule	Percent of orders received on promised date	Time
	Design costs: plan vs. actual Redesign costs: plan vs. actual	Manufacturing costs: plan vs. actual	Shipping costs: plan vs. actual	Cost to process order: plan vs. actual	Number of customer complaints about pricing	Financial
						Volume

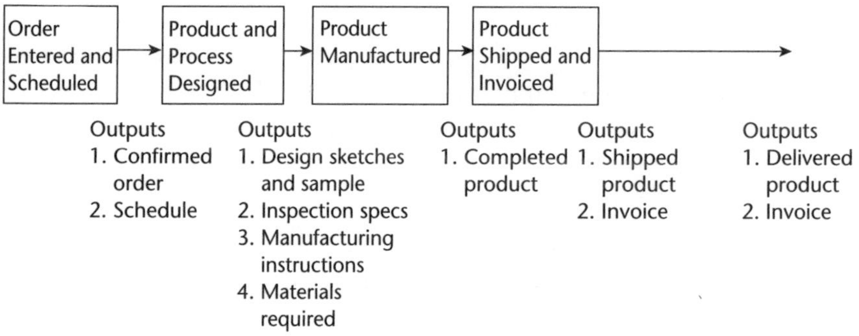

Order Entered and Scheduled	→	Product and Process Designed	→	Product Manufactured	→	Product Shipped and Invoiced	→

Outputs	Outputs	Outputs	Outputs	Outputs
1. Confirmed order 2. Schedule	1. Design sketches and sample 2. Inspection specs 3. Manufacturing instructions 4. Materials required	1. Completed product	1. Shipped product 2. Invoice	1. Delivered product 2. Invoice

- To develop the measures for the "SHOULD" design, you will need the Measures Chain Worksheet and the new subprocesses, their outputs, requirements, and assumptions.

Figure 10.17 is an example of a partially completed Measures Chain Worksheet for the "SHOULD" design of an order fulfillment process.

Step 7: Develop Cross-Functional Role/Responsibility Matrix

Tool: Cross-Functional Role/Responsibility Matrix
The Cross-Functional Role/Responsibility Matrix is a tool to help determine which function will perform which steps in the new process.

When to Use
Create a Cross-Functional Role/Responsibility Matrix if the new process is markedly different from the "IS" process with respect to function roles and/or if a major organizational power shift will occur because of the new process.

How to Use
1. List the process steps (from your Cross-Functional "SHOULD" Process Map) down the left column of the matrix—one per row.
2. List the functions (from your Cross-Functional "SHOULD" Process Map) along the top of the remaining columns.
3. List the outputs of each process step (from your Cross-Functional "SHOULD" Process Map) under the appropriate function.
4. Use the PARIS approach when examining each step to determine:

Who should be the *Performer*?

- The Performer is the person accountable for this task—this is one "doer," or one person who coordinates the work of others in a shared task.
- There is normally one Performer per task. If there is more than one, the matrix must specify what the respective responsibilities are. For example, one function can be the Performer for anything to do with gasoline, another function can do the same task related to diesel.

Who should *Approve* the output?

- The Approver is the person who gives input to the step, or reviews it, or both. The Approver is accountable for results.
- Include as few approval steps as possible, but as many as needed for accountability. Staff groups should set guidelines (enforced, if needed, by line management), but generally should not be in an Approver role.

Who should *Review* the outputs?

- The Reviewer has the right to know what was done and decided. The Reviewer reviews information for other parts of their job (namely, other processes) as preparation for picking up responsibility for later phases of the process and to provide feedback to this area's involvement in earlier parts of the process.

Who should provide *Input* to the task?

- Input happens before the task. Often opinions or information from experts or departments involved in earlier steps in the process or in related processes are sought as input to the task. The Performer doesn't *have* to listen to the input, but clearly teamwork will suffer if the Performer *never* listens. It is up to the person in the role to decide whether to provide input. If input is mandatory, then he or she is Support.

Who should *Support* the task, and in what way?

- The Support person supports the Performer, often with analysis. Generally this represents a fairly significant, resource-intensive task. In the Cross-Functional Role/Responsibility Matrix, provide words around the nature of the support provided.

5. Figure 10.18 shows how roles are derived from process steps.

Time Required
You should be able to create this matrix in an hour, because you already have all the information in existing documents.

Materials Required

- The Cross-Functional Role/Responsibility Matrix Template
- Linear Process Map
- Cross-Functional "SHOULD" Process Map

Table 10.7 is an example of a *partially* completed Cross-Functional Role/Responsibility Matrix for an order fulfillment process.

Step 8: Identify Changes to Performance System

Tool: Human Performance System Checklist
This checklist, along with the Human Performance System Model, should be used by the Design Team during their "IS" process validation session and when they develop the "SHOULD" Map. It will be used again during implementation to help with job redesign efforts. These tools will help them determine the Human Performance System (HPS) factors contributing to disconnect performance for a given job category or group of performers.

When to Use
Use the HPS Checklist as a way to help determine the HPS factors contributing to disconnect performance. The HPS model will also be a helpful reference tool during this activity.

FIGURE 10.18. SAMPLE STEPS FOR COMPLETING THE CROSS-FUNCTIONAL ROLE/RESPONSIBILITY MATRIX

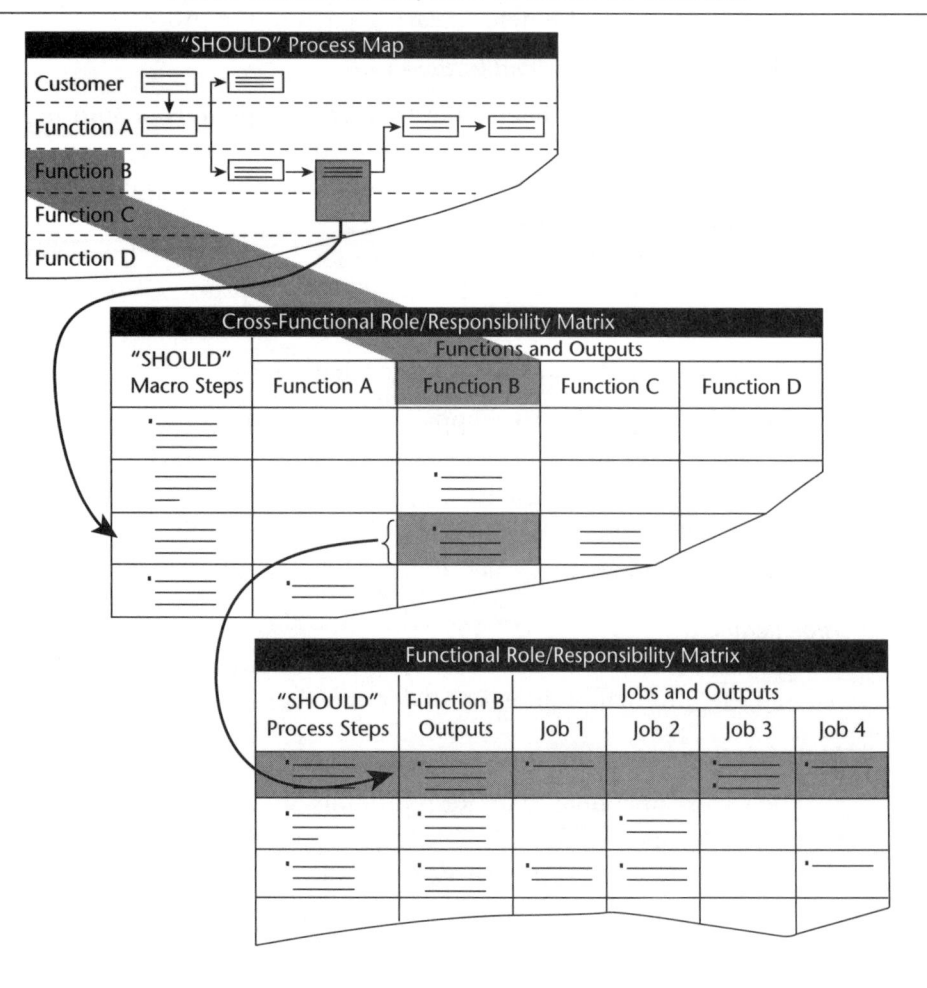

How to Use

Review the job-level disconnects for which the root cause is not clear. Job-level disconnects are represented by:

- Unclear performance expectations
- Inadequate job support (resources or tools)
- Nonsupportive consequences
- Inadequate job performance feedback
- Inadequate training
- Performer incapable of producing required outputs

Using the HPS Model and the HPS Checklist for each job category or group of performers, determine the HPS factors contributing to the disconnect performance.

TABLE 10.7. EXAMPLE: CROSS-FUNCTIONAL ROLE/RESPONSIBILITY MATRIX

Process Step (Macro)	Functions				
	Sales	Credit and Invoicing	Production Control	Production	Assembly and Shipping
			Function Outputs		
1. Order taken	Order form completed Order submitted				
2. Order entered	If credit problem: credit problem addressed, customer apprised of problem, and customer guarantee sought If problem resolved: order resubmitted and customer apprised of status If problem not resolved: order cancelled and customer apprised of status	Customer status checked If existing customer: invoice prepared If new customer: credit checked If credit OK: invoice prepared If credit not OK: order returned to Sales	Order entered Inventory checked If inventory available: order forwarded to Assembly and Shipping If inventory not available: production scheduled		
3. Order produced			If credit problem not resolved: order stopped	Production schedule received Production scheduled Machines set up Materials printed Materials forwarded to Assembly and Shipping	
4. Order assembled and shipped					Order received If production order: materials assembled and shipped and notice of shipment forwarded to Finance

- The questions on the left side of the HPS Checklist are designed to help you determine which of the HPS elements are at work—they can all be or there can be a combination of elements.
- If the answer to a question is "no" or "don't know," complete the Performance System Solution column to begin documenting the steps necessary to resolve the disconnect.
- It may be necessary to meet with individuals in the job categories to get accurate information.

Table 10.8 is an example of a partially completed HPS Checklist for a job-level disconnect.

Tool: Human Performance System Model

This tool, along with the Human Performance System Checklist, will help the Design Team identify job-level disconnects during the "IS" process validation session and will help them document jobs that must be changed once the new process is designed (see Figure 10.19). You will also use this tool during implementation as a reference when preparing employees for the changes they will need to make in their performance.

See Chapter Five for more information on the Human Performance System.

Step 9: Make Recommendations

Tool: Recommendations

Recommendations specify what *must* change to implement the new process successfully. After you develop a list of emerging recommendations, then you will cluster or group the recommendations for ease of reference.

When to Use

Develop and cluster recommendations after designing the "SHOULD" process and the related Cross-Functional Role/Responsibility Matrix.

How to Use

Develop a list of recommendations using the Recommendation Analysis Worksheet shown in Table 10.9.

1. Gather and review the following "SHOULD" Process Design documents:
   - Cross-Functional "SHOULD" Process Map
   - Disconnect list
   - Past implementation efforts data
   - Cross-Functional Role/Responsibility Matrix
   - Step outputs, specifications or requirements, and assumptions
2. Summarize the preceding information into recommendations that include the following:
   - Specific nature of the recommended change
   - Impact of the change on the organization, process, and job
   - Functions (departments) affected by the change
   - Linkage to other recommendations

TABLE 10.8. EXAMPLE: HUMAN PERFORMANCE SYSTEM CHECKLIST

Job-Level Disconnect:
Design Specifications sent to Manufacturing are consistently inaccurate, causing a lot of rework.

	Performance System Troubleshooting Questions	Yes	No	Don't Know	Performance System Solution
OUTPUT	**A. Performance Specifications** Do performance standards exist? (If yes, answer the next two questions.)			X	Meet with Engineering to determine if performance standards exist
	Do performers know the desired output and performance standards?				
	Do performers consider the standards attainable?				
INPUT	**B. Task Support** Can the performer easily recognize the input requiring action?	X			
	Can the task be done without interference from other tasks?	X			
	Are the job procedures and work flow logical?	X			
	Are adequate resources available for performance (time, tools, staff, and information)?	X			
CONSEQUENCES	**C. Consequences** Are the consequences aligned to support desired performance? (If yes, answer the next two questions.)			X	Not aware of any consequences, positive or negative; talk with Engineering and Materials to determine consequences
	Are consequences meaningful from the performer's point of view?				
	Are the consequences timely?				
FEEDBACK	**D. Feedback** Do performers receive information about their performance? (If yes, answer the next question.)			X	Same as Consequences
	Is the information they receive: Timely? Relevant? Accurate? Constructive? Easy to understand? Specific?				
PERFORMANCE	**E. Knowledge and Skill** Do the performers have the necessary skill and knowledge to perform?	X			
	Do the performers know why desired performance is important?			X	Same as Consequences
	F. Individual Capability Are the performers physically, mentally, and emotionally able to perform?	X			

FIGURE 10.19. A MODEL FOR TROUBLESHOOTING OR DESIGNING AN EFFECTIVE HUMAN PERFORMANCE SYSTEM

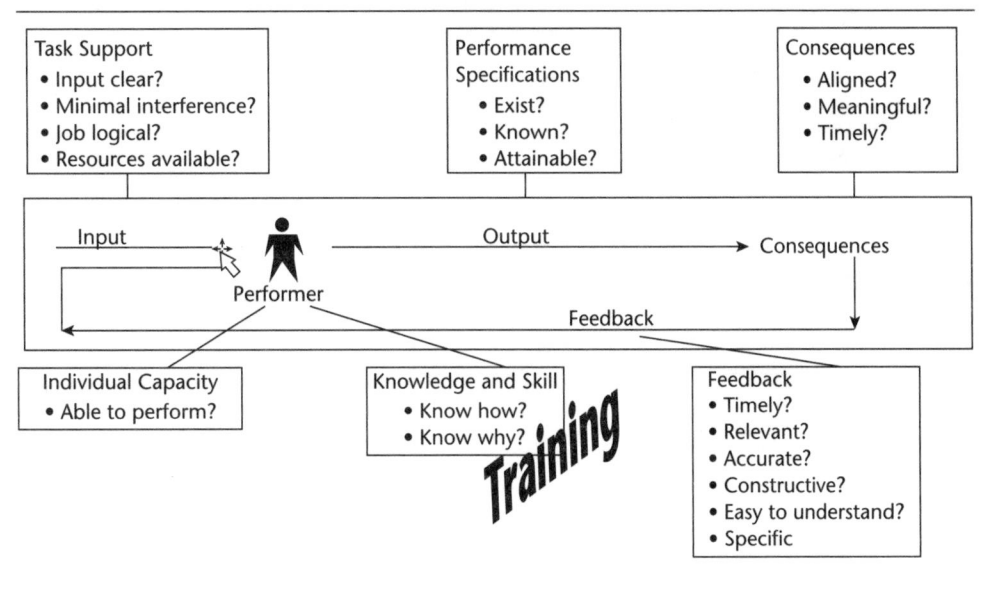

TABLE 10.9. RECOMMENDATION ANALYSIS WORKSHEET

Recommendation	Impact on Project Goals	Time to benefit	Time to implement	Capital requirements to implement	Dollar expense to implement	Staff time to implement	Complexity of change	Disruption to organization	Dependency				Sequence or Phase	Comments
									Precede Recommendation #	Concurrent with Recommendation #	Independent	Follow Recommendation #		

- General estimate of the cost or benefit of the change
- Risks
- Disconnects resolved by the recommendation

3. Organize the recommendations so that the nature and sequence of the change are clear.

   Again using the Recommendation Analysis Worksheet (Table 10.9), develop additional information about each recommendation.

4. Consider the following as you further analyze each recommendation:

   - Impact on Project Goals
   - Time to implement
   - Operating expense
   - Complexity of change
   - Dependencies
   - Time to benefit
   - Capital requirements
   - Staff time to implement
   - Disruption to organization
   - Sequence

   Summarize the information developed for each recommendation using the formats shown in Tables 10.10, 10.11, and 10.12. Group the recommendations into approximately ten preliminary clusters. Typical clusters are:

   - By type of activity or expertise required (such as sales, information technology, or manufacturing)
   - By organization structure or geography (such as sites, regions, business divisions, or countries)
   - By implementation strategy
   - By "SHOULD" subprocesses

Time Required

The time required to develop a list of recommendations will depend on the complexity of the process being changed—plan to spend at least half a day.

Materials Required

You will need the following "SHOULD" design documents:

- "SHOULD" Cross-Functional Process Map
- Disconnect list
- Past efforts implementation data
- Cross-Functional Role/Responsibility Matrix
- Step outputs, specifications or requirements, and assumptions

Recommendation Formats

Following are two examples of formats you can use when documenting "SHOULD" Process Recommendations.

Example 1

Recommendation Summary Description

Revise the incentive compensation system for Sales Representatives to pay commission after the order is shipped, rather than when it is submitted.

TABLE 10.10. EXPECTED RESULTS

Time Saved	Minimum	Best Estimate	Maximum
Faster to customer	3 days	6 days	10 days
On-time delivery (customer satisfaction)	95%	98%	100%
Invoiced sooner (10% of sales)	$70,000/ month	$78,000/ month	$83,000/ month

TABLE 10.11. EXPECTED COSTS

Item	Minimum	Best Estimate	Maximum
Design new system	$3,000	$5,000	$7,000
Implement new system (0.5 hour briefing per Sales Rep)	$1,300	$1,500	$2,000

TABLE 10.12. RISKS

What Could Go Wrong?	Likelihood	Effect	Signal
Sales Reps resist and form union	Medium in view of recent off-site organizing meeting	Reduced flexibility; higher costs	Second organizing meeting
Sales Reps resist and quit	Low — we pay well	Increased costs to hire and train new Reps	Turnover rate

Disconnects/Issues Addressed

Disconnect 15: Submission of incomplete orders causes a need for additional contact with customer, potentially resulting in added processing time.

Example 2

Recommendation Number 19: Process Measures

The process measures established by the Design Team should be implemented and managed.

Description

The process measures that have been identified by the Design Team must be implemented and tracked in order to determine whether the process is achieving its goals for effectiveness and efficiency. These measures will be utilized by the organization and the permanent Process Teams to identify areas for further improvement. These measures should be linked to the individual performer metrics.

Benefits

- Provides the means for ensuring that the process achieves its performance goals
- Identifies potential performance issues or opportunities for continuous improvement

Cost or Effort

- Confirmation of measures described from the process design and identification of tracking vehicles
- Determine responsibility for obtaining, monitoring, and compiling the measurements
- Determine actions required for providing tracking vehicles

Risk

- Lack of acceptance of the measurement system
- Measurement is resisted by performers within the process
- Lack of communication and feedback to continuously measure the process cross-functionally
- Cost of measurement is perceived as too expensive
- Measurement results are "massaged" to reflect expectations rather than actual performance
    Disconnects addressed: 39
    Departments affected: All

(Continued)

Linkage to Other Recommendations

- Provides the means to track effectiveness of the new process
- Provides feedback for continuous process evaluation and improvement

Parties Required for Implementation

- Cross-functional team led by the Project Manager

Key Milestones and Events

- Review, confirm, and enhance measurement system described by Design Team
- Determine which data need to be tracked and assign responsibility for obtaining those data
- Identify and implement methods or vehicles for measurement tracking
- Assign responsibility for analyzing and communicating process measurement data as appropriate

Implementation Strategy

Test measurement system in prototype site

Step 10: Develop Implementation Strategy

Tools: General Implementation Strategy

Use this tool to capture reactions and suggestions received from the Steering Team during their preview of the "SHOULD" Process Design.

When to Use

You will begin to complete the General Implementation Strategy Template during the "SHOULD" Process Design preview session with the Steering Team.

How to Use

1. Explain that this is a high-level first glance at the implementation strategy—details are not necessary at this point. This is designed to jump-start thinking about implementation.
2. Ask Steering Team members for input on the five items in the general implementation strategy:

   What are the guiding principles for implementation?
   What past problems do we need to overcome or avoid?

What is known or already determined about:

Resources?
Timing?
Funding?
Goals or measures?
Degree of operating freedom for implementation?

Who will be involved in implementation, and what will their key roles be?

How detailed does the preliminary implementation plan put together by the Design Team need to be?

You may want to give each member a copy of the template so they can fill in the responses, or you may just wish to capture the input on a flip chart and copy the information into the template later.

Example: Completed Template of General Implementation Strategy

Guiding Principles for Implementation

- Implementation is the responsibility of the receiving organizations (such as districts).
- Funding for pilots will be provided from district expense budgets.
- Funding for development will be provided by Corporate.
- All implementation plans must be approved by district vice presidents.
- Districts will determine the who, what, and when for local resources to be assigned to implementation.
- "IS" Draft Plan must precede other plans.
- General communications will begin upon approval of implementation plans.

Past Problems to Overcome (Avoid)

- Lack of communication about need and vision
  Solution: Cascading information sessions run by district and department managers. Formal communication plan and materials to be developed by Communication and Assessment Team.
- Declaring victory too soon
  Solution: Measure progress reviews versus targets, conducted monthly by Implementation Steering Team.

(Continued)

What Is Known or Already Determined

- Resources

  Implementation Steering Team will determine Project Manager and Team Leaders. District vice presidents will nominate team members.

- Timing

  All recommendations must be implemented in the next eighteen months.

- Funding

  See the preceding Guiding Principles for Implementation.

- Goals or measures

- Degree of operating freedom for implementers

  Implementation Teams (ITs) cannot change the "SHOULD" process. ITs can decide how and when to carry out their plans within negotiated deadlines with other teams.

Scope of Organization to Be Involved in Implementation and Key Roles

- Corporate departments (Information Systems, Human Resources, Field Support, Marketing and Sales)

    Design information systems
    Develop policy
    Provide training programs and instructors

- Districts

    Participate on Implementation Teams (leaders and members)
    Coordinate pilots and feedback activities
    Participate in cross-district training

How Detailed Should the Preliminary Implementation Plan from the Design Team Be?

A high-level plan should contain enough detail to move into implementation.

Tool: Implementation Strategy

This tool will help you develop and analyze alternative implementation strategies for each recommendation.

When to Use

Develop an implementation strategy for each recommendation after you have completed an analysis of all recommendations. You will then be able to analyze each strategy to select the appropriate one to present to senior management.

How to Use

Develop an Implementation Strategy Matrix manually or by using the template.

1. You will need the average readiness and disruption values for each recommendation that you analyzed.
2. Construct a four-cell matrix for readiness and disruption, using Figure 10.20 as a guide. The vertical and horizontal axes should range from 1 to 5.
3. Place each recommendation on the matrix at the point where its average readiness and disruption values intersect. Figure 10.20 shows an example of a completed matrix.
4. Circle the recommendations that you clustered. This will highlight the fact that a cluster may involve the mixture of strategies and require different tasks and timetables. See Figure 10.21 for an example of highlighting clusters.

FIGURE 10.20. EXAMPLE: READINESS AND DISRUPTION MATRIX

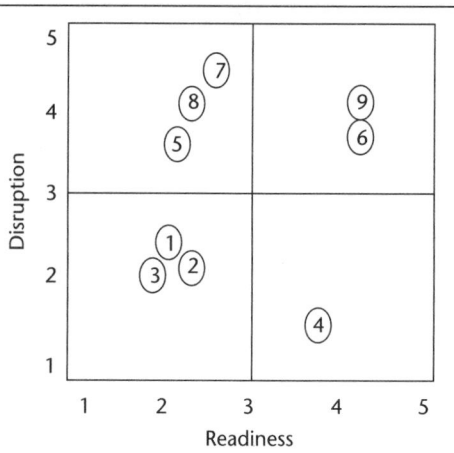

FIGURE 10.21. EXAMPLE: READINESS AND DISRUPTION MATRIX HIGHLIGHTING CLUSTERS

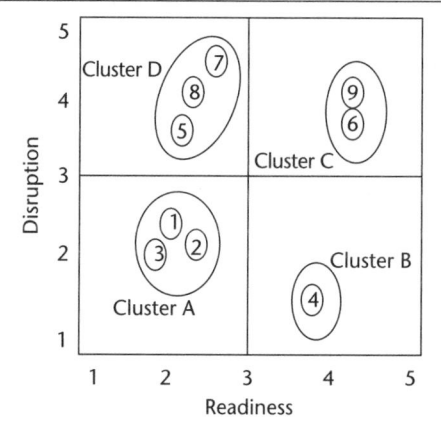

Validate Your Implementation Strategy Matrix

5. Fill out an Implementation Strategy Analysis Worksheet (see Table 10.13) for each recommendation.

Time Required

The time required to develop an Implementation Strategy Matrix will depend on the number of recommendations you must consider—plan on at least a half hour.

Materials Required

- Average readiness and disruption values
- Completed Recommendation Analysis Worksheet (see Table 10.9)

TABLE 10.13.   IMPLEMENTATION STRATEGY ANALYSIS WORKSHEET

Cluster: *[Enter cluster description here]* Recommendations: *[Enter recommendation #'s that are included in the cluster here]* Circle those that apply	If your answer to a question is yes, the shaded strategies below most likely will *not* apply.			
	Immediate	**Inspiration**	**Phased**	**Systemic**
1. Need to allow time for mourning losses?	▓	▓		
2. Time required to design solutions?	▓	▓		
3. Need to test feasibility?	▓			
4. Need to demonstrate feasibility?	▓	▓		
5. Need to cascade through organizational hierarchy?	▓	▓		
6. Need to roll out across geography?	▓	▓		▓
7. Need to spread cost/resources over time?	▓	▓		
8. Need to redesign organization?	▓	▓	▓	
9. Need to alter supporting technical systems (e.g., procedures, specifications, equipment, tool, information systems, training programs)?	▓	▓	Depends on extent	
10. Need to alter company policies, strategies, goals, vision?	▓	▓	Depends on extent	
11. Need to alter key HR systems (e.g., pay, hiring, appraisal, discipline)?	▓	▓	Depends on extent	
12. Need to involve unions, government agencies, external vendors?	▓			
13. Need to train employees in new procedures, skills, etc.?	▓			
14. Need to dismantle existing bureaucracies?	▓	▓		

- Implementation Strategy Analysis Worksheet (optional)
- Implementation Strategy Matrix (see Table 10.14)

Figure 10.22 shows an example of a completed Implementation Strategy Matrix. It shows how nine recommendations plot out in terms of an organization's readiness to implement them and the disruption it believes it will encounter.

TABLE 10.14.   IMPLEMENTATION STRATEGY MATRIX

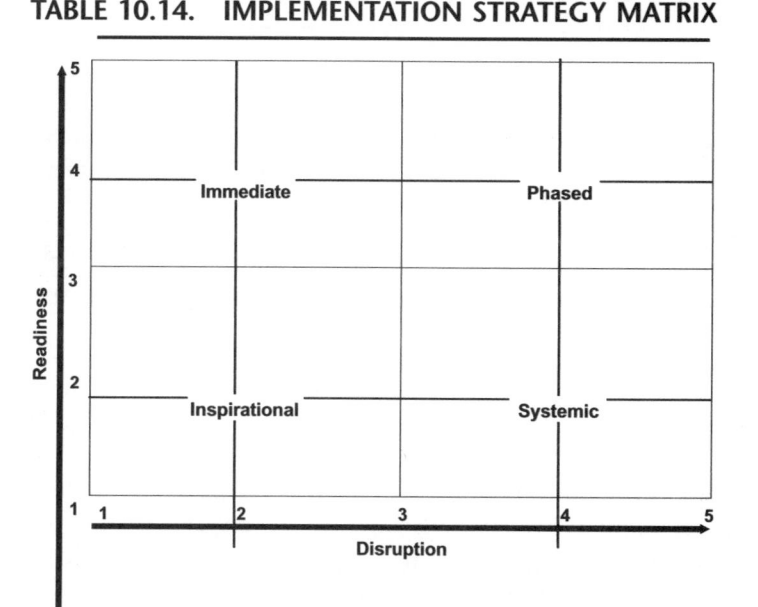

FIGURE 10.22. EXAMPLE: COMPLETED IMPLEMENTATION STRATEGY MATRIX

CHAPTER ELEVEN

OVERCOMING THE SEVEN DEADLY SINS OF PROCESS IMPROVEMENT

*Mistakes are always paid for in casualties and troops are
quick to see any blunder made by their commanders.*

—DWIGHT DAVID EISENHOWER

Companies of all sizes and industries have become aware that they
need to improve business processes such as product development,
order fulfillment, planning, distribution, billing, hiring, and customer
service. Everybody is doing—or at least talking about doing—"Process
Improvement," "process redesign," or "process reengineering."

As with other performance improvement efforts, most organizations
can point to the results of their efforts: cost savings, quality improvements,
and cycle time reductions. However, there has been more sizzle than steak,
more activity than results.

In our experience, most failures to realize the potential return on
Process Improvement investment arise from committing one or more of
what we call the seven deadly sins.

Sin 1: Process Improvement is not tied to the strategic issues the business faces.
One company in the food business is proud of its seventy cross-functional
Process Improvement Teams. When asked about results, executives
mumble vague homilies about "culture change" and "empowerment."
Noble pursuits, no doubt, but what's the increase in shareholder value?

Note: This chapter appeared as "The Seven Deadly Sins of Process Improvement" in
the June 1994 issue of *Chief Executive,* coauthored by Alan P. Brache and Frank Popoff,
chairman and CEO of Dow Chemical. It is reprinted here with the permission of *Chief
Executive.* © 1994 by Chief Executive Publishing, 733 Third Avenue, 21st Floor, New
York, NY 10017. All rights reserved.

Almost every one of an engineering conglomerate's dozens of business units has documented its processes. When asked how they've used these "maps," they admit that they haven't.

Too many Process Improvement Teams either are not centered around critical issues or are convened to address self-selected "backyard" (often intrafunctional) issues that are not high on an organization's overall priority list. We learned during the "quality circle" era that the location of the microwave oven and the color of the walls have little impact on business results.

Process Improvement Projects should be driven by an issue critical to the organization, such as profitability, market share, regulatory compliance, safety, or customer satisfaction. They also should be tied to measurable goals (such as moving from 35 percent to 38 percent share, reducing warranty claims to less than 3 percent of sales, cutting $40 million from the cost of purchased goods, and decreasing product development and introduction time to six months). As these examples illustrate, most Critical Business Issues require us to address cross-functional processes.

In our experience, Process Improvement efforts that are not driven by a measurable strategic issue lose the support of top management and of the worker-level teams. "Become a world-class competitor," "improve efficiency," and "change our culture" are commendable visions that provide no focus for improvement. The number of teams and the number of flowcharts should not be the measures of success.

Our greatest return on investments in Process Improvement comes from its use as a tool for implementing strategy. The CEO must ensure that there's a focused, intelligent strategy to be implemented. Likewise, he or she must ensure that the Process Improvement plan matches the core processes to the Critical Success Factors and to the issues standing between the organization and achievement of its strategic vision. Like any good plan, it should contain action items, names, and dates.

If you're not prepared to tie your Process Improvement effort to your strategy and the critical issues facing your business, don't expect significant results. (A solid Phase Ø, described in Chapter Nine, will help avoid this sin.)

Sin 2: The Process Improvement effort does not involve the right people, especially top management, in the right way. We believe that Process Improvement should not be done by outsiders. CEOs are frequently tempted to hire experts to "do it for us." These consultants present recommendations for improvement. The primary deficiency in this approach is not in the thoroughness of the consultants' analysis or the wisdom of their recommendations. Rather, because the changes come from the outside, they do not garner sufficient commitment from those who have to implement them.

We know of a manufacturing company that recently dismissed a reengineering consulting firm on which it had spent $70 million. While there were pockets of impressive, quick-hit cost reductions, the firm generated so much ill will among the workforce that the company no longer predicts long-term performance improvement.

Process Improvement should be done by the people involved in the process, including customers and suppliers. A value-added role can be played by external consultants or internal consultants from departments such as quality, human resources, and process reengineering. But that role does not entail doing the analysis and redesign. It means providing tools and guidance to the people who work in the process and who will have to live with the changes.

The most frequent cause of shortcomings in a Process Improvement effort is top management's failure to play an active role. "Top management" includes a "sponsor" or "owner" who can make things happen and a Steering Team composed of the department or region chiefs touched by the process. Their role is to provide a strategy that guides the overall Process Improvement effort, to set the direction for each project, to guide the team at key junctures, to remove obstacles, to approve reasonable recommendations, and to manage the implementation of the changes.

We can talk about "empowerment" all we like. However, in an organization such as Dow, no meaningful change will occur without the active participation of functional, regional, and product-line management. If you're not prepared to play an active role, don't invest in process redesign. (If we clearly define the Phase 1 roles and fulfill those roles during Phases 2 and 3, we are unlikely to be tripped up by this sin.)

Sin 3: Process Improvement Teams are not given a clear, appropriate charter and are not held accountable for fulfilling that charter. Let's say you have a Process Improvement Team staffed with highly motivated people at the right levels from the right departments and geographical areas. That's a good start. However, if they do not have a clear sense of their assignment's direction and boundaries, they will flounder, lose their energy, and fail to meet expectations.

A key part of top management's role is to ensure that each Design Team member understands the answers to the following questions:

- What is the driving issue and why has it been selected? (Why are we here?)
- What are the specific project/process goals? (What constitutes success?)
- What is our role and that of others involved in the effort? (Why has each of us been selected? Are we analysts? Recommenders? Implementors?)

- What are the deliverables? (New work flows? Benchmarking information? Action plans? Cost-benefit analysis?)
- What are the boundaries of the process we are to improve? (Where does it begin and end?)
- What, if any, are the constraints? (What is "off-limits"?)
- What is the deadline? What is the schedule? How much time are we expected to spend on this effort?
- What happens to our "regular jobs" while we're involved in this project?
- How will we be rewarded for our contribution? (What's in it for us?)

If you have sponsored a team that is listless, is achieving only modest results, or has spent more than six months and hasn't yet delivered a set of recommended Process Improvements, it may be because it doesn't have a charter that appropriately answers these questions. And that's your fault.

Having established the charter, top management must maintain the pressure for results. At Dow, we emphasize rational problem solving and "managing by fact." In general, the approach has served us well. However, excessive analysis can paralyze a Process Improvement effort, because there's always an additional piece of information that can be gathered or an additional level of root cause that can be unearthed. At some point, the sponsors of an improvement effort have to make it clear that it's time to move on.

If you're not prepared to provide clear direction to Process Improvement Teams and to "hold their feet to the fire," don't be disappointed in their results. (If the Steering Team does a thorough job during Phase 1 and plays its role during Phases 2 and 3, this sin will not be committed.)

Sin 4: The top management team thinks that if it's not "nuking" the existing organization ("reengineering"), it's not making significant improvements. During the past two years, the concept of process reengineering has swept America. Reengineering proponents suggest a fundamental, clean-sheet look at how we do work. So far, so good. However, reengineering often has been equated with reorganizing, downsizing, or installing new computer systems.

Our experience suggests that:

- In itself, reorganization rarely improves performance. Restructuring who reports to whom should follow restructuring how we work. However, improved work processes don't necessarily require structural changes. Indeed, the more you focus on the process, the less important organization structure becomes. We can't estimate the financial and psychological cost of America's obsession with the annual reorganization, but we are confident that the number would be sobering.

- The downsizing mania sweeping business is close to the flash point. Clearly, globally competitive markets demand that we eliminate the waste that in the past we could hide. However, too many companies are using reengineering the same way they used quality—as a back-office waste-reduction tool rather than as a weapon to gain competitive advantage. Downsizing should not be a badge of honor. The most successful Process Improvement efforts enable companies to maintain or grow staff to keep pace with the increased demand they have created.
- Automation often forms part of the solution, but it is rarely the solution. Fix processes first; then talk about computers.

In addition, we don't think that radical change is necessarily healthier than incremental change. Some processes require radical redesign or even re-creation; others do not. The critical business issues ought to determine how revolutionary the change should be. An analysis of current processes can offer significant insights into the design of future processes.

Dow-Europe's top managers sat through a pitch by some process reengineering advocates. Their response was, "Who are these people to tell us how messed up we are and that we ought to throw out everything we've built over the years? We know we have to make significant improvements in quality and cost. However, we're a successful company, and even though we have a long way to go, we think we're doing a lot right. Rather than tearing it down, we'd like to build on it."

Don't measure the success of Process Improvement efforts in terms of how many boxes were changed on the organization chart, how many heads were cut, how much was spent on automation, or how different things are. Measure success in terms of the degree to which you use Process Improvement as a tool to resolve issues and achieve strategy.

If you're not prepared for some in-the-trenches changes, as well as for the breakthroughs that hit the newspapers, don't be discouraged with the small number of "wins" and the time between them.

Sin 5: Process designers don't sufficiently consider how the changes will affect the people who have to work in the new process. Too often, process redesigners follow the "field of dreams" approach—"build an intelligent process . . . and they will come." Our experience indicates that that rarely happens. People don't automatically fall in line with even a brilliantly designed process.

A new process needs to be "sanity-checked" against the abilities of the people who will be affected. An industrial gasses company designed a new financial reporting process that was a work of truth and beauty. The non-value-added steps were eliminated. Work that had been done in series would be done in parallel. Automation would speed the flow. However, the designers uncovered one problem: there were no people in this company or elsewhere who could carry out the steps. The company had to adjust its process to accommodate the real world of human capabilities.

Once the process has been determined to be doable, people in the new process, and those who manage them, need to understand:

- How their jobs are going to change. Will they be expected to use a computer? To complete a different form? To be a member of a team? To make decisions?
- How their measures/goals are going to change. Will they now be measured on customer satisfaction? On how well they function on a team? On performance against budget?

The designers and implementers of the new process must identify how factors in the Human Performance System—resources, tools, training, feedback, and rewards—need to change to support the new process. If a new behavior is expected, it must be supported.

For example, to perform effectively in a redesigned distribution process, distribution managers need daily information on orders, inventories, and letters of credit status; training in new procedures; access to computer expertise; and rewards for how well they interacted with the sales, manufacturing, and finance departments, not just on how well they performed tasks in their "silos."

If you're not prepared to make changes in jobs and job environments, don't waste people's time improving work flows. We can avoid this sin by thoroughly addressing the components of the Human Performance System (see Chapter Five) during Phase 2 and especially during Phase 3.

Sin 6: The organization focuses more on redesign than on implementation. Process redesign is all academic until implementation. The investment in creating the changes pales in comparison with the calendar time, the management time, and the resources required for successful implementation of those changes.

Top management has been defined as a group of people who suffer from attention deficit disorder. When overseeing the implementation of Process Improvements, this disease needs to be in remission. You and the other members of your top management team must remain focused during the time it takes to install the redesign. For a complex process, implementation often lasts nine to eighteen months.

If you visit the executive suite of a telecommunications company we know, you will see a three-by-six-foot cardboard poster. It's a bank check in the amount of $1.3 billion made out to the company. In the memo section, it states, "Process reengineering restructuring charges." It's signed, "The Shareholders." That check helps to keep those executives focused and committed to the changes.

Implementation requires equipping the organization to absorb the change: appointing an implementation leader, establishing detailed action plans, defining roles and rewards for a group that often has six to ten times more people than were involved in the design process, and managing an effort that can be as large as launching a new product or entering a new market.

Implementation usually includes changes to policies, forms, computer systems, job descriptions, and rewards.

The bottom line is, if you're not prepared to scramble some eggs, don't ask people to design an omelet. The implementation (Phase 3) process is designed to ensure that this sin doesn't plague us.

Sin 7: Teams fail to leave behind a measurement system and other parts of the infrastructure necessary for continuous Process Improvement. If an organization doesn't move from Process Improvement (projects) to Process Management (continuous improvement), it has engaged in some needed problem solving but has not realized the potential return on its investment.

We cannot lay the blame for this sin at the feet of the worker-level Design Teams. If they have not created vehicles for the continuous improvement of the redesigned process, it's probably because the effort's sponsors didn't communicate that expectation.

Process Management must rest on a foundation of measures. These ensure that department goals serve the greater good of cross-functional process effectiveness; that they reflect both customer and financial needs, both at the end of the process and upstream; and that they represent the "critical few" meters of process health that should be on the management instrument panel. If your Design Teams create a new process but do not develop a set of measures to go with it, they haven't done the full job.

Once measures have been established, management must monitor performance against them and use this information as the basis for decision making, problem identification, feedback, and rewards. Installing a process-based measurement system isn't easy. However, there's no more potent tool for continuous improvement. And an effective set of process measures provides the link between your overall organization measures (such as return on earnings and market share) and the measures of individuals and teams.

In addition to measures, Process Management usually requires each key process to have a senior-level "owner." The Dow top team has identified the company's eight most critical companywide processes and designated a "global champion" for each. These executives are expected to monitor, report on, and troubleshoot process performance; to coordinate Process Improvement efforts; and to share "best practices" across product lines and geographic areas.

Process Management can also be buttressed by forming permanent Process Improvement Teams, conducting formal process reviews, planning/budgeting by process, and, in some cases, organizing by process.

The question is, How are we going to ensure that we don't lose our focus on this process that we've just (re)designed? A local telephone company answered this question in a powerful way. It was proud of the gains it had made in six or seven years of Process Improvement Projects, but was concerned that it wasn't yet "managing by process" on a daily basis. The top management team concluded that the strongest signal it sent was the way it measured and paid people. That company now pays bonuses to all employees—from top management to unionized frontline workers—based on the performance of the processes in which they work. They've installed a rock-solid basis for continuous Process Improvement.

If you're not prepared to continuously manage processes, don't be surprised if you're asked to continuously fund large-scale ad hoc Process Improvement Projects. (To avoid Sin 7, we recommend establishing the measurement system described in Chapter Twelve and the Process Management infrastructure presented in Chapter Thirteen.)

In most companies, the chief executive no longer asks, "What is Process Improvement?" or "Why should I improve my processes?" Today, he or she asks, "How can I increase the return on my Process Improvement investment?" We believe a large part of the answer is, "By avoiding these deadly sins."

MEASURING PERFORMANCE AND DESIGNING A PERFORMANCE MANAGEMENT SYSTEM

If performance isn't being measured, it isn't being managed.

—Unknown

A Process Improvement Project is not the end; it's the beginning. If an infrastructure for the ongoing management of a process is not established, the process will fall into disrepair as quickly as a rebuilt car engine that is not kept tuned. Process Management is a set of techniques for ensuring that key processes are continuously monitored and improved.

Measurement is the foundation for Process Management and for "managing organizations as systems," which make up the continuous improvement infrastructure described in Chapter Thirteen. The primary tool for communicating direction, for establishing accountability, for defining roles, for allocating resources, for monitoring or evaluating performance, for linking the Three Levels, and for taking improvement action is *measurement*.

The selection of measures and related goals is the greatest single determiner of an organization's effectiveness as a system. For example, one organization we encountered, which manufactured and distributed paint to independent dealers, was losing money and market share. Its basic work flow was quite straightforward: sales representatives took orders from paint dealers. These representatives placed the orders with their regional distribution centers, which then supplied the paint to the dealers. Distribution centers replenished their stock by ordering paint from manufacturing.

During a discussion with the new division president, we discovered that:

- Sales representatives were measured (and compensated) on the basis of their bookings (orders).

- Distribution centers were measured on the basis of "lines per load," which was the extent to which a truck or boxcar was full before it departed.
- Manufacturing was measured on the basis of "yield," which was the amount of paint produced per production line.

If each of these functions—sales, distribution, and manufacturing—is viewed in isolation (in its own "silo"), the measures make sense. However, let's look at the effect of these measures on the performance of the business. As a result of the distribution center measurement system, product ship dates were determined by when the truck or car was full rather than by when the customer needed the product. The result was delays in filling orders. As a result of the manufacturing measurement system, large amounts of a product were produced (so that yield could be optimized) before the lines were switched to another product. Frequently, a distribution center needed its stock replenished to meet current orders at a time when manufacturing was producing a different product. The result, again, was delays in filling orders. In this situation, internal efficiency measures overrode customer satisfaction measures. Who suffered from this measurement system? Initially, the customers; ultimately, the company.

All organizations start with an almost overwhelming network of financial measures in place. Add to that measures driven by past problems, shifting emphases of new managers, and new corporate programs of quality, cycle time, and customer service. The result is a collection of largely unrelated and unmanageable measures, leading in many cases to "measurement gridlock"—managers in a state of paralysis because they can't move performance affecting one measure in a positive direction without (seemingly) moving two other measures in a negative direction.

We discuss measurement in our treatment of goals and management at the Organization (Chapter Three), Process (Chapter Four), and Job/ Performer (Chapter Five) Levels of Performance. However, we believe that measurement is *the* pivotal performance management and improvement tool and, as such, deserves special treatment.

Without measures, we don't get the desired performance. With the wrong measures, we suboptimize organization performance. As you will see, the Three Levels framework enables us to move from gridlock to identification of the "critical few" measures, from a mere collection of measures to a measurement system. The result is the ability to manage all the variables that affect organization performance.

Why Measure?

We have established that an organization is a system and that there are Three Levels of Performance—Organization, Process, and Job/

Performer—that must be managed in order to get consistent, high-level organization output. *We measure so that we can monitor, control, and improve system performance at all three levels,* as shown in Figure 12.1. (In Figure 12.1 and throughout this chapter we show measurement points in the system as meters.)

Without measures, *managers* have no basis for:

- Specifically communicating performance expectations to subordinates
- Knowing what is going on in their organizations
- Identifying performance gaps that should be analyzed and eliminated
- Providing feedback that compares performance to a standard
- Identifying performance that should be rewarded
- Effectively making and supporting decisions regarding resources, plans, policies, schedules, and structure

Without measures, *employees* at all levels have no basis for:

- Knowing specifically what is expected of them
- Monitoring their own performance and generating their own feedback
- Generating their own rewards and understanding what performance is required to receive rewards from others
- Identifying performance improvement areas

FIGURE 12.1. MEASURING THE THREE LEVELS OF PERFORMANCE WITHIN THE ORGANIZATION SYSTEM

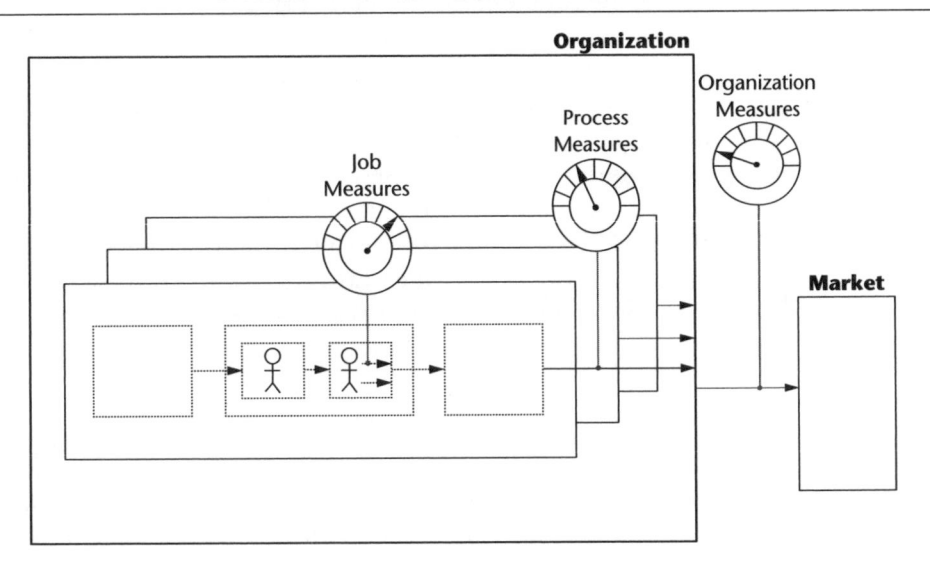

Requirements for Effective Management of the Organization System

Merely establishing measures is not enough; if we are going to manage the organization as a system, we must have:

1. Sound measures that ensure we are monitoring the right things
2. A total measurement system, not a collection of unrelated—and potentially counterproductive—measures
3. A performance management process that converts the data provided by the measurement system into intelligent action

We would like to suggest some guidelines based on our experience in each of these three areas.

Developing Sound Measures

What we want to measure is performance—that is, output—at all three levels. Regardless of the level (Organization, Process, Job/Performer), we recommend that measures be developed following this sequence:

1. Identify the most significant outputs of the organization, process, or job.
2. Identify the critical dimensions of performance for each of these outputs. Critical dimensions of *quality* include accuracy, ease of use, novelty, reliability, ease of repair, and appearance. Critical dimensions of *productivity* include quantity, rate, and timeliness. Critical dimensions of *cost* include labor, materials, and overhead. Critical dimensions should be derived from the needs of the internal and external customers who receive the outputs and from the financial needs of the business.
3. Develop the measures for each critical dimension. For example, if "ease of use" has been identified as a critical dimension of quality for a given output, one or more measures should answer this question: "What indicators will tell us if our customers find our product or service (output) easy to use?"
4. Develop goals, or standards, for each measure. A goal is a specific level of performance expectation. For example, if a measure for ease of use is "number of customer questions/complaints regarding product use," a goal may be "no more than two questions/complaints per month." As continuous improvement efforts bear fruit, goals should become more ambitious.

Table 12.1 shows several examples of measures developed in this way. Important characteristics of this approach to developing measures are:

1. They are output-driven. This is in contrast to the frequent practice of settling on goals and measures because they are topical or easy to measure rather than because they will help achieve a critical output.
2. They are customer-focused: the outputs, critical dimensions, and goals are all determined to a substantial degree by customer requirements.
3. They reflect the reality that most outputs have several critical dimensions and that measures must be multidimensional in many cases. We can no longer get away with thinking that "we can have quality or we can have quantity, but we can't have both." We *can* have both, as well as timeliness. That is the new customer requirement.

Ideally, every measure and goal or standard is developed following this sequence.

Building a Measurement System

Organization effectiveness comes about only when the Organization, Process, and Job/Performer Levels are all headed in the same direction. The key to this is a measurement network that ties the Three Levels together into a system. Such a measurement system makes it possible:

1. To monitor performance at all levels and "troubleshoot" failure. For example, a deficient Organization Level output can be tracked back to a faulty process and process step and a missing or faulty job output, where corrective action can be taken.

TABLE 12.1. EXAMPLES OF "SOUND MEASURES"

Outputs	Critical Dimensions	Measures	Standards
Insurance claims qualified	Accuracy	Percentage of cases of recovery potential identified	75% of cases of recovery potential identified
		Percentage of coverage issues identified later	Additional or corrected coverage issues identified in less than 5% of cases
		Percentage of loss notices entered in correct claim category	All loss notices entered; loss notice entries reported by claim category
	Timeliness	Average loss notice processing/ confirmation time	15 minutes per loss notice
Orders taken	Accuracy	Number accurate orders/total	100%
	Timeliness	Number of minutes	Within 2 minutes

2. For all performers along the chain to see and measure their impact on the critical organization outputs.

The process of building the measurement system requires two stages:

1. Establishing the output linkage from Organization output to Process output to Job/Performer output. (Our mapping technique is particularly helpful in this stage.)
2. Overlaying relevant measures on these outputs following the "sound measures" sequence described above.

To illustrate how a measurement system can be built, let us reexamine Computec, the software and systems integration company we used as our example in Chapters Three, Four, and Five.

Organization Level. The development of the measurement system starts at the Organization Level, determining the critical outputs and goals. One of Computec's strategic goals was to "capture 60 percent of the aerospace project management market within three years."

Because goals at the Organization Level drive all other measurement, it is particularly critical that they:

- Are based on the documented requirements of the external customer and the strategic business requirements of the organization
- Are universally understood within the organization
- Reflect the organizationwide performance to which all subsystems (processes, departments, and jobs) should contribute

Process Level. The first step in linking Process measures to Organization measures is to link the Organization output to the Process Level outputs. In the case of Computec, the Organization output is "project management software." However, management realizes that the key to penetrating this particular market and achieving the market share goal is the introduction of a series of new project management software products. Therefore, a process critical to achieving this Organization Level goal is the new product development process. Computec's first step in determining process measures is to put into place a "SHOULD" new product development process, shown in Figure 12.2. This process map is really an output chain showing the output links from process step to subprocess to final process output.

Once we have established the Organization Level links, we can overlay the appropriate measures, as shown in Figure 12.3. M1 (measure 1) describes end-of-process performance. There can be both M1–External measures relating directly to customer requirements (such as "number of customer complaints") and M1–Internal measures reflecting customer requirements as well as organization business requirements (for instance, "profitable within one year of introduction"). M2 measures are related to

FIGURE 12.2. COMPUTEC PRODUCT DEVELOPMENT AND INTRODUCTION: "SHOULD" PROCESS MAP AND SAMPLE GOALS

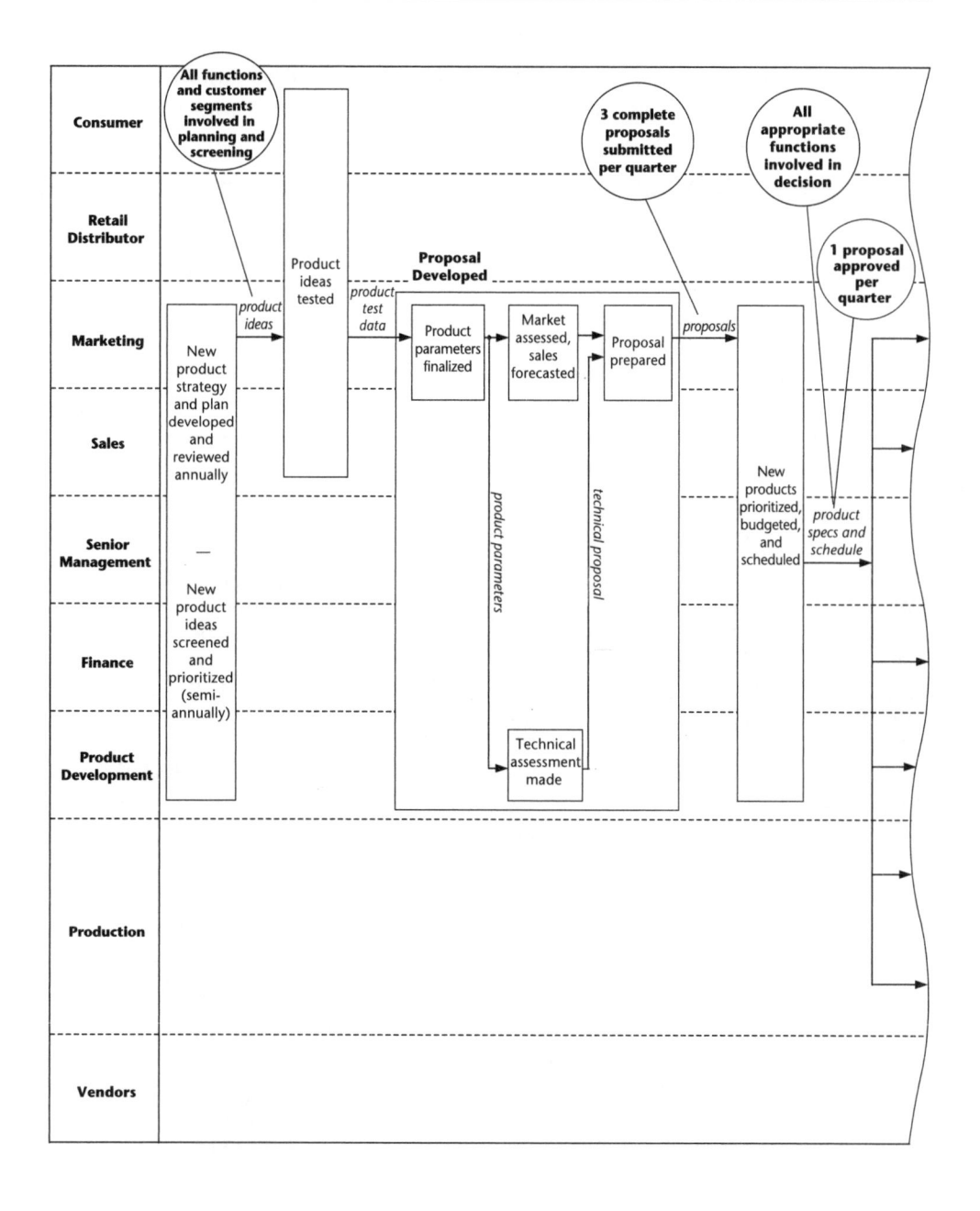

FIGURE 12.2.
(Continued)

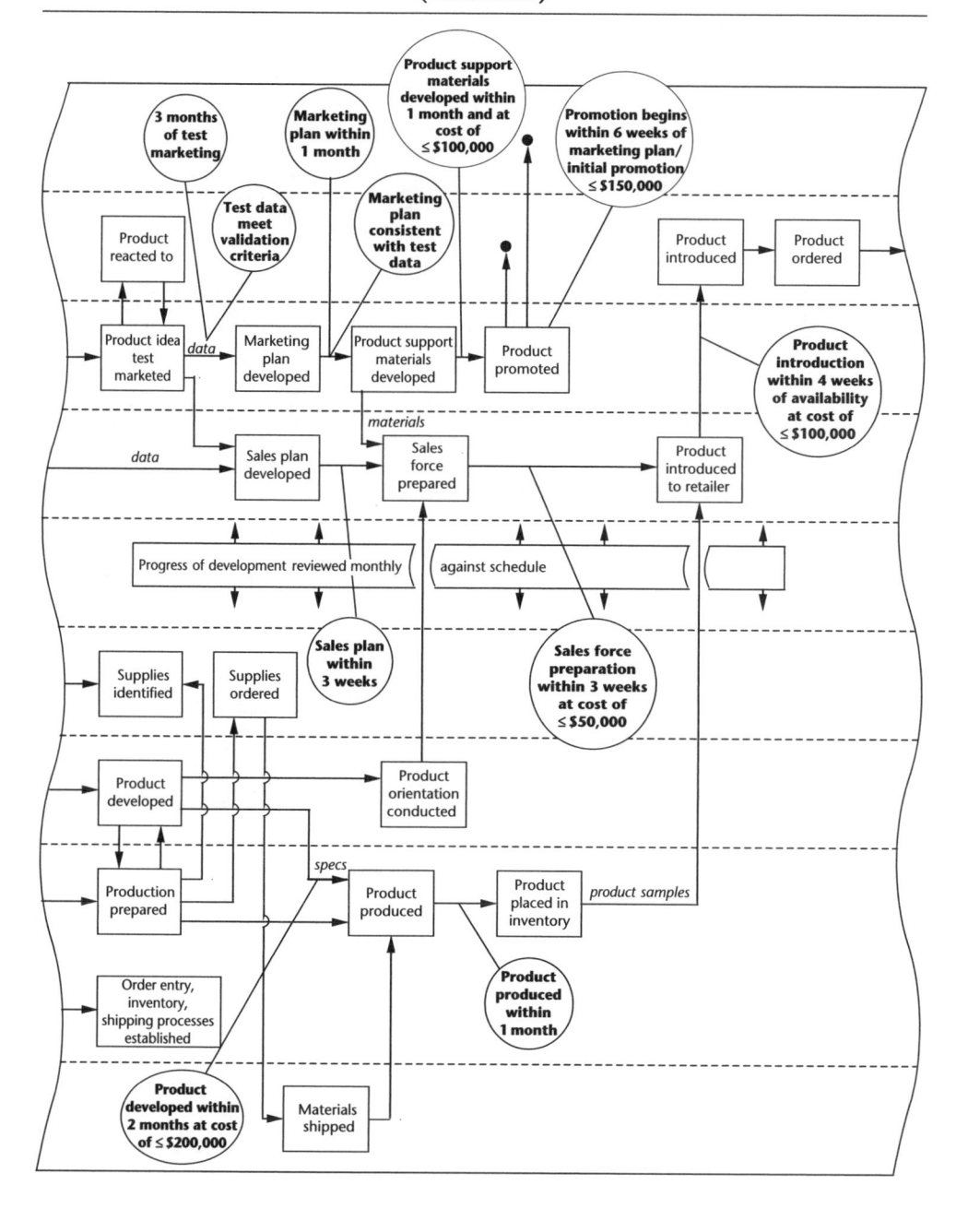

FIGURE 12.2.
(*Continued*)

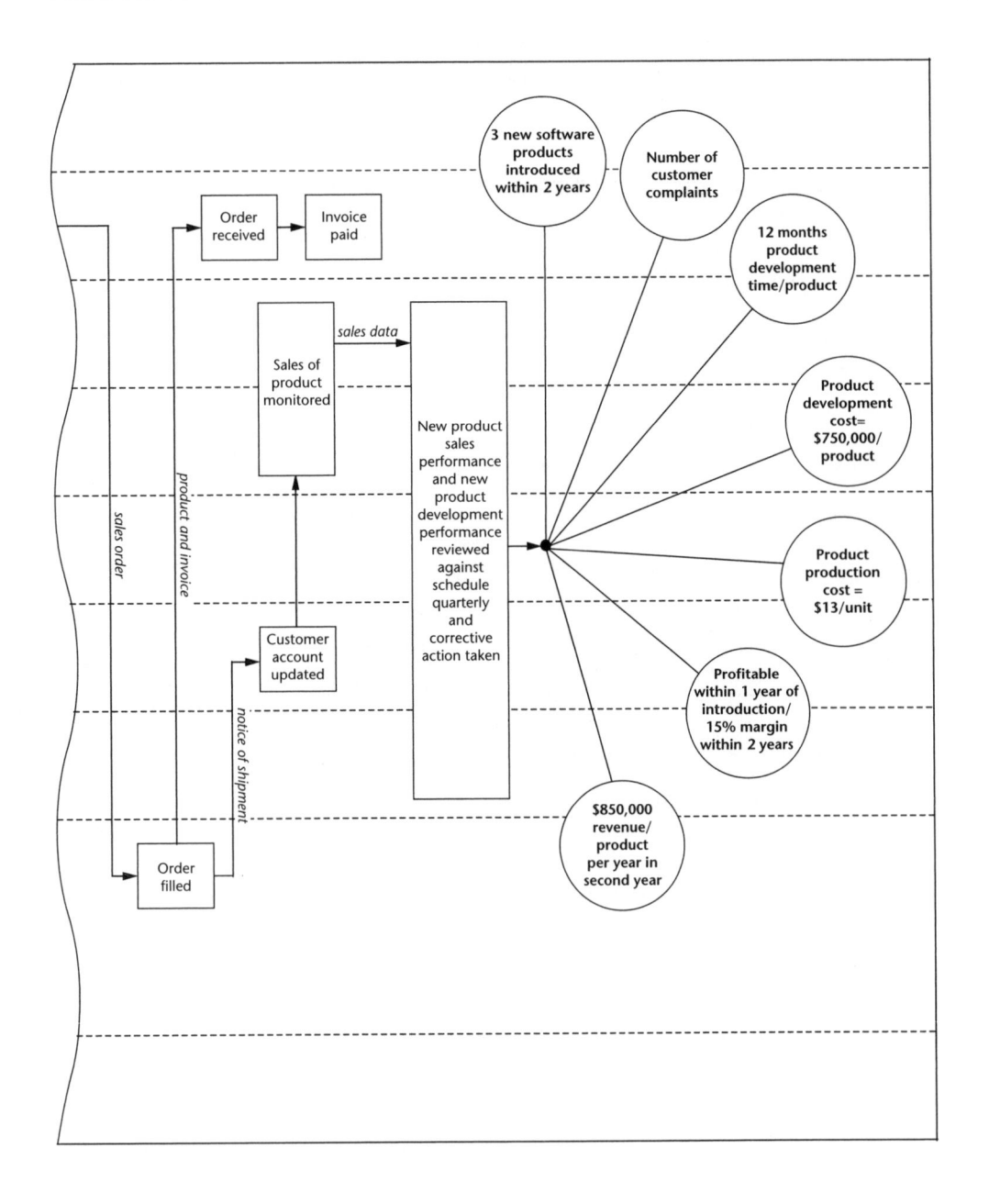

the M1 measures, either internal or external or both. They assess subprocess performance. For example, "three complete proposals submitted per quarter" is an M2 for the "proposal developed" subprocess.

M3s measure the outputs of critical process steps. For example, "test data meet validation criteria" is a measure of the "Product idea test marketed" step. To avoid drowning in measures, we install M3s only for those steps that are so critical to process success that they should be monitored by the Process Management Team (see Chapter Thirteen).

This network of measures is customer- and business strategy-driven; it allows for monitoring and troubleshooting process performance as it affects the desired organization output; and it focuses on the "critical few" indicators of process health.

Once the Process Goals are established, senior management—especially the Process Owner—needs a vehicle for tracking the performance of the process. (Process Owners are covered in Chapter Thirteen. The Computec vice president of marketing most likely would be the Process Owner for product development and introduction.) A simple tracking format appears in Table 12.2.

We have found a need for three types of measures:

- *Regular formal measures,* against which actual performance information is periodically gathered and computerized. For example, we may distribute a monthly printout that shows "revenue per sales representative" and "number of bid wins and losses."
- *Regular informal measures,* against which "back-of-the-envelope" information is periodically gathered. For example, customer service representatives keep a daily stroke tally of the "number of inquiries."

FIGURE 12.3. OUTPUT MEASURES

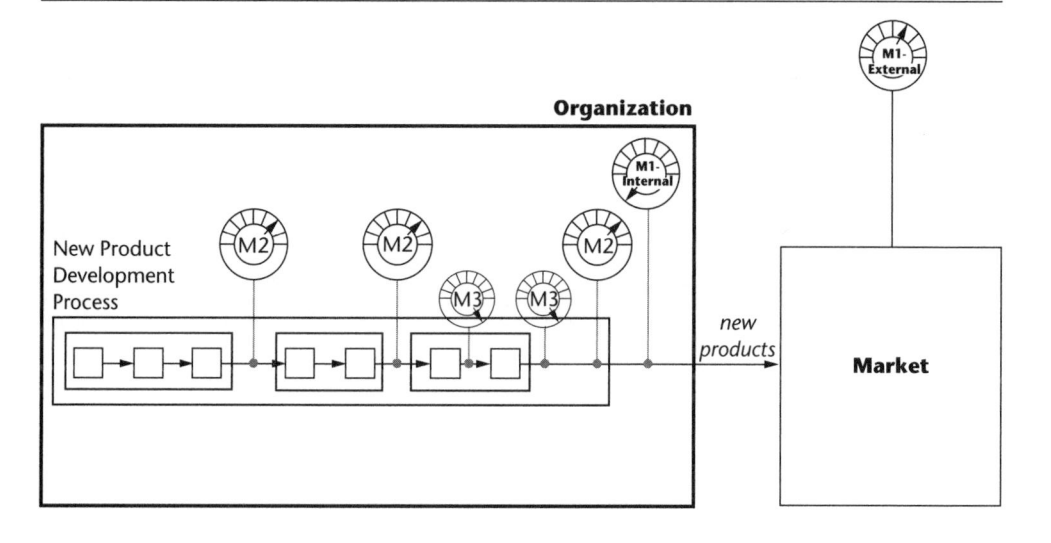

TABLE 12.2. COMPUTEC PRODUCT DEVELOPMENT AND INTRODUCTION: PERFORMANCE TRACKER

Product Idea		PRODUCT DEVELOPMENT AND			
		Test Data Complete	Proposal Developed/ Approved	Product Test Marketed	Product Developed
"Eagle"	Time	(Plan) (Actual)			
	Budget				
	Quality				
"Cardinal"	Time				
	Budget				
	Quality				
"Hawk"	Time				
	Budget				
	Quality				

TABLE 12.2.
(*Continued*)

INTRODUCTION SUBPROCESSES					
Product Produced/ Inventoried	Product Promoted	Sales Force Prepared	Product Introduced	Product Shipped (First 1,000 Units)	Initial Revenue Target Met

- *Irregular measures,* which we employ when there's a special situation. For example, when sales are off, we track "number of sales calls per week," "number of proposals per month," and "average dollar amount per proposal" to help us understand the cause of the downturn. When performance returns, we stop measuring in these areas.

A measurement system needs to accommodate all three types of measures.

Linking Process and Function/Department Measures and Goals. If the Process Goals displayed in Figure 12.2 are to be the primary drivers of function (department) performance, Computec has to be sure that each function's measures reflect:

- Its contribution to overall process (and, in turn, organization) goals
- The contribution it needs to make to other functions so that they can make *their* contributions to process and organization performance

The Process Map format makes it easy to see the contribution each function is expected to make to the process. The meters that fall within each band become the measures or goals for that function. Figure 12.4 shows how the Process Map can be extended to reflect the goals for each function that contributes to the product development process. These goals can serve as the basis for allocating human and financial resources.

If we managed the marketing department, for example, and if the marketing row in Figure 12.4 were complete, we would clearly understand the contribution we were expected to make to the product development process, how that contribution would be measured, our specific goals for a current product development effort, and the resources we could use to meet those goals.

A tool we have used frequently in complex processes (such as product development) is the Role/Responsibility Matrix. This matrix translates the Process Map into a set of responsibilities for each contributing department. By displaying the responsibilities in this format, we can increase the likelihood that no process steps fall between the cracks, that there is no overlap, and that everyone understands who does what. Table 12.3 displays a portion of a Role/Responsibility Matrix for Computec's product development and introduction process. (A Process Role/Responsibility Matrix such as the one shown in Table 12.3 is a different format for displaying the data contained in a cross-functional map. Such a matrix has added value only if a process is very complex or the cross-functional map was not developed in sufficient detail.) While Table 12.3 does not include goals, you may find it useful to include them in the matrix.

Marketing undoubtedly supports a number of processes besides product development and introduction. It also carries out responsibilities that are not in direct support of a major cross-functional process. Table 12.4 shows a portion of a marketing Function Model that would enable its management to track the department's overall contribution to the organization.

FIGURE 12.4. COMPUTEC PRODUCT DEVELOPMENT AND INTRODUCTION: "SHOULD" PROCESS MAP AND SAMPLE FUNCTIONAL GOALS

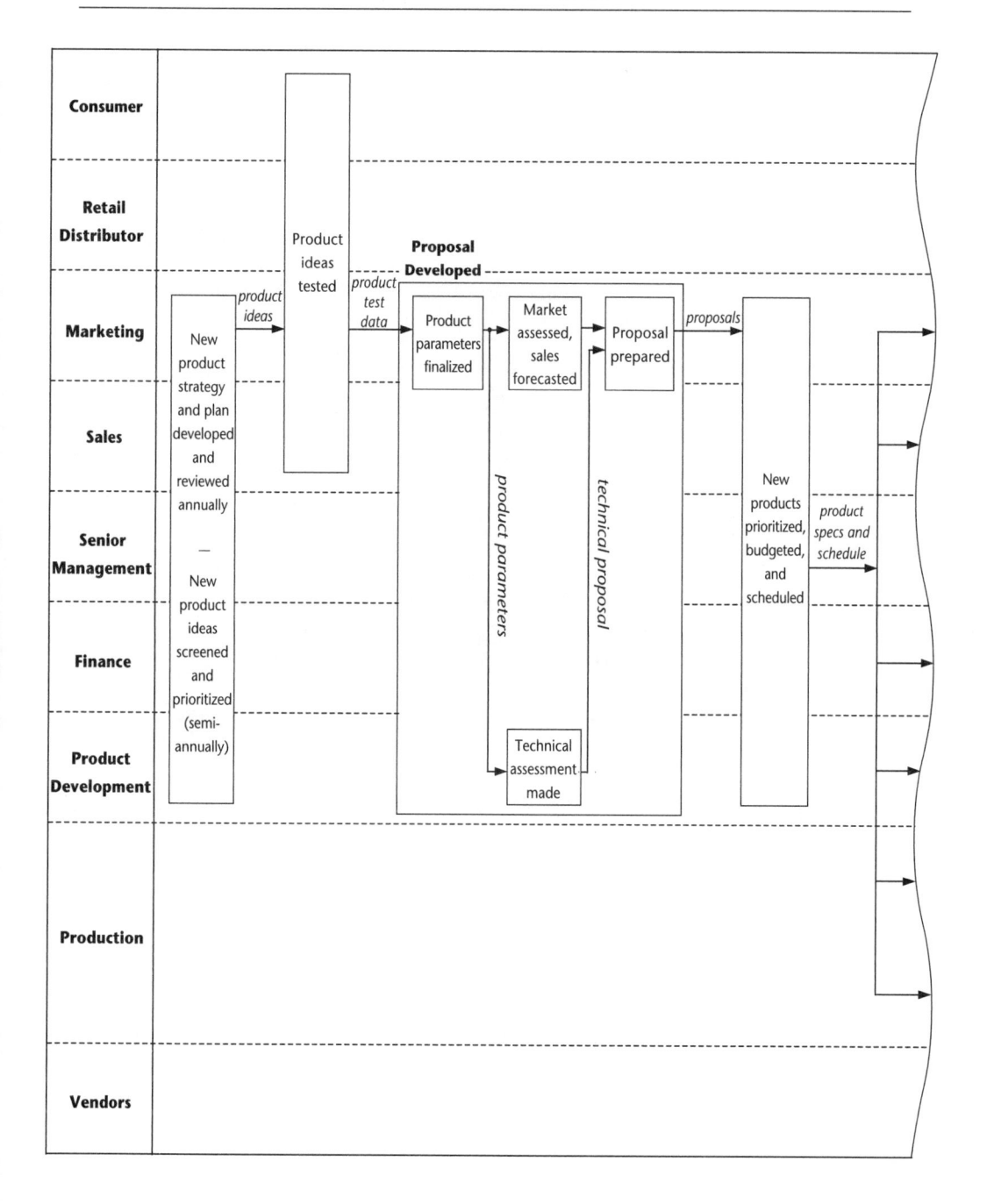

FIGURE 12.4.
(*Continued*)

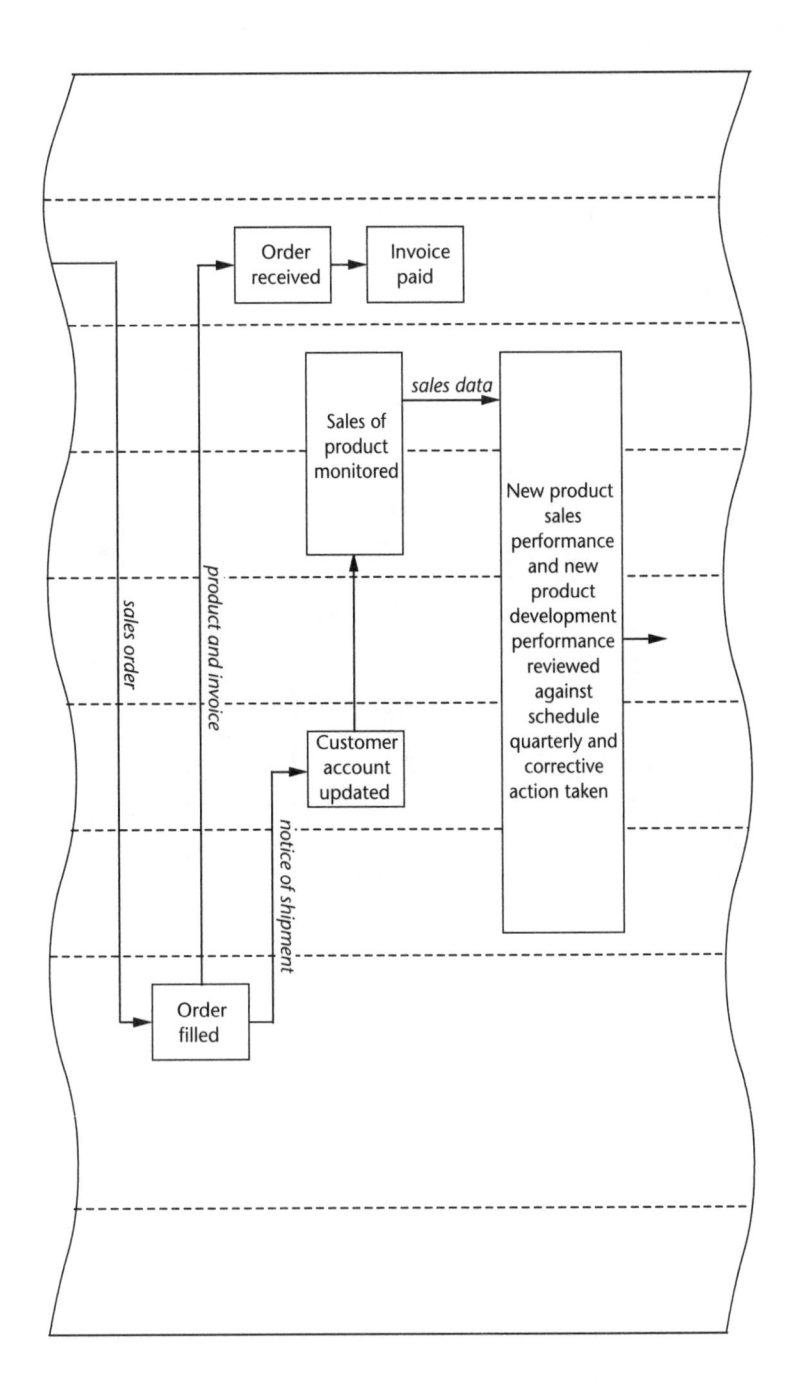

FIGURE 12.4.

(*Continued*)

Function	Measures and Goals					
	Timeliness		Budget		Quality/Other	
	Measures	Goals	Measures	Goals	Measures	Goals
Total Process	Development time	12 months/ product	Development cost	$750k/product	Revenues	$850k/product
					Profits	15% within 2 years
			Unit cost	$13/unit	Number of new products introduced	3 products in 2 years
Marketing	Proposal	4 weeks after idea	Product support	$100k/product	Participation in screening	100% of customers/ departments
	Test marketing	3 months of data gathering			Participation in decision	
	Marketing plan	Within 1 month of test	Promotion	$150k/product		100% of departments
	Product support	Mat'ls within 1 month of plan			Marketing plan	Validated by test data
Sales						
Senior Management						
Finance						
Product Development						
Production						
Vendors						

(table heading: Functional Goals Summary)

TABLE 12.3. ROLE/RESPONSIBILITY MATRIX FOR THE COMPUTEC PRODUCT DEVELOPMENT AND INTRODUCTION PROCESS

Major Process Steps	Functions and Responsibilities				
	Marketing	Sales	Senior Management	Finance	Product Development
1. New product ideas screened and prioritized (semiannually)	• New product ideas solicited and formatted for formal review • Discussion, evaluation, and prioritization of ideas facilitated	• Product ideas submitted • Ideas evaluated, prioritized	• Product ideas submitted • Ideas evaluated, prioritized	• Ideas evaluated, prioritized	• Product ideas submitted • Ideas evaluated, prioritized
2. Product ideas tested	a. Product evaluation questionnaire prepared	b. Evaluation questionnaire reviewed			
	c. Consumer and distributor participants jointly selected for product evaluation				
	d. Evaluation conducted				
	e. Test data summarized				
	f. Test data revised and product ideas selected for a development proposal				
3. Product proposal developed	a. Product parameters described for technical review				b. Product technical feasibility assessed and cost and time estimates developed
	c. Market size evaluated and marketing and sales strategy articulated for each product; marketing and sales cost and time evaluated			d. Product development cost estimates developed	
	e. Sales estimates and break-even point established for each product				
	f. Proposals finalized				

TABLE 12.4.   PORTION OF THE COMPUTEC MARKETING FUNCTION MODEL

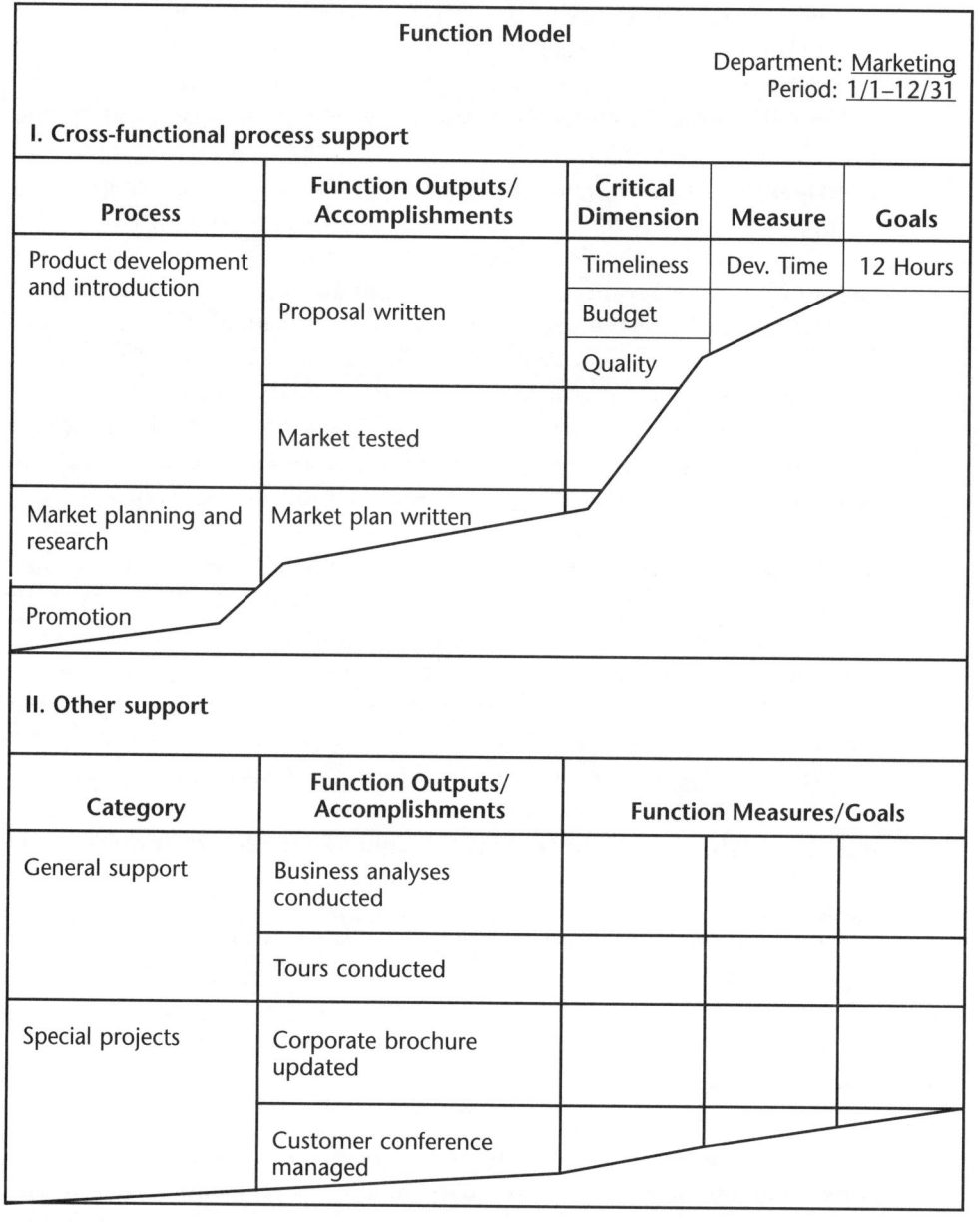

Function Model
Department: <u>Marketing</u> Period: <u>1/1–12/31</u>

I. Cross-functional process support

Process	Function Outputs/ Accomplishments	Critical Dimension	Measure	Goals
Product development and introduction	Proposal written	Timeliness	Dev. Time	12 Hours
		Budget		
		Quality		
	Market tested			
Market planning and research	Market plan written			
Promotion				

II. Other support

Category	Function Outputs/ Accomplishments	Function Measures/Goals		
General support	Business analyses conducted			
	Tours conducted			
Special projects	Corporate brochure updated			
	Customer conference managed			

The Job/Performer Level. Computec's top managers can ensure that the Organization and Process Levels drive day-to-day performance by cascading the goals down to the Job/Performer Level. The first step in that process is to allocate each department's outputs (which were derived from process requirements) among the various jobs in that department. A Function Role/Responsibility Matrix, which is an extension of the Process Role/Responsibility Matrix (Table 12.3), helps organize and display these outputs. Table 12.5 shows how the marketing department's outputs could be distributed among jobs in that department.

Each column in the department's Role/Responsibility Matrix becomes the set of outputs required of the people in a job. At the Job/Performer Level, "outputs" are the accomplishments of individuals who contribute to a function or process output. From the perspective of the function or the process, they are suboutputs. If (as is typically the case) a job supports more than one process, the incumbents' total job responsibility would include the outputs listed under their job title in all Role/Responsibility Matrices.

For the final job description, we use a format called a Job Model. A Job Model is an extension of the Role/Responsibility Matrix. It contains not only the job's outputs but also the measures and goals for each output based on the function measures and goals. (Note that a Job Model directly incorporates the format for developing "sound measures.") Table 12.6 is a portion of a Job Model for the research analyst in Computec's marketing department.

The Job Model represents the final link in a measurement system that ties the Organization Level output to the individual output. Such a measurement system provides a "line of sight" from the individual to the organization output and makes it possible for management to effectively monitor and troubleshoot system performance.

We realize that we have presented quite a few worksheets. Figure 12.5 shows their relationship.

Performance Logic

Another way to make sure that there is a clear link from organization measures to end-of-process measures to upstream process measures to function measures to individual or work team measures is to develop a *performance logic*. A performance logic begins at the very highest level, with the one to three most important indicators of organizationwide health. Many organizations are now using return on net assets (RONA) or economic value added (EVA) as indicators of company or division performance.

Let's say we're using EVA, which is after-tax operating profit minus the total annual cost of capital. We ask what measures influence EVA and we conclude that it is cost of capital, tax, and profit after tax. We then ask

TABLE 12.5. ROLE/RESPONSIBILITY MATRIX FOR THE COMPUTEC MARKETING FUNCTION: NEW PRODUCT DEVELOPMENT AND INTRODUCTION

Major Process Steps	Marketing Function		Marketing Jobs and Responsibilities		
	Outputs	Goals	Research Analyst Outputs	Product Manager Outputs	Vice President, Marketing Outputs
1. New product ideas screened and prioritized	New product ideas solicited and formatted for formal review	• Ideas solicited from all departments and customer segments • Review format follows guidelines • Review each March 1 and September 1	• New product ideas solicited from sales, software design, and product managers • New product ideas formatted for review by process team		
	New product idea screening, evaluation, prioritization facilitated	• All "go" and "no go" evaluations supported by rationale • Priorities consistent with strategic needs • Final screening within four weeks of review			• New product process team convened • New product ideas presented • New product ideas reviewed and prioritized with team
2. Product ideas tested	Product evaluation questionnaire prepared	• Questionnaire meets validity guidelines	• Questionnaire designed	• Criteria for questionnaire developed/reviewed	
	Study participants selected (jointly with retail sales)	• Participants represent all constituencies		• Questionnaire reviewed	
	Evaluation conducted	• All participants agree with decisions • Evaluation within budget	• Participants invited to participate	• Candidates generated and reviewed with retail sales • Final participant list negotiated	

TABLE 12.6. PORTION OF A JOB MODEL FOR THE COMPUTEC MARKET RESEARCH ANALYST

Marketing Department		Market Research Analyst			
Outputs	**Goals**	**Outputs**	**Critical Dimensions**	**Measures**	**Goals**
New product ideas solicited and formatted for formal review	All departments formally polled semiannually for product ideas	Product idea questionnaires developed and administered	Quality—completeness	Percent of customers and departments included in distribution	10% of customers in each market segment 100% of departments
			Quality—ease of use	Percent of complaints or queries regarding questionnaire items	$\emptyset$
			Productivity—timeliness	Frequency of questionnaire distribution	Each March 1 and September 1
			Cost	Dollars per survey	$15,000
		Questionnaire responses consolidated into potential product report	Quality—completeness	Percent of ideas included in report	100%
			Quality—understandability	Number of complaints or queries regarding understanding of report	2/report
			Productivity—timeliness	Time between survey and report	4 weeks

FIGURE 12.5. A THREE LEVELS PERFORMANCE MEASUREMENT/ MANAGEMENT SYSTEM

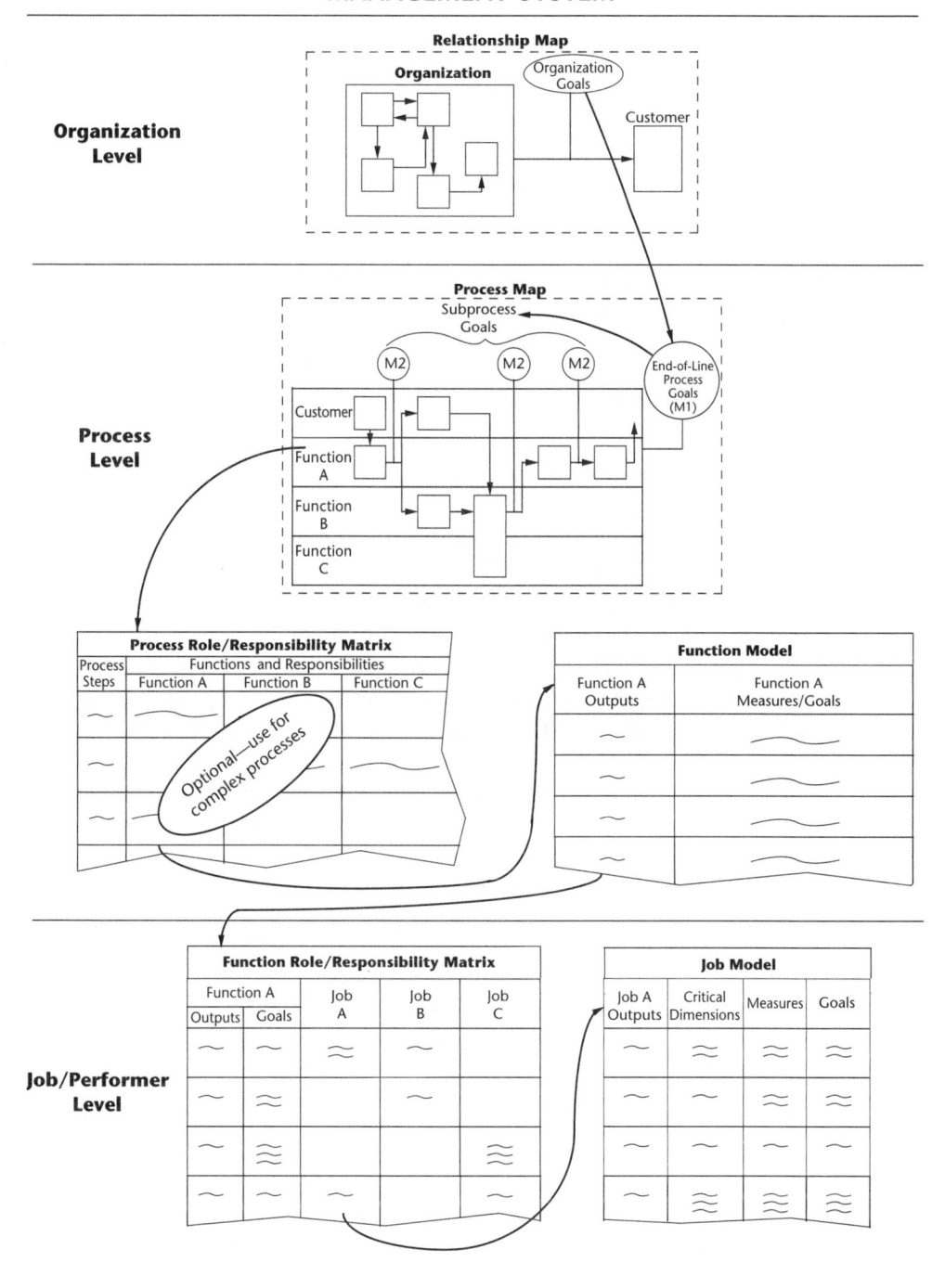

what measures influence each of these. We determine that gross margin and revenue influence profit after tax. Then it gets interesting, as we identify and quantify the variables (expressed as measures) that influence revenue and gross margin. Next, we look at the factors that influence each of these variables. And on it goes.

When this exercise is complete, we have built a hierarchy of measures that extends from the most macro to as micro as needs dictate. This picture, unencumbered by maps or matrices, ensures that we understand dependencies, that we've founded our measurement system on the right indicators, and that we can trace the contribution of every process, every department, and every individual and team to the performance of the organization as a whole.

Using Measures as the Foundation of a Performance Management System

Most managers do not have a valid, integrated, manageable set of measures. Those who do have appropriate and comprehensive measures usually fail to take the next step, which is to use them as the basis for a measurement system, which includes mechanisms for gathering actual performance information, comparing it to the goals, and communicating that information to those who can use it. Those who do have such a measurement system often don't use it appropriately.

To illustrate the last shortcoming, we developed a measurement system for a manufacturing plant that had been performing poorly for some time. The plant manager held daily production meetings that, due to the inadequate quality and quantity of information available to all levels of management, had historically been frustrating finger-pointing sessions. When presented with the first information generated by the new measurement system, the plant manager said, "This is great! Now I know exactly who the SOB is that has been screwing up. I'll have his butt in the next production meeting." This misuse of a measurement system clearly lessened its utility.

Another example is the hotel chain for which we were building a management information and performance appraisal system. A district manager checked into one of the hotels in his district late one evening and was extremely irritated when he observed that the ashtrays in the lobby were not clean per company regulations. The next morning at breakfast, the district manager lectured the hotel manager about the quality of housekeeping in general and particularly about the ashtrays in the lobby. The hotel manager interrupted the breakfast of the housekeeping supervisor and passed on the message from the district manager, with an appropriate level of amplification. The housekeeping supervisor raced to the lobby and cleaned up the ashtrays.

In both of these cases, it is safe to say that the manager's reactions to the performance data (formal reports in the case of the plant manager and informal observation on the part of the district manager) will enhance neither the performance of their subordinates nor, in the long run, that of their organizations.

The plant manager intends to use the information to affix blame and punish offenders. As a result, managers at all levels will be quick to blame others. Avoiding blame will become more important than delivering products. When we pointed this out to the plant manager, he said, "What do I do? This is the only way I know how to manage." We worked with the manager to design an agenda for the production meetings and coached him in asking questions. The focus of the daily production meetings changed from "butt kicking" to problem solving. Over the next three months, the more effective use of performance information enabled the plant manager to reduce the length of production meetings from two hours to thirty minutes. More significantly, the plant accomplished a miraculous turnaround in quality and productivity. Thus, the way information from a measurement system is used is as critical as the nature and extent of the information. Rather than being used to punish, it should be used to answer the question, "Why?"

The second case illustrates two additional side effects of misusing performance information—the tendency of managers to manage behavior rather than results, and to drop down a level and do the job of their subordinates. Rather than triggering the chain of events described earlier, the hotel district manager should have:

1. Interpreted the dirty ashtrays as an indication that the housekeeping process might have broken down. The major concern of the district manager should be the state of the housekeeping process, not a particular ashtray.
2. Shared the "dirty ashtray" observation with the hotel manager and asked him some questions about the housekeeping process:
   - Do you think the housekeeping process is performing up to standards?
   - How do you know if the process is performing up to standards?
   - Do the two of us agree on housekeeping standards or goals?
3. Reviewed, if necessary, the status of the housekeeping process with the hotel manager by asking these questions:
   - Is the procedure manual up to date and being used?
   - Is process performance being tracked, and is that information being used for problem solving and decision making?
   - Are the necessary tools in place and being used?

After collecting these data, the district manager might need to take appropriate corrective action with the hotel manager.

4. Suggested that the hotel manager meet with the housekeeping supervisor to determine where the housekeeping process had broken down,

leading to the dirty ashtrays. They should have jointly answered these questions:

- Are there deficiencies in the process or the process measures?
- Are we inadequately executing the process? If so, are housekeepers properly trained? Do they have sufficient resources?
- Is the housekeeping supervisor properly managing the process?

Based on the answers, the hotel manager should take appropriate action to prevent the problem from happening again.

In both of these cases, the issue is the intelligent use of measurement data to enhance performance.

A Performance Management System. If we want to effectively manage performance at all three levels (and at every tier of the "performance logic" described above), we need:

- To establish appropriate measures and goals (which, at the Process and Job/Performer Levels, includes linking them to those at the higher level)
- To track actual performance, identify gaps between actual performance and the goals, identify the causes of the gaps, and take action to overcome the gaps
- To use measurement information as the basis for management decision making and performance improvement

Figure 12.6 shows these three components of a Performance Management System. To illustrate with a Job/Performer Level example:

Step 1: Define the outputs and performance expectations for each job (goal setting).

FIGURE 12.6. PERFORMANCE MANAGEMENT SYSTEM

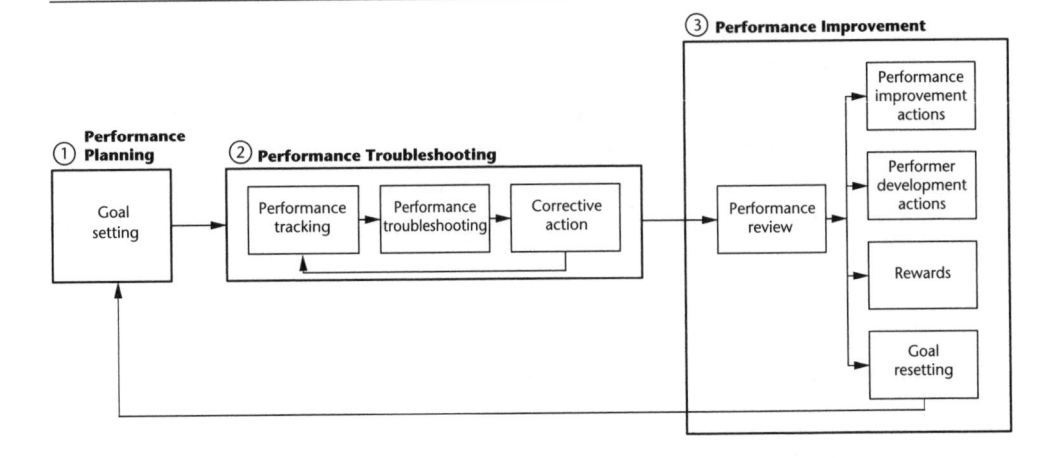

Step 2: Ensure that the job holders are able to monitor their own performance on an ongoing basis and, if off target, to diagnose the situation and take corrective action. In addition, the supervisors and managers of that job holder should be able to track critical components of the job and/or process and troubleshoot off-target performance. However, we want to stress that the job holders should not have to rely on their supervisors or managers for their performance data. It should come directly to them, allowing them to make the necessary adjustments.

Step 3: See to it that the job holders and supervisors or managers periodically (quarterly or semiannually) review performance. This review should be a recap of the frequent discussions between the job holders and managers (described in Step 2), with a focus on performance trends. There should be no surprises for the job holders during this formal review, which should result in a summary performance evaluation and in decisions regarding:

- Action required on the part of the job holders *and* managers to improve performance of the job
- Promotability of the job holders
- Change in compensation for the job holders
- Training and development the job holders need in order to improve their performance on the current job and/or to prepare them for promotion to a new job
- Changes in the goals for the next performance period

In this system, the goals are set periodically and jointly by job holders and their managers. Performance is monitored, "troubleshot," and corrected continuously by job holders and periodically by their managers. For example, sales representatives should constantly be monitoring, diagnosing, and improving their performance as they call on prospects. Their sales managers should monitor the sales and sales activity information continuously. When the managers travel with the reps every other week, they should observe performance, discuss their observations, and make recommendations for improvement.

The performance improvement component (Step 3) should be performed periodically, resulting in longer-term improvement actions, rewards for the job holders, and goals for the next period.

To effectively manage performance, an organization will have a performance management system for all levels of performers, as shown in Figure 12.7. Relating back to our hotel management example, the division manager sets regional goals with the region manager, who sets district goals with hotel managers, and so on. The objective will be to interlock the Job/Performer Levels, assuring that all Job/Performer Levels in the

FIGURE 12.7. COMPONENTS OF AN ORGANIZATION PERFORMANCE MANAGEMENT SYSTEM

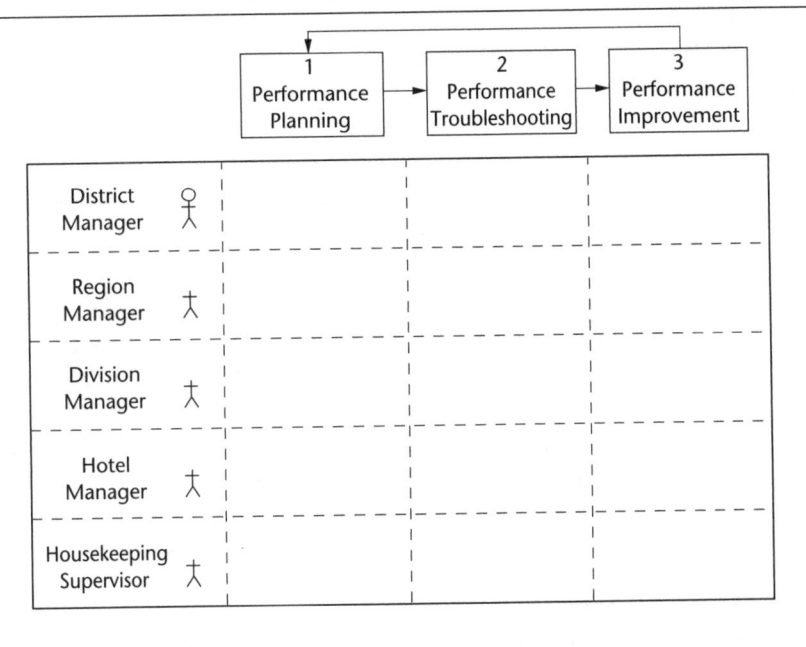

organization are working toward the same Organization and Process Goals. The measurement information monitored at each level is determined to a large degree by the outputs required at each level. Each level of management is monitoring key indicators of the subordinate operation, troubleshooting, and suggesting corrective action. Each level of management periodically reviews performance of the subordinate operation against the goals set in Step 1 and determines jointly with the subordinate manager what action is required to continuously improve performance. Such a system will guard against the misuse of measures and enhance the power of measures in these ways:

1. The performance-planning/goal-setting component clarifies the outputs expected from each level. As a result, managers are less likely to do their subordinates' jobs. To ensure support of cross-functional process performance, top management should review this hierarchy of outputs to ensure that responsibilities are linked at appropriate levels throughout the organization. A process for establishing this output hierarchy at all Job/Performer Levels was a major part of the performance management system we developed for the hotel chain described earlier. The system of Role/Responsibility Matrices, Function Models, and Job Models discussed earlier in this chapter (see Figure 12.5) is an effective way to determine and display desired job outputs.

2. The measurement system discussed earlier in this chapter provides the information that is tracked in the performance troubleshooting component of the system. The job outputs and goals identified in Step 1 determine to a large degree what measurement information (Step 2) should be available to each job holder. The thrust of this component of the Performance Management System is constructive problem solving. This is the proper objective of the production meetings of the plant manager and the field visits of the hotel district manager.
3. Step 2 uses measurement information for short-term troubleshooting. Step 3 uses that information for the long-term development of individuals or teams and for the continuous improvement of the operation.

A measurement system ensures that measures are interlocked at all three levels among all departments and at all levels of performers within each department. A Performance Management System provides a structure for using measures to effectively manage performance.

Summary

Measurement is the key ingredient in Performance Management. Although the topic is large enough to merit its own book, we have limited our discussion to some areas particularly germane to managing organizations as systems.

We believe that the following "truths" about measurement underlie effective management of organizations and human performance:

- Without measurement, performance isn't being managed.
- Without measurement, one cannot specifically identify, describe, and set priorities on problems.
- Without measurement, people cannot fully understand what is expected of them.
- Without measurement, people cannot be sure whether their performance is on or off track.
- Without measurement, there cannot be an objective, equitable basis for rewards (such as raises, bonuses, promotions) or punishments (such as disciplinary action, downgrading, dismissal).
- Without measurement, there are no triggers for performance improvement actions.
- Without measurement, management is a set of uneducated guesses.
- Without measurement, there is no foundation for managing by process.

The bad news is that establishing good measures is not easy. The good news is that straightforward techniques and criteria (some of which are provided in this chapter) can help ensure that the quality and quantity of measures meet the needs of both managers and individual contributors.

Measures alone are not enough. Even the right measures are not enough. To serve as guides and tools, measures have to serve as the foundation of a Performance Management *System*. The components of such a system are described above.

The only barrier to Performance Management is lack of willingness to invest the necessary time in building a Performance Management System. While this investment is not insignificant, our experience has shown that it is more than justified by the short- and long-term payback. In Chapter Thirteen, we present a "managing organizations as systems" scenario that shows the benefits of measures-based Performance Management.

MANAGING PROCESSES AND ORGANIZATIONS AS SYSTEMS

Labor can do nothing without capital, capital nothing without labor, and neither labor nor capital can do anything without the guiding genius of management.

—W. L. MACKENZIE KING

You shouldn't expect most of your managers to exhibit "guiding genius." However, you should expect guiding competence. A competent manager understands the way his or her organization functions and is able to manage the variables that can make it better. Chapter One is devoted to our worldview, which includes the belief that organizations (at all levels) function as adaptive systems. Because your organization operates as a system, you will be most effective if you manage it as a system.

Now that we have presented a methodology for and the pitfalls in Process *Improvement* (Chapters Nine, Ten, and Eleven) and have covered the measurement system (Chapter Twelve) that needs to underlie continuous Process *Management,* we can address Phase 4 of the framework, shown in Figure 13.1.

Process Management

The first part of Phase 4 is ensuring that an individual core process, in most cases one that has been through Phases 1 to 3, is continuously improved.

While most of Phase 2—Process Analysis and Design—is carried out by nonexecutive personnel, Phase 4 is the responsibility of the people who run the business. To effectively carry out this role, executives need:

- To understand the what, why, and how of both Process Improvement and Process Management

FIGURE 13.1. THE RUMMLER-BRACHE PROCESS IMPROVEMENT AND MANAGEMENT METHODOLOGY

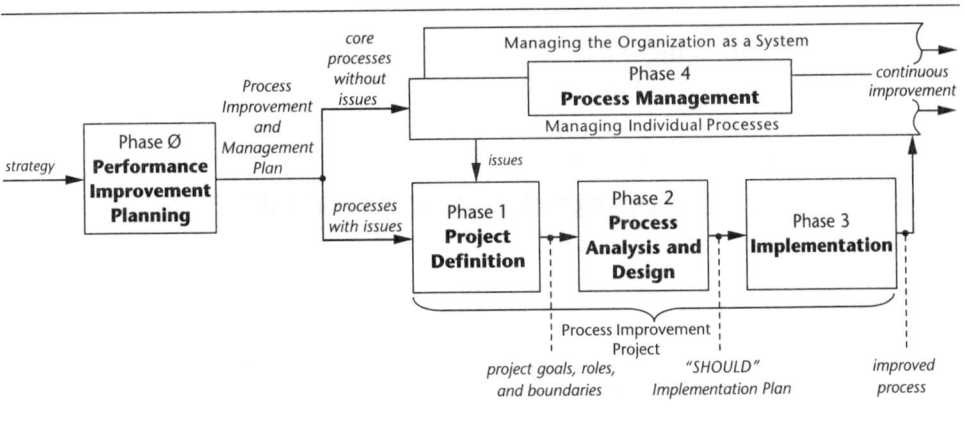

- To develop a Process Improvement and Management plan, which is the primary output of Phase Ø
- To provide the communication, measures, resources, skills, rewards, and feedback (the Human Performance System components) necessary to reinforce Process Management
- To establish the infrastructure and take the actions described below

Selecting Core Processes. While a long-range goal may be to establish a Process Management plan for every process, most organizations begin by identifying the critical few processes that warrant the investment in ongoing Process Management. These processes are those that have the greatest impact on the strategic success of the organization.

Therefore, the seeds of Process Management are sown in Phase Ø, in which "core processes" are identified. During Phase Ø, executives agree upon a specific, up-to-date strategy. They then use Critical Success Factors to identify the core processes from their inventory of primary, support, and management processes.

As you can see in Figure 13.1, some core processes, because they need either substantial or incremental improvement, go through Phases 1 to 3 before entering Phase 4. While the other core processes could be improved, they are not priorities for Process Improvement Projects; they go directly to Phase 4.

A core process is one that influences either a competitive advantage that must be overcome or a competitive advantage that senior management wants to establish, reinforce, or expand. For example, if order-cycle time is a potential competitive advantage, order processing is a strategic process. If the quality of customer service is a competitive advantage, the customer service process is core. If new products are central to the competitive advantage, product development and product introduction are core processes.

These examples of core processes are all primary processes (those that produce a product or service visible to the customer; see Chapter Four). Support and management (purely internal) processes can also be strategic. For example, if the cost of producing a product or service is a competitive advantage, the budgeting and capital expenditure processes may be as strategic as design, material management, and manufacturing. If the ability to quickly respond to the needs of a rapidly changing market is a competitive advantage, market research and planning are probably core processes. Similarly, training, forecasting, and safety management could be core processes.

Process Measures. If we had to select the single action that would make the greatest contribution to lasting Process Management, it would be the development and installation of a process-based measurement system that is linked to Organization Level and Job/Performer Level measures. Chapter Twelve is devoted to this subject.

Process Owners. To ensure that someone with clout is looking at and taking action to improve the performance of an entire cross-functional process, many organizations are appointing an individual as the *Process Owner* of each core process. A Process Owner plays some or all of these roles:

- Monitors process performance and reports periodically to senior management about how well the process is meeting customer requirements and internal goals, as well as about any indications that the process is being suboptimized.
- Chairs a cross-functional Process Management Team, which is responsible for the performance of the process. It sets the goals, establishes the process plan and budget, monitors process performance against the goals, and takes action in response to opportunities for Process Improvement.
- Serves as a "white-space ombudsman," who facilitates the resolution of interface problems among the functions that contribute to a process.
- Serves as the conscience and champion of the process.
- Evaluates and, in highly structured organizations, certifies the process.

Without a Process Owner, the "white spaces" tend to be ignored. As each line manager manages his or her piece of the process, functional optimization or process suboptimization (described in Chapter One) is likely to occur.

Like a matrix manager, who oversees the cross-functional performance of a product or a project, the Process Owner oversees the cross-functional performance of a process. Unlike a product or project manager, however, the Process Owner does not represent a second organization structure. Individuals are not continually torn between their commitments to their vertical (line) and horizontal (product or project) managers. In effective Process Management, reporting relationships remain vertical; the functional managers retain their power. The horizontal dimension is added if the functional managers are judged by their departments' contributions to one or more processes and if Process Owners ensure that interface problems are resolved and that process considerations dominate functional interests. There is one more distinction between a Process Owner and a product or project manager: products and projects come and go; processes are permanent.

Given this pivotal role, the selection of the Process Owner is critical. While not all of these characteristics are essential, a Process Owner tends to be someone who:

- Holds a senior management position
- Holds a position that gives him or her major equity in the total process (the most to gain if the process succeeds, and the most to lose if it fails)
- Manages the largest number of people working in the process
- Understands the workings of the entire process
- Has an overall perspective on the effect the environment has on the process and the effect the process has on the business
- Has the personal ability to influence decisions and people outside his or her line-management responsibility

The Process Owner's responsibility is usually associated with the position, rather than with an individual. For example, we worked with a telephone company in which the vice president of finance was appointed Process Owner for the billing process. When he left that position, his successor became the Process Owner.

We were initially surprised by the low level of conflict between effective Process Owners and the managers of the functions that contribute to the processes. We believe that good Process Owners do not threaten line managers, because they are doing things that nobody has done before. They are adding value without taking anything away from other managers.

Institutionalizing Process Management

In an organization that goes beyond Process Improvement Projects and institutionalizes Process Management, each key process has:

- A map that documents steps and the functions that perform them.
- A set of customer-driven measures, which are linked to Organization Level measures and drive functional measures (see Chapters Four and Twelve). In an institutionalized Process Management environment, functions cannot look good against their measures by hurting other functions and the process as a whole.
- A Process Owner.
- A permanent Process Team, which meets regularly to identify and implement Process Improvements.
- An annual business plan, which includes, for each core process, expected results, objectives, budget, and nonfinancial resource requirements.
- Mechanisms (such as process control charts) for the ongoing monitoring of process performance.
- Procedures (such as root-cause analysis) and vehicles (such as Process Teams) for solving process problems and capitalizing on process opportunities.

To ensure that processes meet these and other performance criteria, some organizations, including Ford and Boeing, have established process certification ratings. To achieve the top rating on a four-point scale, a Ford process must meet thirty-five criteria. These criteria range from the need for the process to have a name and be documented to a requirement that the process be assessed by customers as free of defects. The Process Owner takes primary responsibility for administering the evaluation and certification process.

Institutionalized Process Management is not just a set of certified processes. It is also a culture in which:

- Process Owners, Process Teams, and line managers practice continuous process improvement, rather than sporadic problem solving.
- Managers use their Relationship and Process Maps as tools for planning and implementing change, orienting new employees, evaluating strategic alternatives, and improving service to their internal and external customers.
- The needs of internal and external customers drive goal setting and decision making.
- Managers routinely ask and receive answers to questions about the effectiveness and efficiency of processes within their departments and about cross-functional processes to which their departments contribute. The answers to these questions require a process-based measurement system.
- Resources are allocated based on process requirements.

- Department managers serve as the Process Owners for their intrafunctional processes.
- Cross-functional teamwork is established through the enhanced understanding of other departments, the streamlining of interfaces, and the compatibility of goals.
- Optimum process performance is reinforced by the Human Performance Systems in which people work (see Chapter Five).

When Process Management is institutionalized in an organization, the systems view (see Chapter One) is the framework for addressing performance problems and opportunities. Process effectiveness and efficiency are the end to which policy, technology, and personnel decisions are means.

Managing the Vertical and Horizontal Organizations

Institutionalization of Process Management requires the peaceful coexistence of the vertical and horizontal dimensions of an organization. In most cases, organizing around processes is not practical. While a process organization structure (discussed further in Chapter Fourteen) eliminates the tension between the vertical and horizontal, it merely creates a different kind of white space . . . between processes. Furthermore, it may require additional people, obstruct sharing of learning and resources, and erect career path barriers. In most process-based organizations, functions remain as "centers of excellence."

How does an organization establish effective vertical and horizontal structures? In our experience, the key is measurement. As we suggest in Chapter Twelve, establishing customer-focused, process-driven measures is the first step. In a process-driven environment, each functional manager is still responsible for achieving results, allocating resources, and developing policies and procedures. *The only difference from a traditional (purely vertical) organization is that each function is measured against goals that reflect its contribution to processes.* Line managers have as much authority as in any traditional organization. There is no tug-of-war between two bosses, as in many matrix-managed organizations.

A department always contributes to the greater good. In an institutionalized Process Management environment, that greater good is the processes that serve the organization strategy. Because Process Management fosters symbiotic "we're all in this together" relationships between suppliers and customers, functional managers may need assistance in managing the "white space." That assistance is available from the Process Owner.

In summary, Process Management can coexist quite peacefully with the functional organization because:

- It doesn't change the direction of the business.
- It doesn't (necessarily) change the organization structure or reporting relationships.
- It ensures that functional goals are aligned with process goals.
- It doesn't change accountability or power.
- It changes how the business is conducted only because it ensures that processes (which are there already) are rational.

The Role of Top Management

An organization does not have to implement Process Management all at once. A top manager who is interested in Process Management should begin by instituting a couple of Process Improvement Projects. If these projects successfully address Critical Business Issues, he or she should consider institutionalizing Process Management, at least for the organization's core processes. A top manager's role in institutionalization may include:

- Identifying core processes
- Appointing or serving as a Process Owner
- Appointing permanent Process Teams
- Asking and requiring answers to the questions behind the Nine Performance Variables
- Using process measures as the foundation for performance evaluation, rewards, and troubleshooting
- Chairing a Process Owner panel that conducts process reviews, which are similar to traditional operations reviews
- Installing and managing a process planning system, which resembles typical business planning
- Ensuring that the work environment (rewards, feedback, resources) supports process effectiveness and efficiency

Process Improvement and Management and the Three Levels of Performance

Effective Process Improvement is not limited to the Process Level of Performance. Process Improvement Projects with the greatest impact begin with the identification of a Critical Business Issue associated with a key process. Issue and process identification should be based on strategic goals at the Organization Level. Process Improvement cannot take root if it is limited to the Process Level. All system enhancements have to be reflected in the jobs and the environment at the Job/Performer Level.

Similarly, ongoing Process Management is not just management of the Process Level. An ongoing assessment of Organization Level needs should direct the Process Management priorities. In addition, a cornerstone of Process Management is the monitoring and improvement of the Job/Performer Level. To manage the performance of a process, one must manage the performance of the people who work within that process. To manage people's contributions to process effectiveness, one must manage the variables of the Human Performance System— Performance Specifications, Task Support, Consequences, Feedback, Skills and Knowledge, and Individual Capacity.

Managing an Organization as a System

Everything we've covered up to this point addresses the first part of Phase 4, which relates to actions we might take to manage and continuously improve a single process. At some point, all of the individual Process Management efforts have to be integrated with each other and with the goals at the Organization Level. We call this integration "managing organizations as systems."

Before you begin managing your organization as a system, you should build a logical system to manage. We will illustrate the process with Computec, Inc., the organization we have used frequently as an example. Computec's top managers were concerned about the plateauing of the company's revenues and its loss of market share. They began to address the situation by building an intelligent system.

1. The top team formulated a strategy that addressed the current external (marketplace, competitive, and economic) reality. To develop this strategy, Computec management answered the questions presented in Chapter Six. As part of that strategy, the top team decided to establish competitive advantages in three areas: the extent of Computec's customer service, the appeal of its continuous stream of innovative new products, and the speed with which it fills orders for its packaged software products.

2. The team developed an understanding of the current system by creating a Computec Relationship Map (see Chapter Three). Team members realized that they would benefit by constructing and analyzing this picture of their business system themselves. As a result, they resisted the temptation to delegate this task to an analyst.

3. The top team overlaid the Organization Level (strategic) goals on the map.

4. The team identified the eight Computec cross-functional processes and selected those that had (and still have) the greatest impact on the Organization Goals. On the basis of Computec's intended competitive

advantages, the management team selected four strategically critical processes: product development and introduction (which in Chapter Four we called a *primary process*); order filling (another primary process); purchasing (a *support process*); and operational planning (a *management process*).

5. The team appointed a vice president to serve as the Process Owner for each of the four processes.

6. As a team, top management developed the customer-driven, end-of-line Process Goals for each of the four strategic processes. The management team answered this question: Given our Organization Goals, what performance do we require from this process?

7. The group formed Process Teams, which documented and analyzed the four processes, using the Process Improvement steps described in Chapter Nine. The three key outputs of these teams were a recommended "SHOULD" process (which became the detailed road map for fixing the organization), a recommended plan for moving from "IS" to "SHOULD," and a recommended set of goals for critical segments of the process.

8. The top team integrated the recommendations, so that all four processes could work in harmony. (The management team didn't want the product development process, for example, to be optimized at the expense of the other processes.)

9. The team implemented the "SHOULD" processes, which included changing process flows, changing the assignment of functional responsibilities (and, in some instances, the organization structure), establishing a Performance Measurement/Management System around the Process Goals and the functional goals that they spawned (see Chapter Twelve), and changing job responsibilities and Human Performance Systems as necessary (see Chapter Five). Since changing all four processes at once was more than Computec could handle, the top team phased the implementation.

Evaluating the System

The changes have been successfully implemented. Computec has built a system that works. Now the top team's challenge is to manage the system it has built. However, before the system can be effectively managed, it is necessary to develop a mechanism for measuring and evaluating key components of the system. Toward this end, Computec developed the following:

• A report card for evaluating the performance of each of the four strategic processes. Areas for evaluation include customer feedback, internal requirements (such as performance against budget), ability to respond to change, and extent of continuous improvement. The data for the evaluation come directly from the performance measurement system, which documents actual performance and compares it to the Process Goals (see Step 9).

Figure 13.2 illustrates how process performance information comes together to form the basis of top management's "instrument panel." The dials on the instrument panels of the managers at the next level may consist primarily of subprocess and department measures. At the next level (which may or may not be managerial), the instrument panel may contain measures of individual process steps and jobs. This approach ensures that each level has an instrument panel and that the dials on each of these panels link to those above and below.

• A report card for evaluating each Process Owner in terms of his or her contribution to the effectiveness of the process. The items on this report card are based on top management's clear delineation of the responsibilities of the Process Owner (see the sample list earlier in this chapter). For example, Computec Process Owners are evaluated on how well they keep the rest of the top team informed of process performance and how well they help resolve any "white-space" conflicts between functions.

• A report card for evaluating the vice president of each function on how well that function supports the processes to which it contributes. For

FIGURE 13.2. MANAGING THE ORGANIZATION AS A SYSTEM

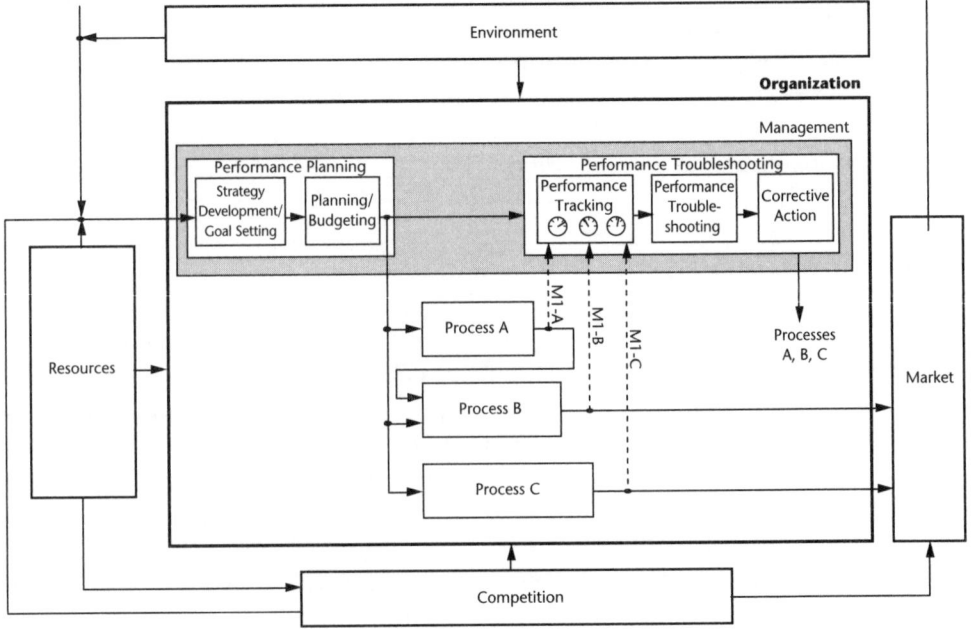

example, the vice president of marketing is evaluated on how well marketing supports product development and introduction. The evaluation is based on the process steps carried out by that function and on the functional goals (in such areas as customer requirements and budget) that evolved from the Process Goals. The Computec Function Models (see Chapter Twelve) were particularly useful in the development of these rating categories.

Vice presidents are evaluated not only on how well their functions achieve their goals but also in "softer" areas, such as degree of cooperation with other functions for the good of the process, responsiveness to changes required for process success, and the degree to which Human Performance Systems support individuals and teams who contribute to process success. The performance appraisals of the four Process Owners assess them both as Process Owners and as leaders of functions that exist to support processes.

The Systems Management Processes

At this point, Computec has created a system that makes sense, and the company has developed mechanisms for evaluating the key aspects of that system: the processes, the Process Owners, and the function managers. Now let's examine the ways in which some of the basic management processes help the senior management team manage Computec as a system.

In the *annual planning process,* the Computec president, Process Owners, and vice presidents:

- Update the strategy and operating plan.
- Identify new Organization Level outputs and Organization Goals.
- Confirm the identity of the strategic processes and update Process Goals to ensure that they reflect Organization Goals.
- Identify the process changes required to meet the new Process Goals. These changes may include modifications to the processes themselves, new goals for process segments, or resource shifts.

In the *annual budgeting process,* the same players:

- Negotiate budgets for the processes, which are based on the Process Goals that were established as part of the planning process. (The Process Owners' commitment to budget allocation is particularly critical.)
- Negotiate function budgets, which are based on the process budgets and on each function's contributions to the Process Goals.

- Roll up the process and function budgets and marry them with the organizationwide budget, which was established in the strategy.

In the *monthly operations-review process,* the top managers:

- Examine product and market performance in terms of customer satisfaction goals.
- Examine product and market performance in terms of revenue and profit goals.
- Examine cost performance in terms of budget goals.
- Examine process performance in terms of the Process Goals established for customer satisfaction, revenue and profit, and cost. Each function's performance is reviewed in terms of the degree to which it is providing the agreed-upon process support. At this step in the review, the team is ready to ask a number of questions:

  - Why is performance better (or worse) than we expected? Is this a blip or a trend? Is this a surprise? If so, why? Is the process flawed? Did functional priorities supersede process priorities? Is our goal setting, planning, or budgeting deficient?
  - Do we need to add to or modify our goals?
  - Do we need to reallocate resources? If so, which process or function gets more? How much more, and from where?

During the operations-review meeting, the president asks the questions. The Process Owners provide most of the answers and are supported by the function heads. The answers lead to decisions, which in turn result in action items that are assigned to individuals. These action items are documented and categorized as changes in policy, changes in goals, changes in resources, changes in processes, changes in reporting relationships, and changes in management practices.

In the *biannual performance review process,* the president provides grades for the processes, Process Owners, and function managers. These ratings serve as the basis for the annual allocation of bonus money. The size of the bonus pot is determined by the profitability of the company. We believe that this scenario has some key distinctions from traditional management:

- Because the measures are customer focused, the customer's voice is heard throughout the performance review process.
- Because the goals are process driven, the top team is able to review the performance of the business comprehensively.
- Because the goals are process driven, the top team can review both the results and the ways in which those results are achieved. Since the team

understands the reasons for the results, it has greater control over the business.

- Because the Process Owner plays a key role in the management process, the voices of "the way work gets done" and of "white-space management" are never drowned out by other considerations.

- Because functional goals are subordinate to process goals, no departmental head can command an inappropriate share of the resources.

- Because the Three Levels are incorporated into the Performance Management process, change is more intelligently managed. The top team is less likely to make strategy or policy decisions without developing an implementation plan that includes actions at the Process and Job/Performer Levels; to initiate systems improvements without determining their impact on the Organization and Job/Performer Levels; or to take action to improve employees' performance, other than in response to the needs of the Organization and Process Levels.

The Systems Management Culture

We have found that the culture of an organization in which systems are being managed differs from the culture of a typical organization. Table 13.1 contrasts the traditional (vertical) and systems (horizontal) cultures. Within a systems culture, we find that managers at all levels are able to answer yes to the systems management questions contained in Table 13.2.

Summary

Managing organizations as systems involves understanding and managing the Nine Performance Variables that serve as the theme of this book. The business system is made up of inputs, outputs, and feedback at the Organization, Process, and Job/Performer Levels. At each of the Three Levels, the system requires clear and appropriate goals, logical design, and supportive management practices.

Performance measures provide the latticework of the system. A Three Levels measurement system provides a window on more than just results. By monitoring and improving those factors that influence results, managers are able to cause more systemic improvement and to understand what's needed to implement change.

Managers become heroes in the systems management culture by understanding their business, collaborating with other departments to get a job done, subordinating the optimization of their departments to the common good of the process, and creating Human Performance Systems that equip people to make their maximum contributions to the system and that reinforce them when they do.

TABLE 13.1. COMPARISON OF THE TRADITIONAL (VERTICAL) AND SYSTEMS (HORIZONTAL) CULTURES

Traditional Culture	Systems Culture
• Functional needs dominate decision making.	• Customer and process needs dominate decision making.
• Functions have minimal interaction with other functions.	• Functions have extensive interaction with other functions.
• Most people understand only the functions in which they work.	• People understand the "big picture" and the business of the other functions with which they need to collaborate.
• People do not know the identity of and linkages with their function's internal customers and suppliers.	• People understand the inputs and outputs that link their functions to other functions.
• Interactions among functions tend to be confrontational.	• Interactions among functions tend to focus on "win-win" problem solving and decision making.
• Functions are competitors.	• Functions are collaborative partners.
• A function's measures isolate it from other functions.	• A function's measures reflect the contribution it should make to its immediate customer and to the system as a whole.
• A function can look good at the expense of other functions.	• A function can look good only through its contribution to the entire organization.
• Only results are measured and managed.	• Results and processes are measured and managed.
• Systems are examined only when there is a problem ("If it ain't broke, don't fix it").	• Systems are continually analyzed and improved ("We're not as good as we could be").
• Information is not regularly shared among functions.	• Information of mutual interest is routinely shared among functions.
• Managers do not allow employees to resolve issues directly with peers in other functions; they expect them to raise issues through the chain of command.	• Managers encourage employees to resolve issues with peers in other functions.
• Employees' involvement in decision making is nonexistent or confined to the function.	• Cross-functional teams at all levels are convened frequently to address critical business issues.
• Employees are rewarded for their functional contribution.	• Employees are rewarded for their organizational contributions.

TABLE 13.2. SYSTEMS MANAGEMENT QUESTIONS

- Does your department have a strategy that is linked to the organizationwide strategy?
- Can you identify all of your department's internal and external customers?
- Do you know all of your department's products and services?
- Do you know your customers' requirements for your department's products and services?
- Do you measure performance on the basis of how well your products and services meet your customers' requirements?
- Can you identify your department's internal and external suppliers?
- Do you establish clear goals for the products and services provided to your department by your suppliers?
- Do you have documentation of your department's role in the cross-functional processes to which it contributes?
- Do you measure your department on the degree to which it contributes to cross-functional processes?
- Do you measure the "upstream" performance of the processes that flow through your department?
- Do you have tracking and feedback systems that effectively and efficiently gather performance information and provide it to the people who need it?
- Do you have the skills to troubleshoot (remove the root causes of) performance gaps in your system?
- Do you spend a large percentage of your time working to improve the interfaces ("white space") between your department and other departments and between subunits within your department?
- Do employees in your department work in an environment where their job design, goals, feedback, rewards, resources, and training enable them to make their maximum contributions to process efficiency and effectiveness?

CHAPTER FOURTEEN

DESIGNING AN ORGANIZATION STRUCTURE THAT WORKS

*Had I been present at the creation, I would have given some
useful hints for the better ordering of the universe.*

—Alfonso X

Managers, at all levels, tend to manage by organization structure. Prevailing wisdom suggests that if an executive can just get the right boxes on the chart, array them in the appropriate hierarchy, and appoint strong people to head them up, the organization will succeed. Toward this end, most large companies embark on a significant reorganization at least once a year.

In Chapter One, we discussed the advantages of seeing an organization from a process perspective, rather than from an organization structure perspective (see Figures 1.1 and 1.3). The distinction between the horizontal view and vertical view is critical when redesigning organizations. The objective of a reorganization is to improve the performance of the organization. However, organization performance is in most cases a result of the effectiveness of the cross-functional processes (the horizontal system). Therefore, the goal of most reorganizations should be to improve the effectiveness and efficiency of the horizontal organization. This suggests that a reorganization should follow a two-step process:

1. Analyze and redesign the horizontal system—the critical cross-functional processes—so that it will meet customer requirements and organization goals.
2. Redraw the organization boundaries (redesign the reporting relationships) to support the effectiveness and efficiency of the horizontal system.

In effect, form should follow function.

Unfortunately, many reorganizations are carried out with attention only to the vertical view—the reporting relations—without a real understanding of the needs of the horizontal system. The worst-case result is that the reorganization ends up optimizing the performance of a particular function and suboptimizing the horizontal system and the performance of the organization. The best-case result is that the restructuring inadvertently benefits the horizontal system. But the need for the horizontal system to be effective is too important to leave to chance. Organization Design means just that: if we want the organization to work, we must design it to do so. And the design work begins with the understanding of the requirements of the cross-functional processes or horizontal system. Work gets done through processes; processes should drive organization structure.

We also believe that Organization Design (one of our Nine Performance Variables) should not start or finish with the organization chart. Organization Design should include:

- A structure at the Organization Level that defines the input-output (supplier-customer) relationships that should exist among functions
- A structure at the Process Level that defines the steps through which inputs should be converted to outputs and identifies the units that should carry them out
- A structure at the Job/Performer Level that defines individual and work-team responsibilities and the environment in which they should be carried out

Let us examine a series of steps for developing an organization structure that works because it encompasses and addresses all Three Levels of Performance.

Designing an Organization Structure

We believe that an effective organization structure results from the following activities and decisions. Starting with Phase Ø (see Chapter Nine) provides input to, accomplishes, or helps set priorities for Steps 1 to 3, which follow. Process redesign efforts (Phases 1, 2, and 3) fuel Steps 3 and 4. Installing an integrated measurement system and taking other continuous improvement actions provides a substantial input to Step 5. So the amount of work that has to be done before Step 5 depends on what has already been done. In the next section, we provide a comprehensive example that illustrates these steps.

Step 1: Establish a Clear Strategy. Your organization's structure should facilitate the achievement of its strategy. If an organization has no strategy, any structure will do. Chapter Six outlined an organization's strategic decisions, which include product and service definition, customer and market definition, competitive-advantage identification, and resource-allocation priority determination. Once these decisions establish a direction, executives can begin to design a structure that will help take the organization down that path.

Step 2: Document and Analyze the Current ("IS") Organization System. Using a Relationship Map (see Chapter Three), display the inputs and outputs that connect the current departments in the organization. Identify any "disconnects" (missing, redundant, or illogical connections), especially those that affect the organization's ability to achieve the strategy.

For example, we worked with a small telecommunications company that identified rapid introduction of new products as one of its potential competitive advantages. When it developed its "IS" Relationship Map, it became clear that it did not have a series of relationships (a process) through which products could be efficiently developed and introduced. Furthermore, product development, while it still appeared on the organization chart, was a department that had recently been the victim of a cost-cutting campaign, and it had no staff—hardly a structure through which the strategy could be achieved!

Step 3: Document and Analyze the Current ("IS") Processes. Using Process Maps and cross-functional Process Teams (see Chapters Four, Nine, and Ten), describe the current flow of the primary, support, and management processes that have the greatest impact on the strategy. Phase Ø helps identify these "critical few" processes. Note any disconnects that currently or potentially weaken competitiveness.

For example, we worked with an aerospace company whose executives determined that they wanted to capitalize further on a current competitive advantage—their ability to substantially customize their product to meet unique customer requirements. A team constructed a map of the process through which customer options became incorporated into products. It revealed significant disconnects that resulted in confused customers, missed delivery dates, and small or negative margins.

Step 4: Develop "SHOULD" Process Flows and Measures. Use the Process Map format to develop "SHOULD" flows for the strategically significant processes analyzed in Step 3. These "SHOULD" processes ought to remove the disconnects identified in the "IS" processes. Then establish a set of process measures, following the format outlined in Chapter Twelve. At this step, you may have to design "SHOULD" subprocesses (further breakdowns) and support (staff) processes.

Step 5: Design the Organization Chart. On the basis of the "SHOULD" Process Maps, determine the most logical departmental groupings and reporting relationships. The goal is to draw organization boundaries that maximize process effectiveness and efficiency. The criteria for selecting the structure that will best serve the process—and, in turn, the strategy—include:

- Maximum product and service quality
- Maximum responsiveness to customers' needs (maximum flexibility and minimum cycle time)
- Maximum efficiency (minimum rework and minimum cost)

To meet these criteria, the organization structure should have:

- The minimum number of interfaces necessary to achieve the quality goals of the process
- Maximum proximity of internal customers and suppliers
- An optimum span of control (number of direct reports per manager)
- A minimum number of layers of management
- Maximum clarity (few, if any, overlapping or fuzzy responsibilities)

In addition, as we discussed in Chapter One, organizations need to be adaptive systems. Instability in markets, competition, regulation, and technology demand Organization Designs that facilitate gathering and processing information about changes in any of these areas, enable the business to react quickly and intelligently to the need for change, and are themselves not overly difficult to change. The best structures are those that help us thrive in an environment of continuous change.

Organization Design, like measurement and managing human performance, is a subject that deserves a book unto itself. However, let us distill our experience into a set of guidelines:

- *Organization Design (defined narrowly as what resources have been grouped together and who reports to whom) is less important than you might think.* If processes are intelligently designed, roles are well defined, and people and machines are equipped to fill the roles, organization structure is almost immaterial. Don't get us wrong; Organization Design can be a significant "disconnect" or a significant "enabler" to a process. However, assuming that a new Organization Design will in itself eliminate disconnects is like assuming that a new house will make our lives run more smoothly. By itself, it won't. If my job has been designed to provide maximum contribution to the process(es) I support, if I understand the what, why, and how of my job, if I'm clear on where I fit in the process (including who my customers and suppliers are), and if I'm driven by what's important (due to my measures and rewards) . . . who cares what my organization unit is called or whether I report to Sally or to Bob?

- *There is no "right" organization structure in all situations.* The strategy and the processes dictate the structure that makes sense for a given organization at a given point in time. Centralization has its advantages; so does decentralization. Functional structures (in which people are grouped by the work they do, like accounting or production) can provide better or worse support for strategy and process than sectored structures (in which people are organized by product, by market, by process, by geography, by shift, and so forth). *We can determine the best structure only by evaluating design alternatives against the criteria listed above. This evaluation is unique to the situation.*

(Throughout this book, we have used "department," "unit," and "function" as synonymous, which they are, in common parlance. In the field of Organization Design, "function" refers to a grouping of similar work. So the human resource and distribution departments are functions; the plastics business unit and the European division are not.)

- A corollary to the preceding guideline: *All organization structures have white space. The mission is not to eliminate white space. The mission is to minimize the extent to which white space impedes processes and to manage the white space that must exist.* If you organize by product, there's white space between products. If you organize by function, there's white space between functions. A popular concept today is the "virtual organization," in which formal structures are replaced with a fluid resource pool that can be nimbly deployed in whatever way is necessary to get a job done (knowing that the next job is likely to be different). However, there is still white space between projects, between processes within today's virtual structure, and between people working in the temporary organization. Process quality is at least as important as in a more stable environment.

- A corollary to both the preceding guidelines: *Organizing by process is not necessarily any better than organizing in some other way.* First, as we state in Chapter Thirteen, organizing by process may eliminate the white space between departments; however, it creates interprocess white space that needs just as much attention. Second, designing an organization structure to serve the needs of one process may suboptimize another process. Third, if we eliminate a function, like finance, and sprinkle financial expertise among the various processes that need it, we are likely to increase headcount. (For instance, a person with financial expertise may be assigned to the "quotation/proposal" process. However, that process requires only 25 percent of his or her time. If he or she had been in finance, the other 75 percent could have been dedicated to other processes.) We may also have lowered technical competence by making it more difficult for finance people to share learning and resources and by eliminating a career path through finance. (We realize that it does open doors to cross-discipline career development.) *Organizing by process isn't bad; it involves trade-offs, just like any other structure.*

• *The best structures help manage change.* As we discuss in Chapter One, organizations need to be adaptive systems. The instability of the current business environment demands organization designs that:

1. Facilitate gathering and processing information about changes in markets, competition, suppliers, regulation, and technology
2. Enable the business to react quickly and intelligently to the need for change
3. Are themselves not overly difficult to change

We are not suggesting that everyone adopt the "virtual organization" described earlier; however, we should embrace its objectives. *An adaptive structure helps an organization thrive in an environment of continuous change.*

• When designing our "SHOULD" process, we don't limit our thinking to those actions that will make the current structure work better (unless the Steering Team has identified the current structure as unchangeable). *To ensure that we don't limit our creativity or build in an Organization Design disconnect, the first iterations of the "SHOULD" process should focus on **what** should be done, not on **who** should do it.*

• *What's most important is how the organization is structured "at the bottom," where work gets done.* Too often, reorganizations focus only on the top couple of layers (the ones visible to the reorganizers), leaving the rest to "sort itself out." We think that's backward; the sequence should be as follows:

1. Design the work to be done (the primary processes).
2. Design the structure to support the primary processes.
3. Design the support and management processes.
4. Design the staff and management structure to support those processes.

In fact, one of the advantages of the process-driven approach to organization structure design is that it provides a vehicle for assessing the value that is added at each level of management. A vice president in one of our client companies evaluated Role/Responsibility Matrices (see Chapter Twelve) in terms of the number of levels of approval. His rule: no more than one level of person should have an "approve" role. When redundant approvals were removed, some jobs had nothing left.

Since, as the second guideline suggests, there is likely to be more than one workable structure, we recommend testing each structure that looks reasonable by simulating the process flow through it. This exercise can be done via the Process Map and/or by a physical "walk-through" of, for example, an order or a new product. This simulation provides the ultimate test of which structure best fits the criteria listed above.

To verify the viability of the organization structure, develop a "SHOULD" Relationship Map that eliminates the disconnects identified in Step 2. This Relationship Map may suggest a refinement of the organization chart and will serve as a key input to the Function Models to be developed in Step 6.

Step 6: Develop Function Models for Each Department. Using the format and rationale provided in Chapter Twelve, define each function in the organization (each box on the new chart) in terms of its outputs and goals. These Function Models should be derived from the Relationship Map's outputs and from the critical process outputs and goals. They should describe the responsibilities with enough detail to:

- Clearly and thoroughly communicate each function's role in the organization
- Ensure that function outputs do not overlap
- Ensure that all process outputs and measures are reflected in function responsibilities
- Serve as a firm foundation for the development of Job Models (see Step 7)

We have found that a Role/Responsibility Matrix (see Table 14.1 at the end of the chapter), which ties each function's key outputs to the steps in a critical process, can provide a useful backdrop for the development of Function Models.

Step 7: Develop Job Models for Each Job. Identify the outputs and goals required from each job in the new organization, using the Job Model format presented in Chapter Twelve. Job Models are particularly critical if the new organization requires new jobs or jobs with new responsibilities. Only through Job Models will the specifics of the new structure be communicated to the people who will make it work.

Step 8: Structure the Human Performance System for Each Job. The failures of many reorganizations are not due to flawed organization charts. Reorganizations fail either because they suboptimize process performance (see Step 4) or because the new structure is not reinforced by the Human Performance Systems in which people work. The Human Performance System (described in depth in Chapter Five) includes the Capacity of the people selected for jobs, their Skills and Knowledge, and the environment in which they work. A manager establishes an environment that supports the new structure by communicating Performance Specifications (the outputs and goals in the Job Model), providing Task Support (clear inputs, necessary resources), structuring Consequences (rewards) that reinforce meeting the goals, and providing regular Feedback on job performance.

Step 9: Establish Management Processes. Once the infrastructure for the new organization has been established at the Organization, Process, and Job/Performer Levels, the system has to be managed. The management process for implementing a new organization structure includes the actions that we introduced in the sections on management in Chapters Three, Four, and Five:

- Goal setting
- Performance management
- Resource allocation
- Interface ("white space") management
- Human Performance System management

Designing an Organization Structure That Works

Ace Copiers, Inc., is a real organization whose name and product have been somewhat modified for presentation here. To establish an organization structure that works, Ace followed the nine-step process just described. An outline of that process, with selected artifacts, follows.

Step 1: Establish a Clear Strategy. Ace Copiers designs, manufactures, distributes, and services office photocopy machines and accessories. During an eighteen-month period, its previous trend of rapid growth slowed, and it lost a significant portion of its market share. Ace introduced only two new products in three years, which was far below the industry average. The development and production of both products went over budget, and neither copier sold well.

These problems motivated Ace's management committee to go through a period of soul searching. They went off to the mountains and returned with a comprehensive strategy. An integral part of that strategy was to introduce two new products during each of the next five years.

Step 2: Document and Analyze the Current ("IS") Organization System. Figure 14.1 displays Ace's original organization chart. Figure 14.2 shows the original Relationship Map and its disconnects.

FIGURE 14.1. ACE COPIERS, INC., ORIGINAL ORGANIZATION CHART

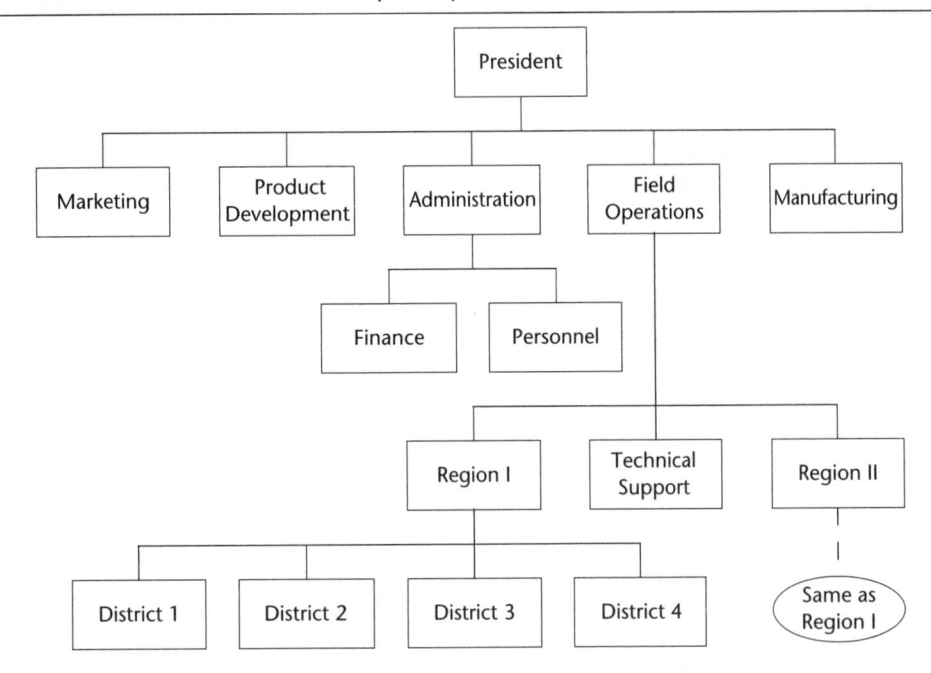

FIGURE 14.2. ACE COPIERS, INC., "IS" RELATIONSHIP MAP AND DISCONNECTS

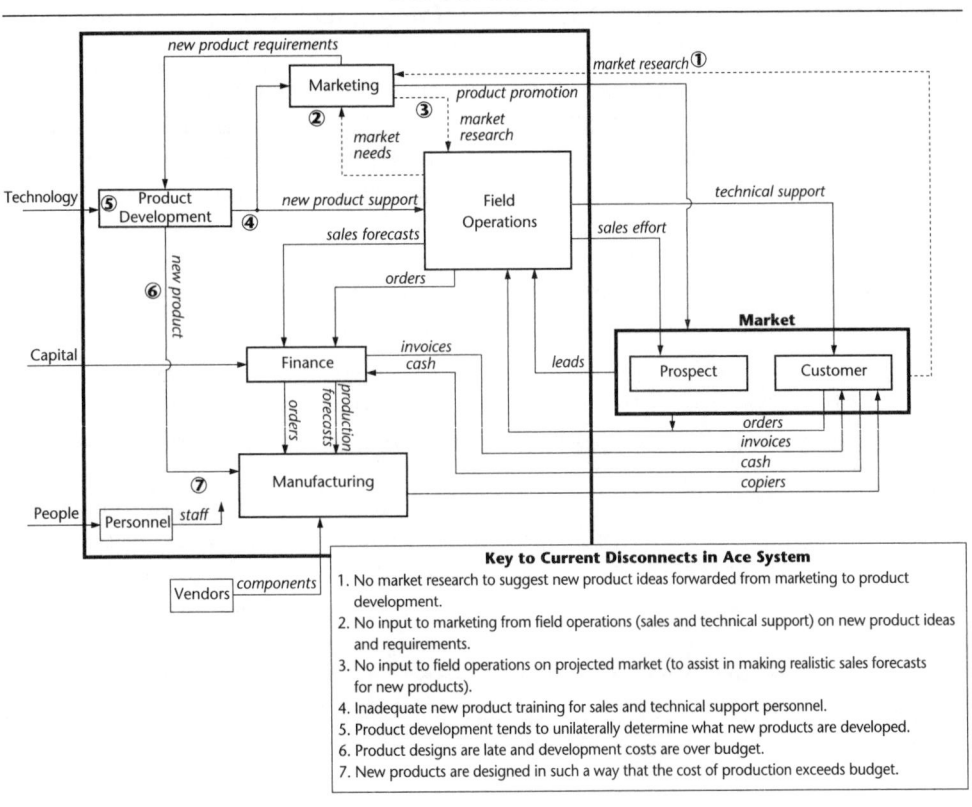

Step 3: Document and Analyze the Current ("IS") Processes. Given its strategy and the disconnects in its system, Ace identified product development and introduction as its most critical process. A cross-functional group developed an "IS" Process Map and identified the disconnects.

Step 4: Develop "SHOULD" Process Flows and Measures. Figure 14.3 displays a portion of the "SHOULD" map that the Ace team developed for product development and introduction. After completing the map, the team developed a set of measures for product development and introduction. Those measures led to a set of standards:

- *New products will achieve sales volume and dollar goals.*
- *New products will be introduced (from conception to field training and production of the first five thousand units) within nine months.*
- *Unit cost of new products will be within established budget.*
- *Development and introduction costs will be within established budget.*

These end-of-line measures and standards spawned submeasures and standards at critical junctures in the process.

Step 5: Design the Organization Chart. As the steps in the "SHOULD" product development process were being entered into the bands in the Process Map, the team members were assigning responsibilities to each function. They decided to split the old product development function into product design (which did the conceptualization) and product engineering (which was responsible for the internal and external configuration of the copier). The new product design function combined with marketing and sales to form an integrated field operations unit.

This field operations structure enabled Ace to make faster product development decisions and to speed up the implementation of those decisions. The establishment of the product engineering function in manufacturing enabled Ace to configure copiers that could be made at a lower cost.

Before the organization chart was finalized, it was tested against other key Ace processes. Ace wanted to make sure it didn't establish a structure that optimized its product development process and suboptimized other critical processes. (If functional isolation can be illustrated by silos, perhaps process isolation can be seen as tunnels.) Figure 14.4 displays the new Ace organization chart. Figure 14.5 displays the new Relationship Map.

Step 6: Develop a Function Model for Each Department. To make sure that the responsibilities of the new functions were clear, the Ace team developed a product development Role/Responsibility Matrix. A portion of this matrix appears in Table 14.1 at the end of the chapter. Measures and

FIGURE 14.3. ACE COPIERS PRODUCT DEVELOPMENT: PARTIAL "SHOULD" PROCESS MAP

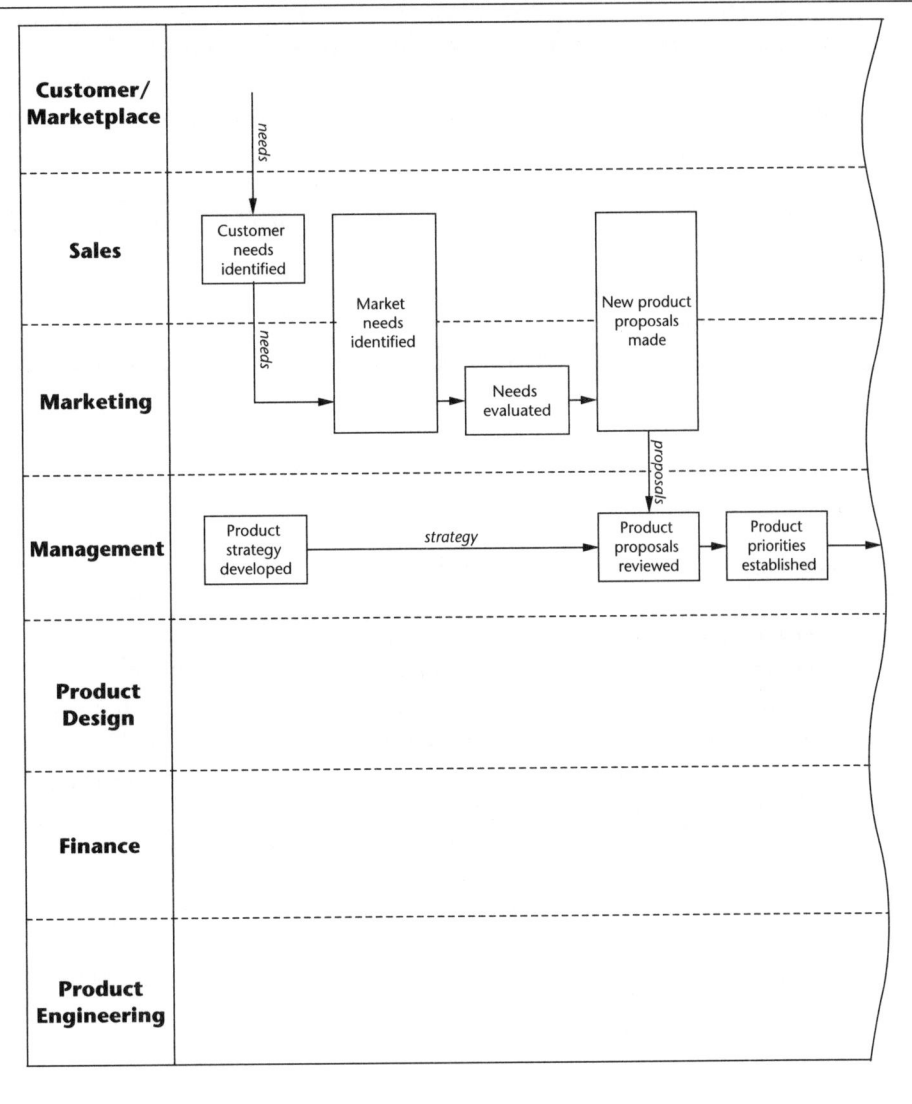

FIGURE 14.3.
(Continued)

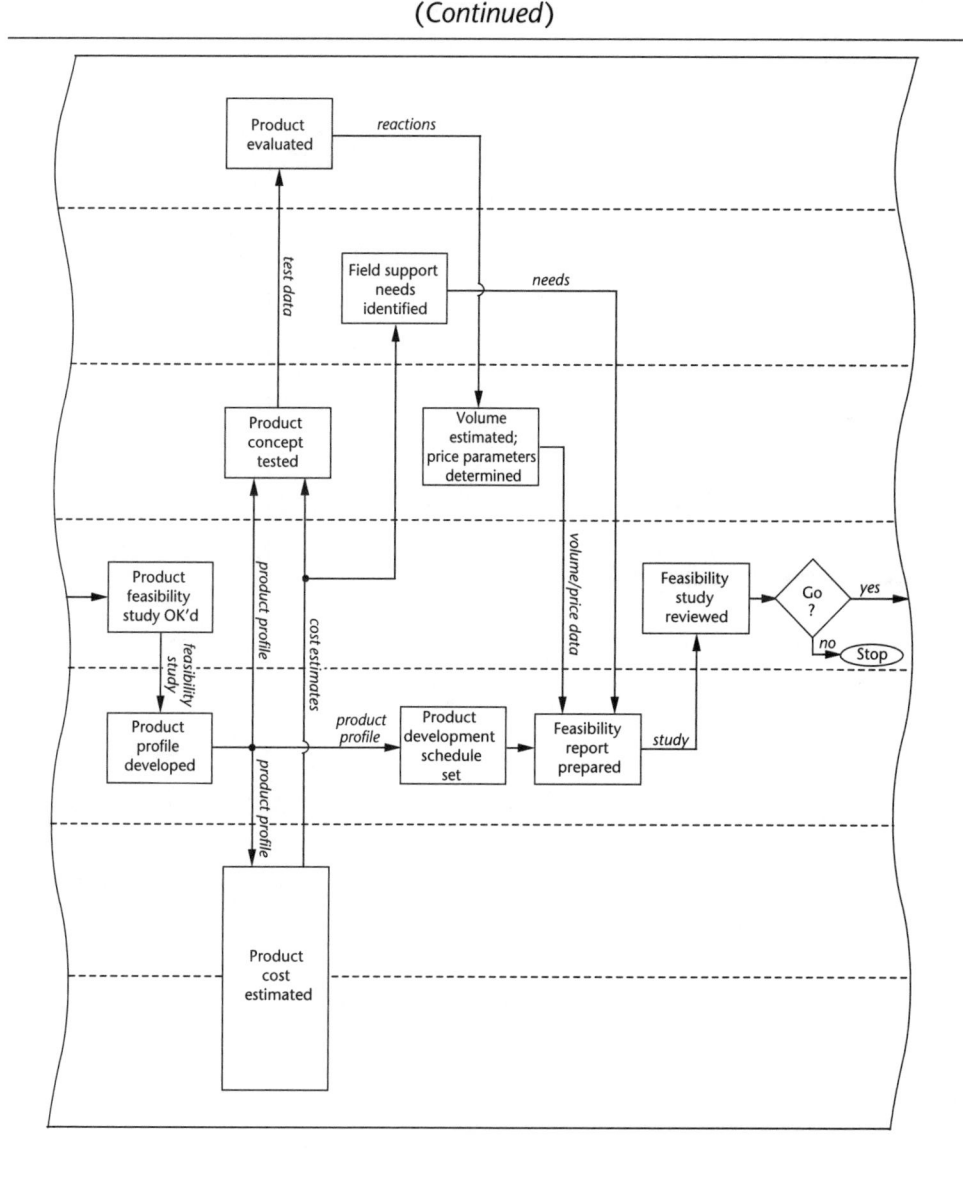

FIGURE 14.3.
(*Continued*)

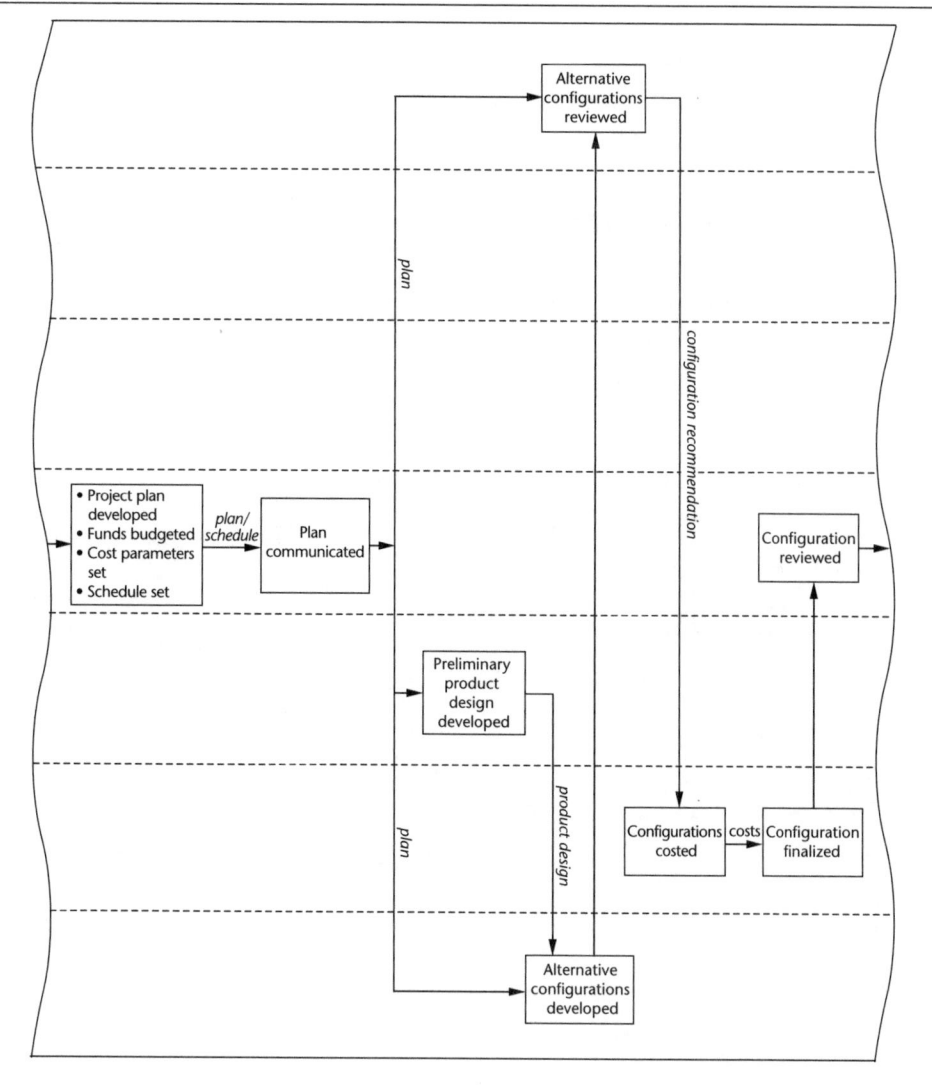

FIGURE 14.4. NEW ACE COPIERS ORGANIZATION CHART

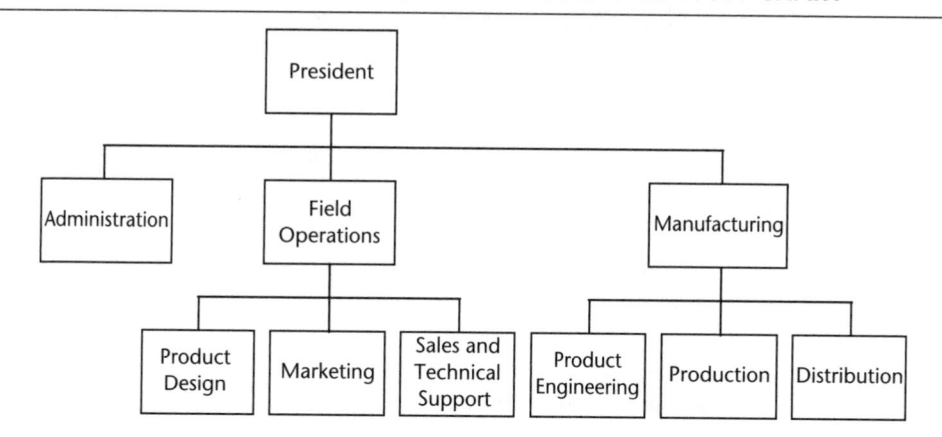

FIGURE 14.5. ACE COPIERS "SHOULD" RELATIONSHIP MAP

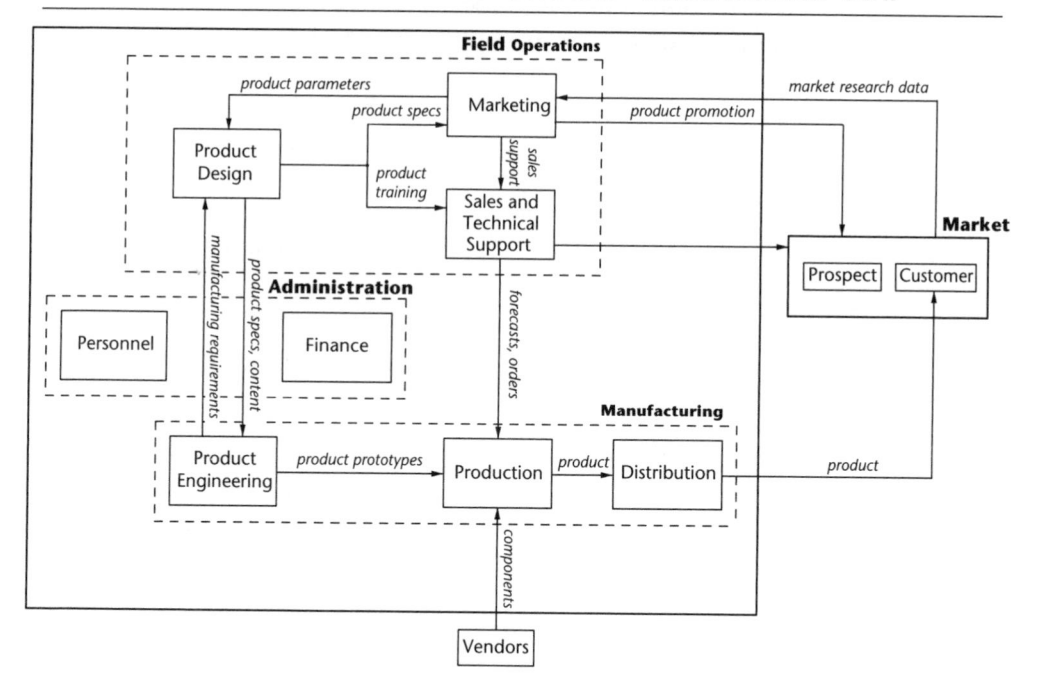

goals were added to the process responsibilities assigned to each function. These responsibilities (outputs) and goals became each department's Function Model (see Chapter Twelve).

Step 7: Develop Job Models for Each Job. Task teams in each department used the Function Model as the basis for developing a Job Model for each job that contributed to the product development process (for instance, sales representative, market research analyst, and design engineer). These Job Models contained the outputs that incumbents were expected to produce to contribute to the function outputs, and the goals they were expected to achieve for each output.

Step 8: Structure the Human Performance System for Each Job. For each job, the required feedback, rewards, and training were specified.

Step 9: Establish Management Processes. Once the new organization was established at the Organization, Process, and Job/Performer Levels, Ace installed an infrastructure for managing all three levels. The top management team created a series of management processes to ensure that goals were continuously set, performance was tracked against these goals at all three levels, resources were allocated so that the product development process was optimized, interfaces were managed, and all components of the Human Performance System were managed. These responsibilities became the core of the managers' performance appraisal.

Summary

Designing an organization structure is more than naming, arranging, and filling the boxes on the organization chart. While clear reporting relationships are administratively essential, getting products and services to customers requires an organization structure that focuses on the nature and flow of work. Toward this end, the first need is to decide what work is to be done (see Step 1). The next need is to understand how work currently gets accomplished (see Steps 2 and 3) and to design the way it should be carried out (see Step 4). Then and only then can a useful organization chart be created. In our opinion, form (structure) follows function (processes).

Our definition of organization structure encompasses the Organization Level of Performance (where strategy is set and customer-supplier relationships are established), the Process Level (where work flows are streamlined and documented), and the Job/Performer Level (where jobs are defined and a supportive Human Performance System is installed). Critical dimensions of the structure at all three levels are performance measures and a management process through which the structure is continuously improved.

We are by no means saying that an organization structure that supports business processes is free of headaches. Managers may still have to contend with trade-offs between response time and cost, for example. However, with critical processes and Process Goals in the driver's seat, they can intelligently make and communicate those trade-offs.

Somewhere along the spectrum between "maximum responsiveness at any cost" and "minimum cost and we'll respond when we can" lies the position desired by most organizations. World-class companies are redefining the spectrum by demonstrating the ability to combine high responsiveness and low cost.

Once an organization's top team has determined its competitive position (as part of strategy formulation), the processes (first) and the reporting relationships (second) can be designed to achieve it. To ensure that the position is attained and then maintained, managers can establish responsiveness and cost goals and can closely monitor performance against those goals.

The good news is that many of the variables that we have historically believed to be in conflict are not trade-offs at all. We have frequently found that a process designed for maximum quality is also a process designed for minimum cost.

TABLE 14.1. ACE COPIERS PRODUCT DEVELOPMENT ROLE/RESPONSIBILITY MATRIX

New Product Development Process Steps	Functions and Responsibilities	
	Field Operations	
	Management	Sales
1. Product needs determined	• Product strategy developed • Product additions reviewed • Products prioritized	• Customer needs identified
2. Product feasibility determined	• Feasibility study OK'd • Feasibility study reviewed	• Field support needs identified
3. Project plan developed	• Cost parameters set • Schedule set • Funds budgeted • Plan communicated	• Plan received
4. Product designed		• Configurations reviewed

Sales
function model

TABLE 14.1.
(Continued)

Functions and Responsibilities		
Field Operations		**Manufacturing**
Marketing	**Product Design**	**Product Engineering**
• Market needs identified • Needs evaluated • New product recommendation made		
• Product concept tested • Volume estimated • Price parameters determined	• Product profile developed • Product development schedule set • Feasibility report prepared	• Product cost estimated
• Plan received	• Plan received	• Plan received
	• Preliminary product design developed	• Alternative configurations developed • Configurations costed • Configurations finalized
↓	↓	↓
Marketing function model	Product design function model	Product engineering function model

CHAPTER FIFTEEN

CREATING A PERFORMANCE-BASED HUMAN RESOURCE DEVELOPMENT FUNCTION

Genius will live and thrive without training.

—MARGARET FULLER

In most organizations, training is a sizable investment, more sizable than senior managers realize. They know the amount of the human resource development department's budget. However, the total investment in training, which includes salaries of participants, is less visible and would be a surprise to most executives. Of more significance is the fact that even fewer of them know the return they are getting on that investment. Can you envision a manager who *could not* cite the return on his investment in a $50,000 telecommunications system? Can you envision a manager who *could* tell you the return he is getting on a $50,000 investment in communications training for managers?

Training is often seen as an employee benefit (like company picnics or contributions to the insurance plan), which is not expected to provide a tangible return. Isn't training just part of enlightened management, intrinsically good and unquestionably valuable in immeasurable ways?

No. Training should be treated like other investments:

- If the return on a given training investment is not easily quantified, how can a manager describe the specific benefits to the organization of that training effort?
- How is the investment in training to be assessed (and compared to other potential investments) *before* the investment is made?
- If top managers are committed to spending a certain percentage of revenue on training, how can they be sure that they are investing in the right training?

The answer to all three of these questions is the same. With the exception of situations in which an employee is being developed for a new job, the purpose of training is to improve current performance. Therefore, training should be assessed in terms of its impact on performance.

Two Views of Performance Improvement

There are two views of performance. In the prevailing view, people exist in a vacuum. If managers want to establish or improve a certain performance *output*, all they need to do is arrange for the proper training *input*. Figure 15.1 shows this limited perspective. When people in the human resource development department hold this view, their response to a request for training tends to be "You got it. When do you want it? Do you have enough money for a multimedia program?"

Unfortunately, the world of performance is not simply "skills and knowledge in, performance out." This reality leads to the second view of performance: the systems view. In the systems view, represented by the Nine Variables that serve as the theme of this book, human performance is a function of:

- *The Job/Performer Level,* where job outputs are defined and the Human Performance System establishes the environment in which people work
- *The Process Level,* where work flows are defined
- *The Organization Level,* where the strategy provides the direction, and the organization configuration provides the structure in which people work

Every trainee (or potential trainee) is a performer who functions within all Three Levels of Performance and is influenced by each of the Nine Performance Variables. As Table 15.1 shows, Skills and Knowledge (which is all training can provide) is one small part of one of the Nine Performance Variables. Without the perspective of the Three Levels, training is likely to be prescribed when training is not needed. When not supported by the Human Performance System, by work processes, and strategy and structure, training that is needed is nevertheless sure to fail.

The systems (Three Levels) view has significant implications for the human resource development (HRD) function, particularly because

FIGURE 15.1. THE "VACUUM" VIEW OF PERFORMANCE

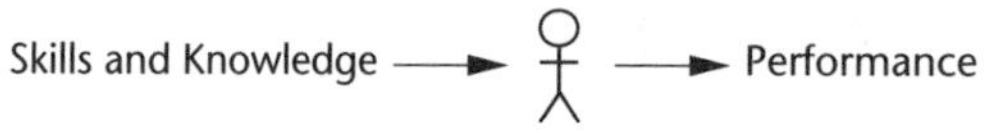

Skills and Knowledge ⟶ 🧍 ⟶ Performance

Performance Levels

TABLE 15.1. TRAINING'S ROLE IN THE NINE PERFORMANCE VARIABLES

Performance Needs

	ORGANIZATION LEVEL	PROCESS LEVEL	JOB/PERFORMER LEVEL
GOALS	**ORGANIZATION GOALS** • Has the organization's strategy or direction been articulated and communicated? • Does this strategy make sense in terms of the external threats and opportunities and the internal strengths and weaknesses? • Given this strategy, have the required outputs of the organization and the level of performance expected from each output been determined and communicated?	**PROCESS GOALS** • Are goals for key processes linked to customer and organization requirements?	**JOB GOALS** • Are job outputs and standards linked to process requirements (which are in turn linked to customer and organization requirements)?
DESIGN	**ORGANIZATION DESIGN** • Are all relevant functions in place? • Are all functions necessary? • Is the current flow of inputs and outputs between functions appropriate? • Does the formal organization structure support the strategy and enhance the efficiency of the system?	**PROCESS DESIGN** • Is this the most efficient and effective process for accomplishing the Process Goals?	**JOB DESIGN** • Are process requirements reflected in the appropriate jobs? • Are job steps in a logical sequence? • Have supportive policies and procedures been developed? • Is the job environment ergonomically sound?
MANAGEMENT	**ORGANIZATION MANAGEMENT** • Have appropriate function goals been set? • Is relevant performance measured? • Are resources appropriately allocated? • Are the interfaces between functions being managed?	**PROCESS MANAGEMENT** • Have appropriate process subgoals been set? • Is process performance managed? • Are sufficient resources allocated to each process? • Are the interfaces between process steps being managed?	**JOB MANAGEMENT** • Do the performers understand the Job Goals (outputs they are expected to produce and standards they are expected to meet)? • Do the performers have sufficient resources, clear signals and priorities, and a logical Job Design? • Are the performers rewarded for achieving the Job Goals? • Do the performers know if they are meeting the Job Goals? • Do the performers have the necessary knowledge/skill to achieve the Job Goals? • If the performers were in an environment in which the five questions listed above were answered "yes," would they have the physical, mental, and emotional capacity to achieve the Job Goals?

training is one of management's favorite performance improvement solutions.

HRD is often asked to bring about major organizational change with the small lever shown in Table 15.1. A review of the Nine Variables framework shows that job performance is a function of Job Goals, Job Design, and Job Management, where Skills and Knowledge is but one of six factors. In our thirty years of experience, we have seldom seen a job performance "problem" that could be significantly improved by manipulating the Skills and Knowledge (Training) factor alone. *Senior management should either provide HRD with a longer lever or realize that HRD's influence on organization performance is important but very limited.*

The Three Levels context and tools have implications for all areas of HRD. We will devote the rest of this chapter to exploring four of these areas:

- Determining training and development needs
- Designing training
- Evaluating training
- Designing and managing the HRD function

Determining Training and Development Needs

Our basic assumption is that HRD is in the performance improvement business. The question that should be asked in planning and implementing all HRD interventions is how this activity affects the performance of the business.

HRD can discover training needs in two ways: reactively (in response to requests for training) and proactively (as a result of planning to meet organization needs through training). The Three Levels approach can help identify training needs in both situations.

Reacting to Requests for Training. When responding to a request for training, the HRD professional must realize that the requester probably has not conducted a thorough analysis and most likely does not know the limitations of training as a performance improvement intervention. All he or she knows is that there is a feeling of pain. The HRD needs analyst's primary objective has to be to understand the performance context of the request. Only through that understanding can he or she determine whether any training is needed and, if so, the specific objectives that the training should meet.

As Section A of Figure 15.2 shows, the ideal response to a request for training follows an "outside-in" process. It begins at the Organization Level and moves through the Process Level to the Job Level. Sometimes

FIGURE 15.2. TWO APPROACHES TO TRAINING-NEEDS ANALYSIS

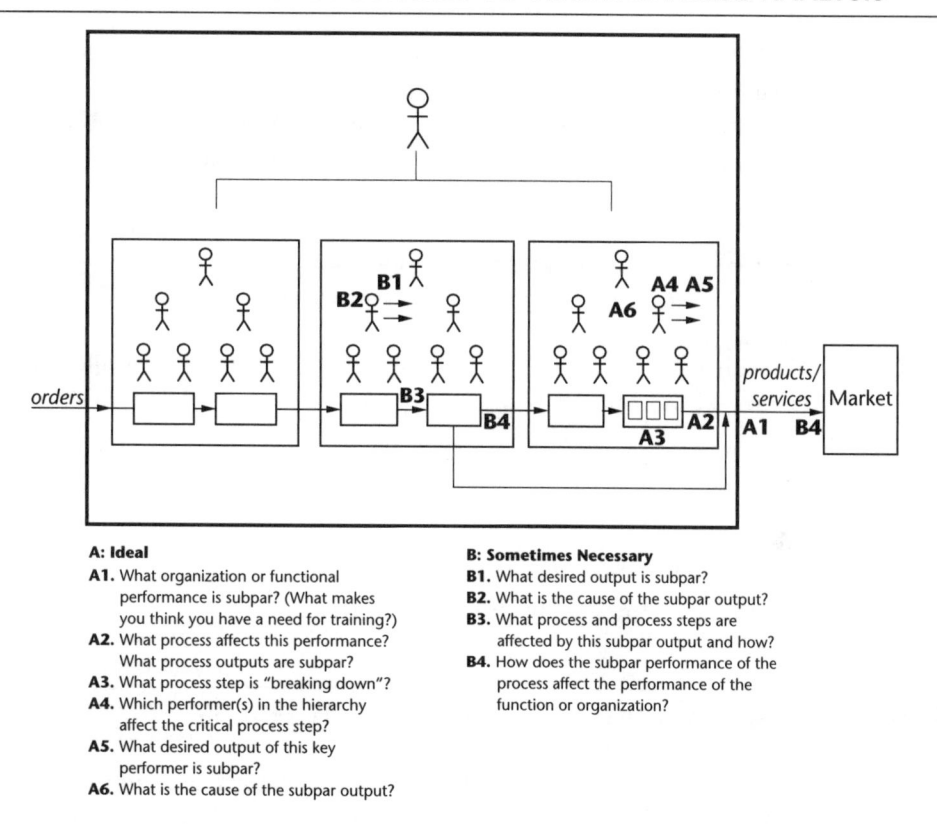

A: Ideal

A1. What organization or functional performance is subpar? (What makes you think you have a need for training?)

A2. What process affects this performance? What process outputs are subpar?

A3. What process step is "breaking down"?

A4. Which performer(s) in the hierarchy affect the critical process step?

A5. What desired output of this key performer is subpar?

A6. What is the cause of the subpar output?

B: Sometimes Necessary

B1. What desired output is subpar?

B2. What is the cause of the subpar output?

B3. What process and process steps are affected by this subpar output and how?

B4. How does the subpar performance of the process affect the performance of the function or organization?

political factors prevent the HRD analyst from beginning at the Organization Level. Under these circumstances, we recommend the less ideal (but still performance-based) "inside-out" process displayed in Section B.

The ideal needs-analysis process is more likely to get at the real issues behind the training request and is more likely to unearth performance needs that cannot be met by training. However, it may be more risky because it goes beyond what is normally expected of the HRD function. It also tends to be more time-consuming. The "sometimes necessary" approach, while less countercultural and time-intensive, may not address the most significant organization need. While the analyst does verify the need for training before proceeding with any development, he or she is locked into the assumption that the person identified by the requester represents the greatest performance improvement opportunity.

To illustrate the ideal process, let us examine a request for training. Sharon Pfeiffer, the vice president for operations at Property Casualty, Inc. (PCI), the partially fictionalized company introduced in Chapter Eight, has asked Stephen Willaby, the director of HRD, for a comprehensive training program for incumbent claim representatives. She tells him that claim reps' training is a high priority for her this fiscal year and that she will provide the funding from the operations budget.

If Stephen sees the vice president's request as a trigger to conduct a training-needs analysis, he will most likely use one of these three techniques:

- A training-needs survey, in which reps and their managers are asked to identify the skills and knowledge required to perform the claim rep job
- A competency study, in which a group of claim reps and claim managers are asked to identify the general competencies of an effective claim rep (analysis, computation, and written and oral communication)
- A task analysis, in which effective claim reps provide a list of the tasks they perform while doing their job

Any of these three approaches is better than developing a program without a needs analysis. They gather some real-world information, they can be done quickly and inexpensively, and they are not risky for Stephen. However, these methodologies share a significant weakness: none of them is tied directly to the organization, process, and job *outputs* that are the reason the claim representative job exists. Knowledge and skills, competencies, and tasks are all *inputs* to the results that PCI expects the reps to produce.

The failure of these three techniques to focus on performance outputs would be misguided if Stephen were being asked to develop entry-level training for claim reps. In this situation, however, his input focus is worse than misguided. At best, it is wasteful; at worst, it is dangerous. Because the vice president has requested the course for incumbent reps, we can assume that she wants to improve current performance. The course or curriculum that results from any of these three needs-analysis techniques *may* address the true performance needs that spawned the request; but is this training buried in a sea of material that covers parts of the claim rep job that are being performed satisfactorily? Is training *of any kind* for claim reps the solution to Sharon's concern? Is the claim rep job the one that should be addressed? *What's the real performance need?* If Stephen were to take the ideal approach outlined in Section A of Figure 15.2, he would:

1. Identify, at the Organization Level, the Critical Business Issue—the performance problem or opportunity of concern to the vice president. Are there too many errors in processed claims, causing complaints from claimants and extensive rework? Are the payout amounts to

claimants too high? Does Sharon see an opportunity for PCI to establish a competitive advantage in the area of claim processing time?

2. Identify, at the Process Level, the business process that has the greatest
   impact on the Critical Business Issue. Let's say that it's the claim adjudication process.
3. Use a Process Map (see Chapter Four) to document the adjudication
   process and to identify any gaps between desired and actual performance of each process step.
4. Identify the job(s) that have an impact on the performance of the
   process steps in which there are gaps. Perhaps those jobs are claim rep
   and claim supervisor.
5. Develop a list of the desired outputs of reps and supervisors. Identify
   which of the desired outputs are not being produced.
6. Identify the causes of any subpar outputs. Possible causes (covered in
   depth in Chapter Five) include missing or inadequate Performance
   Specifications, Task Interference, missing or unaligned Consequences,
   missing or inadequate Feedback, lack of Skills or Knowledge, and lack
   of Individual Capacity.

Stephen would develop training only for the Skills and Knowledge
needs. Ideally, he would have the charter to recommend changes in nontraining (environmental) areas as well.

During this six-step process (a distillation of the fourteen-step performance improvement process described in Chapter Eight), Stephen would
most likely visit the claims office that is performing best (in terms of measures related to the Critical Business Issue) and two or three other offices.
In each office, the required information could be gathered by interviewing the office manager and by interviewing and observing effective and
ineffective claim supervisors and reps.

The PCI request was actually made by an insurance company executive. Fortunately, the real Stephen arranged for a Three Levels analysis.
As it turned out, the job that was having the most impact on the Critical
Business Issue (excessive claim payouts) was claim supervisor. Thus, not
only did claim reps not need training, *they were not even the performers with
the greatest opportunity for improvement.* Claim supervisors needed improvement in two of their job outputs: qualifying claims and assigning claims
to claim reps. Training was part of the solution, but the primary need was
for a system of measurement and feedback. If the director of HRD had
responded unquestioningly to the request of the vice president for operations, he would have developed an impressive training program for claim
reps—an impressive waste of PCI's money.

Proactively Planning for Human Resource Development. HRD professionals
certainly should not try to do away with training requests. However,

they should not be driven by training requests. The way out of the purely reactive mode is to initiate HRD plans. The steps in an HRD planning process are:

1. Identify major clients (by business unit or department, with a senior manager as the contact in each client organization).
2. Develop an HRD plan with the client contact. Begin by identifying the client organization's anticipated operating needs for the next eighteen months. These needs should be based on the business unit's strategy or the department's contribution to the strategy. On the basis of these needs, identify the training that will be required to meet them. The plan should outline what both the client and the HRD function are going to do to meet the plan.
3. Consolidate all of the business-unit HRD plans into a plan and budget for the HRD function.
4. Review progress toward the plan with the client every six months.
5. Review progress at the end of the year and update the plan for the next year.

If an unplanned training request comes into the HRD function, an HRD representative and the client contact should discuss whether it represents an addition to or a replacement for something in the plan. If it is an addition, required resources can be negotiated with the client.

Even if HRD is limited to training interventions, this simple planning process results in clear priorities, which are based on the customer's long-term needs. It places the needs in the overall performance context of the business, and it enables the HRD department to make its resource decisions on a firmer business footing.

Designing Training

The "vacuum" view of performance leads to subject-matter-driven training and development. Training programs tend to address the hot topic of the day, or perceptions of what "they" need.

Here is a typical example of a subject-matter-driven training design. An HRD department was asked to train a large group of new people, whose job was to interview applicants for unemployment compensation. The design assignment was given to Matthew, a training specialist. He began by identifying subject matter areas relevant to the new interviewer. He examined existing bodies of knowledge concerning interviewing techniques and psychology. Matthew identified interviewing technique subject matter areas, such as developing the types of questions to ask, using questioning and probing skills, and interpreting answers. While exploring interviewing psychology, he uncovered subject matter areas that focused on an interviewee's behavior and personality makeup. After a considerable amount of apparently relevant subject-matter research, Matthew developed a three-day course that made extensive use of videotape and role-play exercises.

The Three Levels view, by contrast, leads to performance-driven training and development based on the needs-analysis approach already described. Performance-driven training design (which fits well with the techniques described by others as Criterion-Referenced Instruction or Learner-Controlled Instruction) suggests the approach used in the following example. Gwen, the educational technologist who was given the new-hire interviewing/training assignment, began by determining what the new interviewer was expected to do on the job. Specifically, she identified all the decisions the interviewer was expected to make, particularly the final decision (output) of the typical interview. From this analysis, Gwen learned that in all cases the interviewer's output was to decide where to refer the interviewees. There were four possibilities: Office A, where the applicants would receive unemployment compensation; Office B, where the applicants would be referred to jobs (because they were able to work and didn't qualify for compensation); Office C, where the applicants were interviewed by a psychiatrist (because they had psychological problems that would interfere with job placement); and Office D, where they were interviewed by the chief interviewer (because the applicants presented special problems or didn't clearly belong in one of the other three offices). On the basis of this information, Gwen concluded that the task of the new interviewers was primarily one of categorizing, or sorting. They were expected to decide which of the four offices to send applicants to. Thus, she decided that the subject matter of the training should consist of the following steps, presented in this sequence:

1. The four alternatives for the final decision
2. The criteria for each alternative (the conditions under which an applicant should be sent to each office)
3. The information required to make the final decision, on the basis of the criteria
4. Techniques for asking questions to elicit the required information

The resulting one-day course did not require elaborate instructional design or expensive media. It concentrated on teaching the interviewers to discriminate among the offices to which various applicants could be sent.

Without going through an exhaustive or overly formal analysis, Gwen addressed all Three Levels: she determined what the *organization* needed from the interviewer, she examined the interview *process,* and, on the basis of this information, she identified the skills and knowledge needed by the *performers.* Unlike Matthew, who based his course on an academic and generic model of interviewing skills, Gwen let the subject matter of the course be driven by the real world of her organization. Gwen's design was based on *performance.*

Evaluating Training

Evaluating training in a vacuum is a waste of time. A training program may have well-stated learning outcomes, appropriate media, excellent materials, and effective instruction. However, if the training addresses the wrong performance area, is not reinforced by Consequences and Feedback, is not supported by a well-designed work process, or is not linked to the direction of the organization, it is not worth the investment. With typical methods of evaluation, a workshop could win awards for instructional design the same week that the company files for Chapter 11 protection. Performance impact evaluation, by contrast, does not allow a course to look good without its also having a significant impact on the performance of the business.

Figure 15.3 shows where four types of evaluation fit into our basic systems diagram. All four types of evaluation are valid. The ideal course is liked by trainees, teaches what needs to be taught, provides skills that are used on the job, and provides skills that have a positive impact on the performance of the organization. However, most evaluations are of Types I or II, which are "upstream" from the performance that ultimately matters. Performance impact evaluation focuses on Types III and IV.

FIGURE 15.3. FOUR TYPES OF EVALUATION

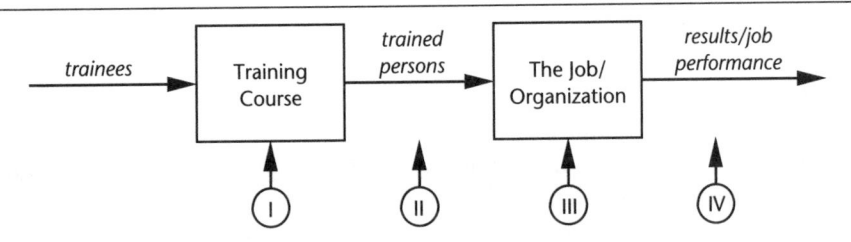

Type I.   Are the trainees happy with the course?
Type II. Does the training course teach the concepts?
Type III. Are the concepts used on the job?
Type IV. Does the application of the concepts positively affect the organization?

One use of performance impact evaluation is to help avoid or eliminate unneeded training. For example, if the director of engineering has requested a workshop in report writing, it would be readily apparent how to evaluate trainees' satisfaction (a reaction questionnaire) and learning (a test). If, however, the requester would be unable to determine whether the new writing skills were being applied on the job and, more important, whether their application was having any effect on the engineering department's performance, the training would be a questionable investment.

Another use of performance impact evaluation is to identify areas in which management needs to support the training. For example, a training course on quality control would be fairly simple to assess with Type I and Type II evaluations. As Types III and IV are discussed, the HRD specialist and the client may realize that if management does not take action to support the use of the quality-control techniques (by providing resources and rewards), the best training in the world will have no effect on performance.

If the HRD analyst has determined the training needs, as just described, evaluation (especially Type IV) should not present a problem. Because the training needs directly affect documented organization performance problems or opportunities, the training can be evaluated in terms of its impact on those problems or opportunities. The questions that appear in Column A of Figure 15.2 provide the framework for performance impact evaluation.

Designing and Managing the HRD Function

The Three Levels approach to determining training needs, to designing training, and to evaluating training suggests a different kind of HRD department. As a matter of fact, this type of HRD function can transform itself from a training operation to the organization's *performance department*.

A performance department differs from a traditional training function in a number of ways. Its people:

- Understand that their mission is to improve performance, not to provide skills and knowledge.
- Only conduct training and development that are linked to organization performance needs.
- Only conduct training and development that are supported by the environment in which the trainees work (the Human Performance System).
- Evaluate training and development according to their contributions to organization performance needs.

- Conduct diagnoses that go beyond training—and development-needs analysis. They are interested and skilled in unearthing nontraining problems, such as Task Interference, poor Feedback, and unsupportive Consequences.
- Recommend solutions to both training and development and nontraining and development needs.
- Understand the business at all Three Levels of Performance and the influence of all Nine Performance Variables.
- Understand that the department is a business and must be run as a business.

To expand on the last item in the list, the performance department is an organizational subsystem; it is subject to the systems laws described in Chapter One. As a business, it also has a clear strategy (including a specific identification of products or services and customers) that is linked to the organizationwide strategy, and it is structured to run as a performance business whose subfunctions carry out needs analysis, design, development, delivery, and evaluation. Figure 15.4 shows one configuration for a performance department.

You should not infer from Figure 15.4 that a performance department must include a minimum of twenty people; a number of functions can be performed by the same person. As a matter of fact, the department in Figure 15.4 could be staffed by as few as three people.

Moving from the Organization Level to the Process Level, we see that the performance department includes the traditional training processes: course development, course delivery, and course evaluation. However, it also includes processes for organization, process, and job-needs analysis and for nontraining interventions (designing measurement systems, feedback systems, and consequence systems).

At the Job/Performer Level, the performance department structures jobs to include analysis, design, planning, evaluation, and consulting, as well as development and delivery responsibilities. Lastly, the manager of the performance department creates a Human Performance System that supports a holistic performance mission. Since the manager wants the performance department's staff to identify performance improvement opportunities and design multifaceted solutions, he or she doesn't measure the staff on "number of classroom days."

Frankly, we don't care whether it is the HRD department that assumes the role of performance department, as long as somebody does. We focus on HRD because that tends to be the natural place for this expertise and set of services to reside. However, we have worked with organizations where HRD fulfilled the traditional training role, and comprehensive performance diagnosis and improvement were the mission of a separate department.

FIGURE 15.4. MODEL OF A PERFORMANCE-FOCUSED TRAINING FUNCTION

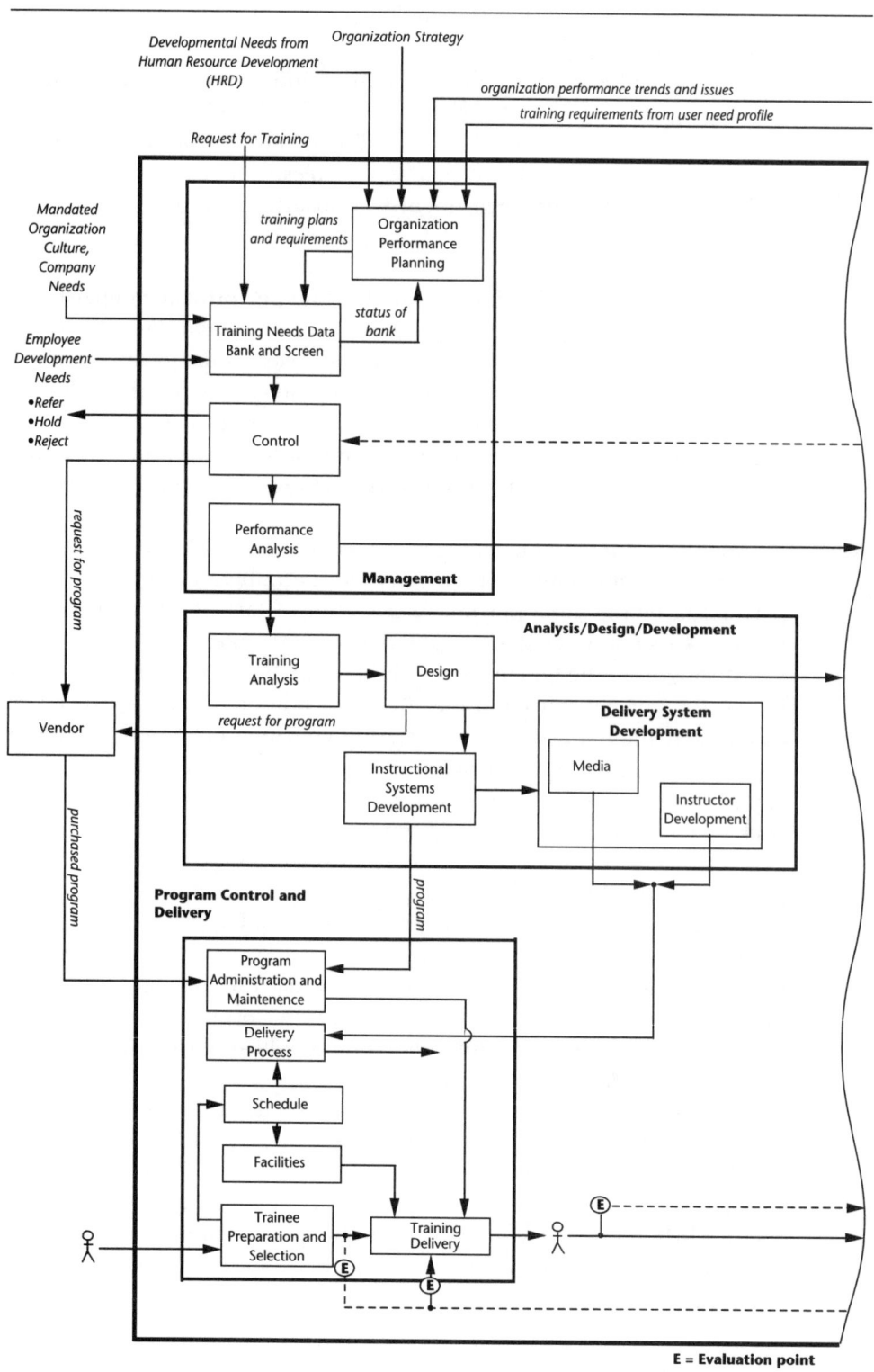

E = Evaluation point

FIGURE 15.4.
(*Continued*)

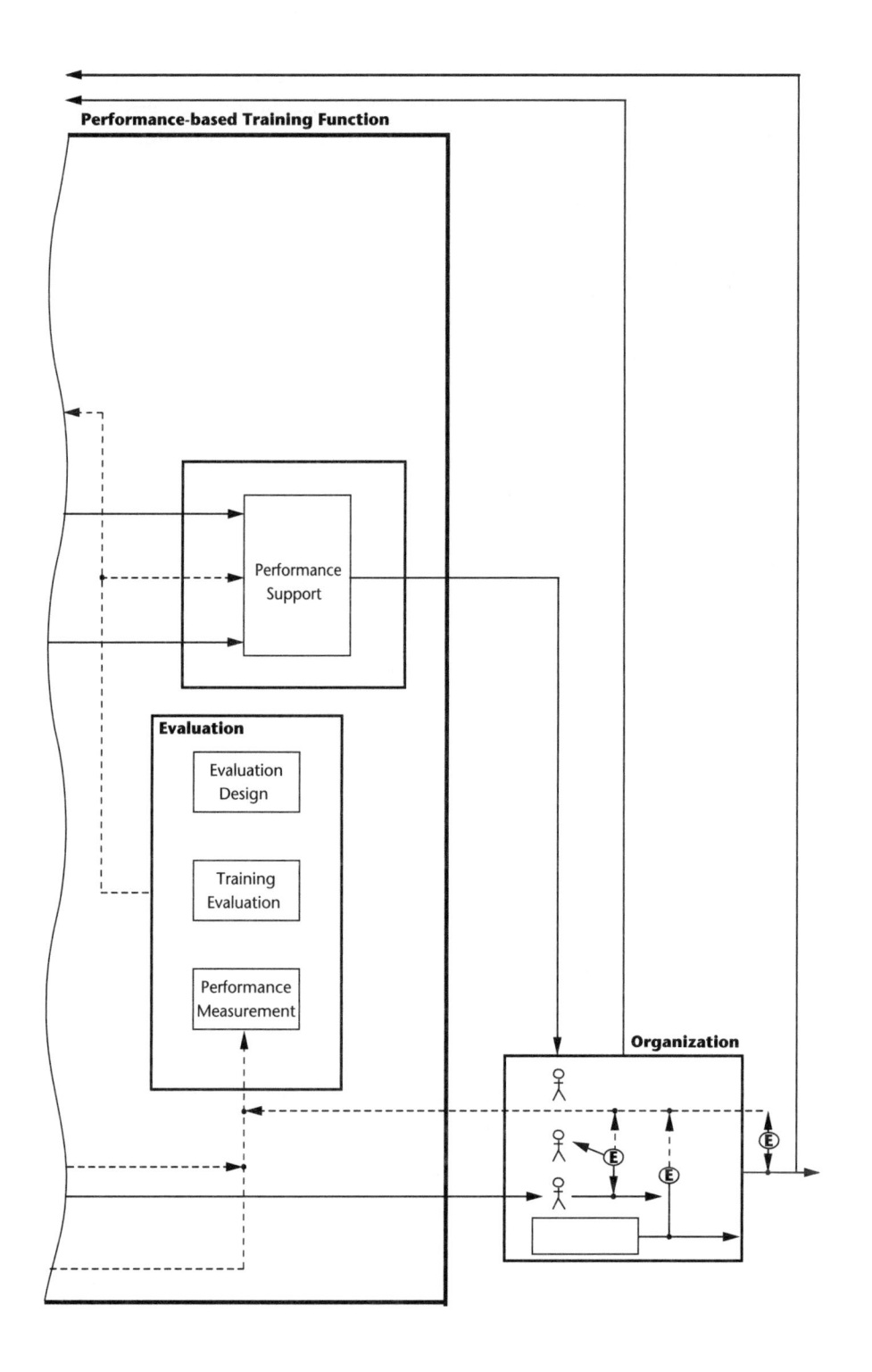

Summary

We believe that HRD functions are uniquely positioned to become their organizations' performance departments (or, at least, performance-based HRD departments). Reflecting the Three Levels–based systems view, rather than the limited and potentially counterproductive "vacuum" view, performance departments realize that training is a very small lever with which to move the world, no matter where the fulcrum is placed. Their people identify needs and evaluate contributions at all Three Levels of Performance. They are as comfortable at the Organization and Process Levels and in nonperformer components of the Human Performance System as they are in the classroom, and they are credible businesspeople who are making a demonstrably significant contribution to the company's competitive advantage.

CHAPTER SIXTEEN

DEVELOPING AN ACTION PLAN FOR PERFORMANCE IMPROVEMENT

A journey of a thousand miles must begin with a single step.

—LAO TZU

Say you believe that the systems view of an organization represents the way work gets done. You are determined to manage each component of the system you manage. You agree that the tools at all Three Levels of Performance should be at the heart of any comprehensive effort to formulate and implement strategy, improve quality, productivity, cycle time, and cost, and design an organization that works. You have vowed to use the questions that support each of the Nine Performance Variables as the basis of your management system. However, you may feel a bit overwhelmed. At this point, your primary question is most likely "How do I start?"

One way to begin is by initiating a Three Levels project. Before there can be any widespread commitment to the Three Levels as a way of life in an organization, the approach must demonstrate its worth. The best way to make a short-term contribution and to show long-term potential is by applying the Three Levels tools to a strategic issue facing your organization. The following steps represent an initial Three Levels effort. They are stated in a way that should enable you to use them as the basis for an action plan. Throughout the description, "you" refers to the top team in the organization, which can be the entire enterprise or any meaningful component thereof.

Step 1: Organization Level

The way to start is to develop a strategy for the business. Developing strategy doesn't necessarily mean embarking on a six-month planning journey. It may require only a couple of hours to confirm and perhaps update your vision and direction. If you and your colleagues haven't reached consensus on the answers to the questions provided in Chapter Six, any improvement effort runs the risk of being ill-directed.

Once the strategy is clear and up-to-date, we recommend conducting what Chapter Nine describes as Phase Ø, Performance Improvement Planning. During this effort, the strategy and a "super-system" map (see Chapter One) help identify one or more Critical Business Issues (CBIs), which represent opportunities to establish a competitive advantage or eliminate a competitive disadvantage.

Phase Ø will also help identify the process which, if improved, will have the greatest impact on the highest-priority CBI.

Although you should certainly start with an opportunity with which you are comfortable, we suggest that you resist the temptation to pick an easy or minor issue just to see whether the approach works. The Three Levels tools can address an issue of any complexity; as a matter of fact, they are most helpful when an issue is multifaceted. The approach will prove its worth only if it is applied to an issue of significance.

Step 2: Process Level

Having identified a CBI and a process, we recommend that you lead a Process Improvement Project (PIP). A PIP begins with Phase 1, in which you and others on the top team define the goals, roles, and boundaries of the project. During Phase 2, which involves both senior management and people who work in the process, the current process will be documented and analyzed, the future process will be designed (as radically as dictated by the goals specified in Phase 1), and measures will be developed. Detailed action planning and implementation occur in Phase 3, which includes action at all Three Levels of Performance.

The steps and tools used in Phases 1, 2, and 3 are described in Chapter Nine.

Step 3: Job/Performer Level

A key aspect of Phase 3 involves the identification of one or more jobs critical to the successful implementation of the process improvements designed during Step 2. For each job, have the Process Team (along with job incumbents and supervisors) describe the outputs and goals required by the new process. Then ask the team to identify the environmental support that must be provided to the people in these jobs.

To display the outputs and goals, we recommend that you use the Job Model format presented in Chapter Twelve. To identify the resources, feedback, rewards, and training that should support the new job responsibilities, we suggest that you use the Human Performance System questions listed in Chapter Five.

This three-step process will enable the participants and others to see the benefits of addressing all Three Levels of Performance. They will work with some of the pivotal Three Levels tools—the Relationship Map, the Process Map, the Job Model, and the Human Performance System questions. Most important, they will resolve a critical issue facing the organization and will create a foundation upon which continuous improvement (see Chapter Thirteen) can be built.

We don't, however, want you to think that the Three Levels can be used effectively only in a "bundled" fashion. A second answer to "How do I start?" is by applying one or two of the Three Levels tools in a targeted application. In addition to the more comprehensive projects described earlier (especially in Chapter Seven), organizations have successfully applied individual Three Levels tools in ways such as these:

- Relationship and Process Mapping were used to realign an entire telecommunications company to increase the focus on the customer.
- Relationship and Process Mapping were used to strengthen and formalize the historical "handshake" relationship between an electronics manufacturer's U.S. headquarters and a foreign subsidiary, which is projected to quadruple its revenues in three years.
- Relationship Maps were used in an aerospace company's orientation training to quickly show new employees where they fit into the big picture.
- Organization, Process, and Job measures were used in a paper mill to get everyone from the mill manager to the machine operators rowing in the same direction.
- Role/Responsibility Matrices and Job Models were used to clarify the responsibilities of branch managers in a consumer loan business and to clarify the responsibilities of four levels of management in a fourteen-hundred-store retail organization.
- The Human Performance System was used by a publishing company to diagnose and remove some of the causes of high turnover among its salespeople.
- Job Models and the Human Performance System were used as the basis for the design of a performance appraisal system in a government agency.

Summary

Our files contain data on hundreds of performance improvement projects spanning thirty years. They all include applications of Three Levels tools, and they range from the macro (establishing speedy cycle time as a competitive advantage in an international electronics company) to micro (improving the performance of machine operators in a snack-food manufacturing company). We continue to find new ways in which all three categories of users—executives, managers, and analysts—are applying the Three Levels as:

- A *set of tools* for diagnosing and eliminating deficient performance
- An *engine* for continuously improving systems that are performing adequately
- A *road map* for guiding an organization in a new direction
- A *blueprint* for designing a new entity

However, Three Levels Performance Improvement is more than issue-specific interventions. The tools enable managers and individual contributors to bring about many of the culture changes that are frequently discussed but rarely pursued systematically. These culture changes include:

- Ensuring that a customer orientation drives all activities
- Establishing accountability by objective performance measurement
- Minimizing departmental conflicts
- Implementing a participative style of management
- Creating a work environment that leads to both better performance and a higher quality of work life

We believe that any reader takes no more than a handful of meaningful ideas or tools from even the best of management books. In our opinion, the most significant ideas we have presented are the following:

- Organizations behave as adaptive systems. To effectively, nimbly, and proactively adapt to the demands of a rapidly changing environment, all system components—inputs, processes, outputs, and feedback— must be managed.
- An organization's strategic and operational effectiveness is the product of Three Levels of Performance—the Organization Level, the Process Level, and the Job/Performer Level. As a result, every improvement effort must be seen through the lens of the Three Levels.
- The three Performance Needs that must be met at each of the Three Levels are Goals, Design, and Management. Failure to manage the

Nine Performance Variables is failure to manage the business holistically.

- Cross-functional processes are particularly critical to the quality, productivity, cycle time, and cost of any business.
- Managing people should include addressing the needs of all components of the Human Performance System in which they work.
- At each of the Three Levels, there are tools that can help in documenting, analyzing, and improving performance.

We are performance improvement practitioners. We are interested in a theory only if it helps us get results. We have found that the Three Levels framework provides us with a unifying theory of performance improvement. More important, it has led us to the tools we have described and illustrated.

The approach we have described in this book does not represent a quick fix. We have never encountered a tool that brings about comprehensive, lasting organization change without the investment we have described. The Three Levels viewpoint will enable you to better understand your organization and the variables affecting its performance. With this understanding as a foundation, you can use the Three Levels technique to bring about top-to-bottom performance improvement. We believe that the challenge can be met.

INDEX

INSTRUCTOR'S GUIDE

The Instructor's Guide for the third edition of *Improving Performance: How to Manage the White Space on the Organization Chart* contains chapter-specific teaching materials. It is specifically for use by university instructors and is not based upon or similar to Rummler-Brache's process improvement and training certification workshops for companies. (See pages 111–115, Step 2 of Project Definition, in Chapter Nine for additional information on Rummler-Brache training.) The Instructor's Guide is available free online. If you would like to download the Guide, please visit www.wiley.com/go/college/rummler.